Further praise for

WHERE THE MONEY IS

"With the style and pacing of a good novel, Rehder portrays the great variety of bandits he pursued in his more than 30 years with the FBI . . . this should become a standard in the genre." —*Publishers Weekly*

"In addition to his many insightful comments about the criminal mind, Rehder packs plenty of action into this crime-fighting memoir."
—*Booklist*

"While devouring Rehder's accounts of pursuing both amateur and professional bank robbers, readers will become armchair experts themselves. Before the book ends, Rehder covers every classification of bank heist imaginable." —*St. Louis Post-Dispatch*

"Who knew bank robberies could be so interesting? This collection of essays centering on memorable bank robbers tracked—and in most cases captured—by retired FBI agent Rehder reads like fiction."
—*Library Journal*

D0851379

✦✦✦ WHERE ✦✦✦
THE MONEY IS

TRUE TALES FROM THE BANK ROBBERY
CAPITAL OF THE WORLD

WILLIAM J. REHDER
& GORDON DILLOW

W. W. Norton & Company ✦ New York London

Printed in the United States of America
First published as a Norton paperback 2004

For information about permission to reproduce
selections from this book, write to
Permissions, W. W. Norton & Company, Inc.
500 Fifth Avenue, New York, NY 10110

Manufacturing by Courier Westford
Book design by BTDNYC
Production manager: Julia Druskin

Library of Congress Cataloging-in-Publication Data

Rehder, William J.
Where the money is : true tales from the bank robbery capital of the world /
by William J. Rehder, Gordon Dillow.— 1st ed.
p. cm.
ISBN 0-393-05156-0 (hardcover)
1. Bank robberies—California—Los Angeles—Case studies. 2. Robbery
investigation—California—Los Angeles—Case studies. 3. Thieves—
California—Los Angeles —Case studies. 4. Rehder, William J. 5. United
States. Federal Bureau of Investigation—Officials and employees—
Biography. I. Dillow, Gordon. II. Title.
HV6661.C2R45 2003
364.15'52'0979494—dc21

2003002224

ISBN 0-393-32575-X (pbk.)

W. W. Norton & Company, Inc.
500 Fifth Avenue, New York, N.Y. 10110
www.wwnorton.com

W. W. Norton & Company Ltd.
Castle House, 75/76 Wells Street, London W1T 3QT

1 2 3 4 5 6 7 8 9 0

To Gaye, Michael, Erik, and Hilary Rehder

To my wife, Tule, and
Louise and Troy Dillow, my mother and father

CONTENTS

ACKNOWLEDGMENTS AND AUTHORS' NOTE   9

1 ✦ **SMITTY'S MISTAKE**   13

2 ✦ **EVERYBODY LIKES EDDIE**   48

3 ✦ **CASPER**   99

4 ✦ **THE HOLE IN THE GROUND GANG**   150

5 ✦ **INSIDERS**   196

6 ✦ **SHOOT-OUT IN NORTH HOLLYWOOD**   246

EPILOGUE   285

ACKNOWLEDGMENTS AND
AUTHORS' NOTE

This book was a team effort. It could not have been accomplished without the considerable talents and dedication of each member of the team. Among them are our literary agents, Eric and Maureen Lasher, who from the beginning provided us with faith, confidence, friendship, and wise counsel. Also special thanks to W. W. Norton, particularly editor in chief Starling Lawrence, and Morgen Van Vorst, who believed in the project and knew just what to leave in, and what to take out.

Special thanks go to the following FBI employees, past and present, who provided help and inspiration during my thirty-three-year Bureau career: FBI communications specialist Linda Webster, a friend, sidekick, confidant, office mate, and "little sister" for over eighteen years. Friend and partner Joe Chefalo, big, strong, utterly fearless, one of the finest FBI agents ever to carry the credentials, a guy who put the fear of God and the FBI into any number of kidnappers and Klansmen and bank bandits. Carl Schlatter, my mentor and West Coast father figure when I was a young agent; and Charlie Ogle, my first supervisor on the LA FBI Bank Squad, now seventy-five years old and still as gruff but incisive as ever. There are also those very special Bank Squad guys from whom I learned something new every day: Jerry Crowe, Frenchie LaJeunesse, Biff Flanigan, Art Thatcher, Tom Powers, Jim Hall, Myron Hitch, Frank Calley, Bernie Connors, J. C. Fishbeck, Pat Hill, Mike Mench, Steve Powell, Bill Elwell, Dan Bodony, and Bank Squad supervisors Mark Llewellyn, Ken Jacobsen, and Bob Mack.

There are others no longer present to read these words but whose memories remain vivid in my heart. First among them are my parents, Ann and Bill Rehder, whose worry about me being an FBI agent finally gave way to pride. Also LA Bank Squad agent Wayne Bourque, who for eight courageous years carried a full caseload while battling the cancer that would eventually take his life. Other friends, gone but not forgotten, include Bank Squad agents Bob Linker, Ed Plevak, Dick Cromwell, Carl Pilkvist, Jim Keenan, and Tom O'Quinn; and LAPD Robbery Homicide Bank Team detectives Dave Lively, Joe Chandler, and Bob Kestler.

We are also most grateful to the following FBI employees past and present who have provided us with their time and personal recollections recounted within the book: Dan Gordon, George Schroder, Andy Chambers, Brenda Cotton, Biff Flanigan, Jack Trimarco, Paul Chamberlain, John McEachern, and Jerry Hines. Likewise, we thank past and present LAPD Robbery Homicide Bank Team detectives John Licata, Brian Tyndall, Greg Grant, Tom Gattegno, and Steve Laird, as well as former LAPD Burglary Special Detail detectives Dennis Pagenkopp and Doug Sims. Special thanks are also due to John Wiley, the UCLA law professor-turned-federal prosecutor (and now California Superior Court judge) for his friendship, time, recollections, personal notes, editorial advice, and constant encouragement. Thanks also to Charlie Fine, Stephen Wolfe, Jerry McNeive, Donald Re, and April Smith.

We also want to express our admiration and heartfelt thanks to all of Bill's colleagues on the LA FBI Bank Squad, the LAPD Robbery-Homicide Bank Team, and former detectives of the Los Angeles County Sheriff's Central Robbery Detail. These few lines of appreciation will never convey the gratitude felt for their camaraderie and dedication to excellence.

Finally, we thank our beautiful wives and best friends, Gaye Rehder and Tule Dillow, for patiently reading through the many drafts, and being our first and best critics.

This is a work of nonfiction; everything in it is true. However, the names of a few minor characters, and all criminal informants, have been changed to protect their privacy or their safety. Errolyn Ramirez is a pseudonym. The observations and opinions expressed in this book do not necessarily reflect those of the Federal Bureau of Investigation.

WILLIAM J. REHDER
GORDON DILLOW

WHERE
THE MONEY IS

1

SMITTY'S MISTAKE

December 1966, a cold, gray, miserable morning in Cleveland; there was no other kind of December morning in Cleveland. I was dirty and dog-tired after working all night, fueling up on crankcase coffee out of paper cups and chasing down bum tips and bad calls all over the rustbelt urban catastrophe that was the city's East Side. Now I was crammed into a dark, fetid, roach-infested little room in an ancient three-story brownstone walk-up, with a half dozen other guys carrying guns, trying to make a howling junkie named Smitty come out from under the bed.

It was strange. But I knew then that this was what I wanted to do with my life.

Some sixteen hours earlier, Smitty had made a bad mistake. Recently paroled from state prison on a robbery beef, and now badly in need of financing, he had tucked a gun into his waistband, put on a stingy-brim hat and a pair of sunglasses—sunglasses, in December, in Cleveland— and then clomped down the stairs of his building and onto the sidewalk. Shivering in his threadbare black jacket, he walked six blocks east, along streets lined with crumbling row houses and boarded-up windows, to a small branch office of the Cleveland Trust Bank, near the corner of East 105th and Superior, in the city's Hough District. Despite the cold, he stayed outside for a while, pacing back and forth, back and forth, back and forth in front of the bank, practicing his lines and try-ing to get his nerve up.

I can do this, he told himself. No, I gotta do this.

I gotta rob this bank.

If Smitty had been much of a thinking man, he could have come up with a million reasons not to do it—and all of them put together couldn't compete with that one desperate, overpowering reason why he had to. He'd already pilfered and boosted and stole as much as opportunity and his limited abilities had permitted, and it was never enough. Even the lousy forty bucks that he'd squeezed out of his girlfriend the day before was gone, the shit that he'd scored with it just a dim, warm, happy memory. Now the warning signs of detoxification sickness were already there, like the first foul breath of the flu, and he knew it would only get worse, and then infinitely worse.

His body was making an argument that his mind couldn't win. The argument was: Feed me. There is money behind those doors, and what that money will buy is what I need. So give it to me, you miserable motherfucker, or I will make you—us—so sick that you will sorely wish you had.

In the junkie's world, need trumps fear every time. Smitty touched the butt of the gun under his jacket for reassurance, and then walked into the bank.

The word "bank" can be deceiving. This was not the headquarters of Chase Manhattan or Bank of America. It wasn't one of those quiet, dimly lighted, cathedral-like places with red velvet ropes on gleaming brass stands and walls paneled in deep, rich wood, a place where men in three-piece suits with watch fobs hanging across their bellies sat behind mahogany desks, shepherding dollars measured in millions. This was a small branch bank in a bad part of town, an enterprise dedicated to cashing payroll and welfare checks and issuing low-five-figure busi-ness loans and nickel and dime mortgages. The desks were gray steel, the walls sheetrock, the lighting tubular fluorescent. Linoleum, not car-pet, covered the floor; the carpet wasn't made that could have withstood even a single winter of commercial foot traffic in Cleveland.

But if the branch occupied a low rung in the banking ladder, it was still a bank, and therefore full of money. On an average day there would be about a quarter of a million dollars in cash stashed in the vault and stacked in the tellers' drawers; on payday Fridays and the first of the month, when the government checks arrived in people's mailboxes, that amount might swell to half a million, easy. And it was all there for the taking.

Of course, Smitty's ambitions didn't run that high; he only wanted a little something to get him through the day.

There was a short line at the teller counter, and Smitty waited, trying to stay calm; the sunglasses notwithstanding, no one paid any particular attention to him. There was no guard. Although the bank was robbed about once a year, on average, the losses were always relatively small, less than what a security guard's annual salary would be. Bankers, of all people, understood cost versus return, and besides, the last thing the bank wanted was for an untrained, minimum-wage security guard to start trading bullets with a bank robber. It would be bad for business.

Finally it was Smitty's turn. He walked up to one of the teller stations, opened his jacket to show the butt of the gun in his waistband, and said, in a low voice and with as much menace as he could muster, "This is a robbery. Gimme all the money, both drawers. No alarms."

The teller was a stout woman of middle age, with prior robbery victim experience, so she did exactly what she'd been trained to do. She didn't panic, didn't scream, didn't do anything that might set this guy off. She followed his instructions, slowly and deliberately taking the stacks of loose and strapped bills out of both of her drawers, upper and lower, and putting them on the counter, while Smitty whispered, "Come on, come on, hurry up," and started stuffing the money into the waistband of his pants. The teller made sure to grab the three bills—two tens and a twenty—that were sitting in a segregated portion of her top drawer and hand them over. They were "bait bills," indistinguishable from any others except that their serial numbers were recorded: if the guy later got caught with the bait bills in his possession, it would be strong evidence against him. And despite the robber's warning about no alarms, with her hand out of Smitty's line of sight, the teller also pressed together the two buttons on the silent alarm system under the counter, which notified a central alarm center that a robbery was under way and also activated the surveillance cameras mounted on the wall above the exit doors.

Within thirty seconds the teller had emptied the drawers. Smitty stuffed the last strapped stack into his waistband, then backed away from the counter and headed for the door, tucking his head down to hide his face from the cameras that he knew were clicking away.

So far, so good. He had the money, and except for the one teller, no one in the bank had seemed to even realize a robbery was going down. But as anybody who's ever done it will tell you, there's a high pucker factor when you do a bank lick. It's hard enough to stay cool when you're inside, and you have your business to attend to. But by the time you hit the exit door, and you see the light and smell the fresh air, such as it is, your entire universe starts narrowing down to one overriding ambition: Putting as much distance as possible between yourself and the scene of the crime. It's a physical sensation; every nerve ending in your body is urgently advising you: *Run, don't walk! Run! Get away! Get away!*

Even professionals have a hard time keeping it in check—and Smitty was no professional. The instant he cleared the bank doors, he broke into a run. Which made for a memorable picture: A frightened, desperate-looking man in a stingy-brim hat and sunglasses—once again, sunglasses, in Cleveland, on a miserable gray afternoon in December— loping down a sidewalk with one hand clutching a bulge in the front of his pants and his head swiveling back and forth over his shoulders to see if anyone was gaining on him. Even in a rough, mind-your-own-business neighborhood like the Hough, it was the sort of thing that bystanders tended to notice. The guy couldn't have made his immediate status any more obvious if he'd been carrying a sign that said: "I just robbed somebody, and now I'm running away."

Short term, though, it was Smitty's lucky day. Because rustling and crinkling inside his pants as he finally climbed the stairs to his grim little apartment was some $4,000 in cash, an impressive figure for a one-on-one bank robbery—that is, one bandit holding up one teller. I can almost see the look of wonderment and joy spreading across his face as he stood in his room, drenched in fear sweat, his breathing short and labored, fishing the money out of his pants and dropping it on the sagging Murphy bed as he counted it up: "Five hundred, twelve hundred, two thousand, three thousand—Oh, sweet Jesus!—four thousand dollars."

By Smitty's low standards, it was a bonanza, a miracle, manna from heaven. It was a hundred times bigger score than he'd ever had knocking over liquor stores and mom-and-pop groceries—and a hell of a lot safer, too, the way he figured it. You hit a mom-and-pop and you just never knew if crazy old Pop would fight for his money, maybe pull a .38 out from under the counter and put a cap in you, or chase you down the street, shouting and waving his arms because you'd stolen his lousy forty or fifty bucks. With that kind of crazy shit, a guy could actually get hurt. But the bitch in the bank had just handed it over—no fuss, nobody chasing you, a clean getaway, a ton of money.

The guys in the joint had been right: Robbing a bank was easy.

Smitty raked the bills on the bed into a pile, took out a couple hundred bucks and stuffed it into his pocket, then peeled back a corner of the filthy linoleum and carefully laid short stacks of bills on the floor before putting the linoleum back down and tamping the bulge with his foot. You didn't want to venture out in the Hough District with that kind of roll on you; thieves were everywhere. He put on his jacket, locked the door, and thumped down the stairs to find his connection and score some shit. He was happy, and pretty soon he'd be happier.

It probably never even occurred to him just how big a mistake he'd made.

Sure, Smitty had learned a little something about bank robberies during his prior stretch in the joint. He wasn't a total mutt; he had audited the cellblock classes at the Extension University of Crime at Ohio State Penitentiary in Mansfield; he could listen and learn. For one thing, he knew enough to make the teller empty not only her top cash drawer but her lower reserve cash drawer as well, the one where she kept the larger stacks of bills, so if she caught a big transaction she wouldn't have to go through the hassle of going back to the vault and signing out more cash. That had significantly increased the take. He also knew that no matter what he told her, the bitch would probably hit the silent alarm button and turn on the cameras, so he'd have to try to hide his face on the way out. Yeah, he probably should have kept his cool outside the bank, and not done the Jesse Owens number, but hey, it worked, right? He'd gotten away; it was over, it was history. Like most small-time career criminals, Smitty's worldview permitted no unpleasant musings on the mistakes of the past or the consequences of the future; he was pretty much restricted to the happy now.

So he didn't think back to those moments when he had paced back and forth in front of the Cleveland Trust Bank, those little moments of destiny when he had failed to notice—or at least appreciate the significance of—the small decal sign posted right on the front door, for all the world to see. It was the same notice that was affixed to the front door of every federally insured financial institution in America, the one that said:

> The FBI investigates any robbery, burglary, or larceny in this institution—Federal Bank Robbery & Related Crimes Statute, Title 18 USC Section 2113.

Smitty's big mistake was that he hadn't given nearly enough thought, if any, to exactly what that meant in immediate, practical, personal terms.

What it meant was that by robbing a bank, Smitty the small-time thieving hype had moved up, albeit briefly, from the minors to the bigs.

And it meant that his ass belonged to us.

✦ ✦ ✦

While Smitty was making his big mistake, I was five miles away in the old Standard Office Building on Ontario, hunched over a gray metal desk in the bull pen of the Cleveland FBI field office, putting the finishing touches on another in a literally endless stream of applicant background investigation reports—and wondering if I'd made a big mistake of my own.

Whenever anyone applied for a federal job that would give him access to national security or criminal intelligence information—in the FBI, the U.S. Attorney's office, the federal judiciary, the State Department, the Atomic Energy Commission, whatever—he (or she) had to undergo a background security check by the FBI. Mostly that involved having an FBI agent interview friends and associates of the applicant and ask a long series of by-the-book questions: "Has (name of applicant) ever made disparaging remarks about the United States government?" "Have you ever heard (name of applicant) advocate the overthrow of the United States government?" "Have you ever had reason to believe that (name of applicant) has engaged in deviant or depraved sexual behavior?" And on and on.

For FBI agents it was stultifyingly tedious and unrewarding labor, the lowest kind of scut work. So naturally whenever possible it was dumped on the newest, greenest agent in the office.

In the Cleveland FBI field office in December 1966, that was me.

Just three weeks earlier I had completed my fourteen-week training program at the FBI Academy. And so far it wasn't working out quite the way I thought it would when I signed up.

I hadn't come naturally to a law enforcement career. Unlike a lot of guys who carry a badge, I wasn't descended from six generations of Irish cops; it wasn't in my blood. In fact, growing up in a safe, quiet suburb of St. Louis, in an *Ozzie and Harriet*–style family, I had never encountered a criminal, and had hardly ever even spoken to a cop. The only youthful interest I'd shown in becoming an FBI agent was in Catholic high school, when we were all assigned to give a classroom speech on "The World's Most Interesting Job." Out of the blue I had picked "FBI Agent," and as I researched the topic, mostly through Bureau-approved books and publications (almost everything written about the FBI at the time was Bureau-approved), it really did sound kind of cool.

But actually joining the FBI wasn't the stuff of my boyhood dreams. I majored in accounting at St. Louis University, and then went to St. Louis University Law School, fully intending to become a practicing attorney—although I wasn't sure I really wanted to do that, either. It wasn't until my senior year in law school, when the FBI Special Agent in Charge of the St. Louis field office came out to give our class a sales pitch about the FBI, that I started to think, yeah, that might be something different. My pal, Jerry McNeive, who'd been a classmate all through high school, college, and now law school, thought so, too. We both decided to sign up.

My parents, God bless 'em, were horrified. Twenty years of education, eleven of them *Jesuit* education, for gosh sakes, with a law school degree almost in your pocket—and you want to be a glorified cop? Lord, where have we failed? You'll never make any money. And it could be dangerous!

Which I guess is what I was hoping for: danger, adventure, a chance to see the world, or at least a little more of it than I would see in Warson Woods, Mo. I went in for an interview, filled out reams of paperwork, underwent an extensive background check—performed, no doubt, by the newest, greenest young agent in the St. Louis FBI field office. I was accepted; so was Jerry. A few weeks later, after we had passed our bar exams, we flew out to Washington, D.C. At 9:00 A.M. on July 25, 1966, we reported for duty at FBI headquarters in the Justice Department Building.

There were thirty guys in our New Agents class—literally, thirty guys (there were no female FBI agents at the time) all between the ages of twenty-five and thirty-five, all attired, as ordered, in dark suits and white shirts and dark ties. About three quarters of us were law school graduates. Although the popular conception was that FBI agents had to be lawyers or CPAs, that wasn't necessarily true. You had to have a college degree of some sort—the FBI was the only law enforcement agency in the world that had that requirement—but our class also included some former cops, some former military officers, and civilian Bureau clerical employees who wanted to move up to Special Agent status. Of course, throughout the FBI selection process we'd been told, again and again, that for every one hundred applicants only one was selected for FBI training. So naturally, we all thought we were pretty hot shit.

There was a welcoming speech from an FBI big shot, and they passed out our FBI badges, which were tucked into cheap tan vinyl cases. The gold badges were a little strange. I'd always thought of a law enforcement officer's badge as a big, shiny, heavy thing, but these were tiny, just an inch and a half across. Jerry and I assumed that these were just replicas, sort of junior G-man badges that would be replaced by the real, more substantial thing if and when we completed our training and became bona fide Special Agents. (All FBI agents are called Special Agents.) But no. That was the badge. With the tiny badges in our left hands, we raised our right hands and swore the oath: "I (state your name), do solemnly swear . . ."

After a few more days of orientation and paperwork, they put us on a bus and shipped us south to the Marine base at Quantico, Virginia, for four weeks of firearms and defensive tactics training. For the next three and a half months we would alternate between field training in Quantico and classroom instruction at the Old Post Office Building in Washington, D.C. (In later years, the Quantico facilities would be expanded and all FBI training would be conducted there.)

A lot of the Quantico training was fun, and even exciting. We lived in six-man rooms on the upper floors of the main building, Hochmuth Hall, an old, Colonial-style structure that also contained classrooms, a gym, administrative offices, and a chow hall. (The chow was surprisingly good.) Much of our time was spent on the firing ranges, or in Hogan's Alley, a mock city street with a bar and a bank and a movie theater—named, of course, the Biograph, after the Chicago theater where John Dillinger was shot by FBI agents—where we would practice crime scene investigation and arrest scenarios, sometimes shooting at pop-up targets bearing the images of Dillinger or Machine Gun Kelly or other famous gangsters. I had never shot a gun in my life before I got to the Academy, but I was soon better than proficient with almost every small-arm weapon you could name: Smith & Wesson .38s, Colt .45s, 12-gauge shotguns, .30-caliber carbines, even Thompson submachine guns. I never became a gun fanatic, but hey, there's not a red-blooded boy in America who wouldn't get a visceral thrill from cranking off a drum of .45s from a Thompson.

I also got to meet some admirable FBI men, tough, real-life street agents turned instructors I just naturally looked up to—legendary agents like "Big George" Zeiss and Hank Sloan and Charlie Donnelan.

They and some others like them were the bright lights, the guys who made learning to be an FBI agent interesting, and fun. They went a long way toward making up for the fact that much of the Academy classroom material was boring, and boringly taught by FBI headquarters time-servers who were counting down the days to their pensions.

Sure, I could summon up some interest in fingerprint techniques and investigative and interrogation procedures, and federal law concerning kidnapping and extortion and bank robbery. But it was hard to spend an afternoon listening to some agent-in-name-only drone on about federal laws on the illegal use of a railroad pass, or interstate transportation of defective refrigerators, or any of dozens of other minor violations that the FBI was charged with investigating. And, of course, it would all be on the test.

Yet I knew that would eventually pass. I was still proud to have been selected for the FBI, proud that I was doing well in the Academy. But I was also twenty-five years old, with a law degree—which is a pretty good working definition of a guy who thinks he already knows everything.

And for me there were some troubling things about this organization I was joining.

For one thing, we learned quickly that whatever else it was, whatever its image, the FBI was first and foremost a bureaucracy—it wasn't called a "Bureau" for nothing—and that individualism was not encouraged or held in high esteem, at least not in the upper reaches of the organization. For every conceivable activity, from putting gas in a Bureau car to putting a Bureau bullet in a bad guy, there was a fixed and immutable procedure—with requisite paperwork, in quintuplicate—and you deviated from the procedure only at your peril. Even in class we were required to sit in alphabetical order. Centralized control and absolute uniformity was the goal.

That extended to personal appearance. Dark suits, white shirts, dark ties, and haircuts that harkened back to the 1950s were the order of the day, every day; facial hair of any kind was strictly prohibited, and sideburns were not allowed to extend below the tragus—which, as every FBI agent and ear, nose, and throat specialist knows, is the cartilaginous protuberance situated in front of the meatus of the external ear. In short, any hint of personal flair was not permitted. I found that out early on, when I got tired of wearing a white shirt and decided to wear a pinstriped shirt to class instead. I thought it looked pretty sharp, but the training supervisor disagreed. He yanked me out of class, demanded to know if I was having some kind of a "laundry problem," and strongly suggested that I either get with the white shirt program or get the hell out. So much for the pin-striped shirt.

(The Bureau's insistence on rigid personal appearance standards, no matter what the circumstances, would occasionally create ludicrous situations. For example, in the late 1960s, youthful-looking FBI agents in various cities were assigned to monitor anti-war demonstrations for violations of federal law, such as burning draft cards. The idea was that they would dress up in the fashions of the day—tie-dyes, bell-bottoms, that sort of thing—and meld quietly and anonymously into the crowds. Unfortunately—or fortunately, depending on how you feel about federal agents infiltrating public demonstrations—given the Bureau regulations, they might as well have been wearing FBI windbreakers and had their credentials and badges hanging around their necks. All the bell-bottoms and tie-dyes in the world couldn't make you blend into a 1968 peace and love crowd when your hair was prohibited from venturing so much as an eighth of an inch south of your tragus.)

But the rigidity and uniformity went deeper than surface appearance.

Working for the Bureau, I discovered, wasn't just a job; it was an all-encompassing way of life, an entire culture of its own. Standards of personal behavior were ruthlessly enforced, on duty and off. An FBI Special Agent was expected not to drink coffee or other stimulating beverages on duty, and preferably not at all. If a Special Agent must consume alcohol, he must do so in moderation, and of course never while on Bureau business. A Special Agent must not gamble or accumulate excessive debt. Ideally, a Special Agent would be married and a solid family man; if not, he was expected to be morally upright in his relations with members of the opposite sex. Fornication was not the Bureau Way.

And on and on. A Special Agent was expected to be perfect and above reproach in all things, privately and professionally. Even the smallest infraction, such as being a pound or two overweight on your annual physical exam, could earn you a "letter of censure" that would sit like a festering sore in your personnel jacket and could permanently affect your promotions and pay raises; if your name continued to appear on what was known as the "fat-boy roster," you'd be subject to monthly weigh-ins and further discipline. More serious violations, such as using a Bureau car to pick up your dry cleaning on your lunch hour, or washing down lunch with a beer, could get you fired—or, if you were lucky, earn you a disciplinary transfer to, say, the field office in Butte, Montana, where you could freeze your ass off while pondering the beauty of the world's largest open pit copper mine.

Sometimes you didn't even have to break a rule to get punished; anything that embarrassed the Bureau was enough to ruin you as an agent. If, for example, some car thief with more balls than brains hot-wired your parked and locked Bureau car while you were six blocks away interviewing a crime witness, and if that incident somehow became an amusing little story in the local paper—BOLD CROOK KIDNAPS FBI CAR— well, it may not have been your fault, and maybe there was nothing you could have done to prevent it. But you could still kiss your career goodbye. Or at least kiss Butte, Montana, hello.

I could understand ruthless punishment of actual corruption, no matter how small. And I wasn't a natural rebel by any means—the pinstriped shirt episode notwithstanding. But much of the Bureau culture seemed like petty, mean-spirited bullshit, a culture based on fear. Even in the Academy I could see that the FBI was full of by-the-book bureaucrats who lived in constant mortal terror of making some small misstep that would ruin them; especially at headquarters and at field supervisory levels, fear pervaded the FBI like a shit mist.

Like I said, I was young, single, looking for adventure. I wasn't sure that joining such a rigid, hidebound organization was the right way to find it.

And then one afternoon at the end of our training, the FBI culture went from merely troubling to flat-out weird. That was the day I met, for the first and last time, the man who in the FBI table of organization outranked God: J. Edgar Hoover.

It's difficult for people today to understand just how large the figure of J. Edgar Hoover loomed in those days, not only in the Bureau but in the American consciousness as well. Like every other kid in America, I had grown up on movies and radio shows and newspaper stories about Hoover and his G-men and their battles with gangsters and Nazi saboteurs and Communists lurking in our midst, and like every other kid in America, I had assumed that the tales were true—which in part they were. For entire generations, and by his own careful design, J. Edgar Hoover, he of the bulldog face, the steely eyes, the slicked-back hair, and the sharp-looking suits, was the living embodiment of all that the FBI stood for, a virtual superman in the war against crime and evil.

And you have to give the man his due. In 1924, at age twenty-nine, Hoover had taken over a small, incompetent, corrupt federal agency called the Bureau of Investigation, a governmental afterthought whose three hundred agents weren't allowed to carry guns or even make arrests. Over the next forty years, with boundless energy and by sheer force of will, Hoover had built it into the most famous, prestigious, and incorruptible law enforcement agency in the world, with 7,500 special agents and the most efficient forensic and identification capabilities in existence. If Hoover wasn't a great man, he certainly had done great things.

But the longer he stayed on, the more his power grew—allowing him to defy even presidents if it suited his purposes—and the more isolated and dictatorial he became; eventually he constructed a cult of personality unlike anything ever seen in American government, before or since. He surrounded himself with sycophants, generously rewarding toadyism and savagely punishing anyone inside or outside the Bureau who appeared to threaten his absolute rule. FBI headquarters became a kind of echo chamber, repeating Hoover's words and beliefs back to him without challenge or alteration. While Hoover was alive no FBI press release, no matter how trivial the subject, failed to mention the director's name; usually it was the only name mentioned. In Hoover's mind, he *was* the FBI.

His hypocrisy was legendary: he would fire an agent for using a Bureau car to pick up a kid at school, or taking a free meal "on the arm" from a restaurant owner, but the same rules that he drafted and ruthlessly enforced on his agents didn't apply to the director. He routinely took taxpayer-financed junkets to resorts and race tracks under the guise of "inspection tours," and cheerfully used Bureau personnel to make improvements to his private residence. He dined every working day for more than twenty years at Harvey's Restaurant in Washington, D.C., and not once was presented with a bill. He fulminated publicly and privately against "degenerates" and "perverts," but there were persistent rumors that Hoover and his closest friend and companion, Assistant to the Director Clyde Tolson, had what would later be known as a "don't ask, don't tell" thing going on. (Those rumors were never confirmed, and it could be that Hoover, a lifelong bachelor, was simply asexual; later allegations that Hoover was a flamboyant cross-dresser strike me as so much bullshit.)

In short, Hoover ruled the FBI like a mad king, doling out favors and punishments by whim, sometimes with nothing more than the raise of an eyebrow or the wave of a hand. For an FBI agent, just being in the same room with him could be terrifying. And on this particular afternoon we, the young men of 1966 New Agents Class No. 2, had a particularly dangerous assignment:

We had to shake J. Edgar Hoover's hand.

At the time, the "welcome aboard" handshake from the director was the only form of graduation ceremony that new agents received; no family or friends were permitted to attend. It was perilous, because if for some reason Mr. Hoover didn't think you acted like or, even more important, looked like his concept of an FBI Special Agent, then you would be out—and never mind all the time and money the Bureau had just spent training you. We'd all heard the story about the poor bastard a few training classes before us who in his few brief, terrible moments with the director had somehow managed to make a bad impression.

Afterward Hoover had whispered to the training counselor—a sort of FBI drill instructor who marshaled the class through its training cycle—that the man "looked like a truck driver." And that was the end of him. The fledgling agent was booted out before his career even began, and the training counselor got a letter of censure in his file for letting that ugly, truck-driving sonofabitch get through FBI training in the first place.

So the tension level that afternoon was high. We stood in a line—arranged, as always, in alphabetical order—that started in Hoover's outer office, under the stern and faintly disapproving gaze of Hoover's long-time personal secretary, Miss Helen Gandy, and snaked out the door and down the hall. Our training counselor, a jittery, by-the-book, schoolmarmish sort even in the best of times, was a nervous wreck. He kept moving up and down the line like a finishing school headmistress at the debutantes' ball, straightening a tie here, picking off some lint there, and making sure that, as ordered, we'd all brought handkerchiefs, so that before entering the director's office we could wipe off our right hands. Mr. Hoover, we'd been somberly informed, hated sweaty hands; a moist, clammy handshake could get you bounced out of the Bureau even faster than looking like a truck driver.

Finally the door to the inner sanctum opened and in single file we paraded inside. We'd all been thoroughly briefed on what to do: In turn, stride directly and purposefully toward Mr. Hoover, who will be standing near his desk, stopping exactly 24 inches in front of him. While looking directly into his eyes—there was no room in the FBI for shifty-eyed, swivel-headed, nervous-looking Special Agents—extend a dry, freshly wiped right hand in Mr. Hoover's direction. As Mr. Hoover grasps your hand, say in a low, clear voice, "Mr. Hoover, it's an honor to meet you. My name is (insert name here), from (insert hometown here)." Mr. Hoover will say, "Welcome to the FBI," after which he will release your hand and you will exit the office and walk directly out into the hallway.

Do not—repeat, do not—fuck up.

The new agents went in and then moments later came out, most of them looking relieved, a few frightened and unsure whether they'd passed the test. As the line snaked forward, I found myself in what appeared to be a large office, with a polished mahogany desk, the walls covered with photos. I say it appeared that way because I really couldn't see it very well in the dark. The drapes were shut tight against the afternoon sun, and all the lights had been turned down. The only exception was a ceiling-mounted spotlight that shone down on an American flag.

And there, standing next to the flag, on an 8-inch-high portable raised dais, bathed in a bright cone of light, was Yahweh himself.

I don't know what I'd expected. But after all I'd heard about him, seeing J. Edgar Hoover in person was a shock.

The suit was still sharp, with the silk tie knotted just so, and the bulldog face was still instantly recognizable. But Hoover was old, seventy-one, just five years short of his death, and shorter of stature than his public image—hence the raised dais he was standing on, the better to look down on his new subjects. And as my place in line moved closer, I could see that Hoover's face was jowly and deeply lined, dusted with a thick coat of pancake makeup—so much so that he didn't even look human. The truth is that standing in the brilliant spotlight, in that gloomy, darkened office, J. Edgar Hoover looked for all the world like a wax statue of himself at Madame Tussaud's.

It was downright spooky. I mean, what kind of a guy dusts himself with makeup and stands on a box under a spotlight in a darkened room in the middle of the afternoon just to bestow handshakes on some new employees? As far as I knew, not even presidents did that—maybe not even the Pope. And everyone took it so seriously, as if this sort of Hoover-worship was simply the natural order of things.

I felt as if I'd stepped through the looking glass. And I wasn't at all sure I'd be able to thrive on this side of the mirror.

Still, the handshake went exactly as ordered. I wasn't about to throw away the past fourteen weeks in the Academy with any ad-libs; I stuck with the script. Even without pre-wiping, my hand was completely dry.

"Mr. Hoover, it's an honor to meet you. I'm Bill Rehder, from St. Louis, Missouri."

His eyes didn't register anything, positive or negative. They seemed to look right through me.

"Welcome to the FBI."

And that was that. I had passed the final, unofficial test. I had shaken hands with the waxlike figure of God while managing not to look like a truck driver or sweat all over His palm.

I was a Special Agent of the FBI.

Now I was in Cleveland, making $8,000 a year—less than I could have been making as a lawyer—and spending my days trying to find out if guys angling for a job as meat inspectors with the U.S. Department of Agriculture had ever disloyally remained seated during the playing of "The Star-Spangled Banner."

Cleveland hadn't been my first choice, or my any choice. Bureau policy was to send new agents to a second-tier field office—in other words, not New York, L.A., or Washington, D.C.—for one year, and whatever hopes and desires the new agent might have had, had no bearing on the issue. They had needed a fresh young body in the Cleveland field office, which covered all of northern Ohio, so Cleveland was where I went.

True, life in the field office was a little looser than at the Academy or at FBI headquarters in Washington. No, you couldn't have a Mr. Coffee in the office, but you could swill down all you wanted at the coffee shop down the street as long as you didn't let the SAC (Special Agent in Charge, the top man in the field office) see you. And you didn't necessarily have to wear a white shirt—although if Mr. Hoover or the inspectors from headquarters came out for a field inspection, the white shirts had to come back on. Best of all, the field agents themselves seemed like good guys, serious street agents, not at all like so many of the nervous, by-the-book bureaucrats and paper-pushers who seemed to gravitate to FBI headquarters.

But after a couple of weeks it still wasn't very exciting. I had an "honor commitment" to stay with the Bureau for at least three years after graduating from the Academy, but I doubted it would go much beyond that. (For my friend Jerry McNeive, it didn't; he left the Bureau after three years and went on to a successful career as a corporate attorney.) I figured that eventually I would go back to St. Louis and unbreak my dear old mother's heart by settling down and becoming a lawyer.

Then I got the Call.

"Hey, Rehder!"

It was Irv Foley, a young Special Agent with a year or two on the job.

"We got a bank robbery in the Hough. The SAC wants you to help us work it."

It's funny what destiny can look like. You always think it's going to be something grand and awe-inspiring, a thundering voice from heaven, a light on the road to Damascus. Maybe sometimes it is.

But sometimes destiny can assume the miserable, forlorn shape of a bank-robbing shitbird named Smitty.

✦ ✦ ✦

By the time Irv and I got there, the scene of Smitty's big mistake looked like a car lot for beat-to-shit four-door Dodge sedans with whip antennas and puke-beige paint jobs—which is to say, Bureau cars. Including us, there were eight FBI agents on the scene, plus a couple of Cleveland city police detectives and assorted Cleveland P.D. patrol units. It was a massive show of federal force for a $4,000 bank holdup; it was also standard operating procedure. Because in 1966, the FBI looked at bank robbery, any bank robbery, as virtually a personal affront, an insult to the power and majesty of the U.S. government in general, and the Federal Bureau of Investigation in particular.

Which wasn't surprising. After all, J. Edgar Hoover's fledgling FBI had made its bones on bank robbers in the 1930s: John Dillinger, Baby-Face Nelson, Alvin Karpis—the last of whom was personally arrested by Hoover, in a carefully staged production, after a congressman had publicly ridiculed the director for never having arrested anyone himself. In a sense it was Dillinger and his fellow bank robbers who had created the FBI, and ever since then the capture of—or, better yet, the killing of—bank bandits by his Special Agents had never failed to give Director Hoover a case of the warm fuzzies.

A shooting in Cleveland at about this same time illustrates the attitude. Two agents were staking out an apartment building in a poor, white, working-class neighborhood where a suspected armed bank robber was holed up. They had called for backup before going in, but before the backup arrived, the guy comes strolling out of the building and down the front steps, not a care in the world. He turns left on the sidewalk and then suddenly, up ahead, he sees the Special Agent—or rather, he sees a guy in a suit and tie, which in that neighborhood could only mean either a detective or a G-man.

So the robber does a one-eighty and starts running the other way, but then up ahead he sees another guy in a suit and tie—that is, the other half of the stakeout duo, Special Agent Jerry Davis, a former parole officer who was one of the few African Americans to break the FBI's long-standing, Hoover-imposed color barrier. (There were some political battles that, thankfully, even Hoover couldn't win.) Jerry draws his Bureau-issue Smith & Wesson Model 10 .38-caliber and yells at the guy to stop, but the guy apparently decides that he just doesn't want to go to jail that day. He draws his own piece from under his jacket and starts bringing it up. So Jerry, standing there in an Academy-perfect, two-handed combat stance, lets one round go, hitting the bank bandit in the chest.

One bullet, one bandit; if the guy wasn't dead when he hit the sidewalk, he was inexorably on his way. But the kicker is that later, when the 8 by 10 black-and-white autopsy photos came back, the overhead shots at the morgue showed the guy lying on his back on the slab with a neat, perfectly round, 38/100ths-diameter hole directly over his heart; if he'd been a Quantico pistol range target, that hole would have been dead center in the 10-ring. And when the Cleveland SAC, Charley Bates, saw that gruesome glossy, he put it in a picture frame and sent it off to FBI headquarters with the inscription: "Dear Director Hoover: This is how we handle bank robbers in Cleveland."

Well, in the later, kinder, gentler FBI, that kind of bloodthirsty stunt probably would have earned the SAC a letter of censure and an order to attend remedial sensitivity-training classes. But Hoover was absolutely delighted with the trophy photo of the dead bank robber lying on the slab—and with the sentiment behind the inscription. From that point on, Bates was a made man in the Bureau. (Charley later went on to become SAC in San Francisco, and personally headed the massive Patty Hearst kidnapping investigation.)

So, no, it wasn't surprising that eight FBI agents rolled out for a bank robbery in the Hough District. That was how we handled bank robbers in Cleveland.

Irv had filled me in on the way over. As junior members of the team, and the last agents to arrive at the scene—the other agents had gotten the call over their Bureau car radios—we most likely would be assigned to do the quadrant searches, that is, the door-to-door search for potential witnesses and evidence. Meanwhile, the other agents would interview the victim teller and other employees in the bank. If we were lucky, during our man-on-the-street interviews we might find somebody who'd seen the bandit running away; if not, we'd still build up paper for the case file by taking down the names and addresses of every single person we interviewed, whether they'd seen anything or not.

Paper was important. If the investigation went south on us, and somehow the bandit got away, a nice, fat case file was career insurance, its very bulk demonstrating to headquarters that the Cleveland field office of the FBI and its dedicated Special Agents had left no stone unturned in their relentless search for the perpetrator. Or, in the more likely event that we caught the guy, a thick case file would make a solid, satisfying *thump* when it landed on the desk of the prosecuting Assistant U.S. Attorney, reassuring him that the evidence against the defendant was stacked up eight ways from Sunday, and also providing a useful prop with which to intimidate any eager young defense attorney or federal public defender who might entertain thoughts of actually taking this miserable loser to trial. Either way, the fatter and longer the file, the better off we were. We even had a saying for it: "In length is strength." So pile it on.

I didn't mind. If it was paperwork, at least it was paperwork in the field, not behind a desk. Irv and I got out of the Bureau car and went inside the bank.

The victim teller, the one who'd actually been accosted by the bandit, was sitting in a threadbare upholstered chair by the manager's desk, waiting to be interviewed. Sometimes victim tellers would tremble and cry as they recounted what happened, but this gal was tough; she looked more angry than scared. Toward the back, the dozen other bank employees and a half dozen customers who'd been in the bank during the holdup stood in little clusters, talking in low voices and also waiting to be interviewed. It would turn out that none of them had really seen anything; they didn't even know the robbery had taken place until the guy was already out the door. As bank robberies go, this had been a relatively low-stress affair: no pistol-whippings, no shots fired, no "On the floor, motherfuckers!", no hurried pawing and sexual assault of a female employee (yes, it happens).

Still, most of the witnesses had the shaky, disbelieving look of someone who's just been narrowly missed by a speeding car in a crosswalk. A man with a gun had just robbed the bank; their thoughts were on what might have been.

Special Agent Bernie Thompson, a former military officer with a Kentucky hill country drawl that the Academy hadn't erased, was the case agent and had been first on the scene; he drew the other agents around him for their assignments. There was Bill Fallon, a tall, crisp-

looking veteran agent who later would become an SAC, and Everett
Hayworth, a beefy, middle-aged veteran agent from the old school—and
the only FBI agent I ever knew who routinely carried a switchblade
knife and a sap to supplement, if necessary, his .38. (A few years earlier,
two brain-dead punks had tried to mug Ev on his way to work, not realizing that he was an FBI agent, and Ev had pulled out that sap—an 8-
inch stiff leather bludgeon filled with lead shot—and beat the living shit
out of both of them.) Several other agents also were there, and Irv of
course. And me.

It played out the way Irv predicted. The veterans would interview the
bank employees, and watch over the local police crime scene technician
who would dust the counter for latent prints. Bernie Thompson wanted
Irv and me to do the quadrant searches. We had a rough description of
the suspect: Black male, twenty-five to thirty-five, average height,
weight, black jacket, no distinguishing facial characteristics. Our job
was to look for anybody who might have seen the guy, and, if we picked
up anything hot—"Oh yeah, I saw a guy with a gun and a fistful of bills
run right into that apartment building over there"—to hightail it back
to the bank to get the others. Bernie didn't want any hotdogging on our
parts.

(We didn't realize it at the time, but a local TV station had picked up
the news of the bank robbery off their police scanner and had sent a film
crew, this being an era when the TV news guys could still muster some
enthusiasm for a bank robbery. The camera crew was filming through
the bank window, and caught Irv and me standing there as Bernie was
pointing us to our assignment areas with a classic "He went thataway!"
pose. The guys I roomed with, none of whom were in law enforcement,
saw it on the news that night. Hey, Rehder's on TV! They thought it was
pretty cool—and, secretly, so did I.)

So we headed out. The bandit was last seen leaving the bank and
running south on 105th Street, so Irv, the senior man, took the southeast and southwest quadrants, which were more likely to produce a witness. I headed north on 105th Street, straight into the teeth of a cold,
soot-filled wind blowing in off Lake Erie. I'd only taken a few steps
when suddenly it struck me that this wasn't an exercise in Hogan's Alley
at the Academy. This was the real thing—and it was a million miles
away from anything I'd ever known in the white-bread suburbs of St.
Louis.

In any American urban center, no matter what its racial or ethnic makeup, there are good, decent, hardworking families—and the cop who forgets or denies that is doomed to inflict a world of misery on the people he deals with and also, ultimately, on himself. But the Hough District was also home to every social pathology on the inner-city menu: crime, drugs, prostitution, poverty, overcrowding, neglect, despair. Ten years earlier it had been a lower-middle-class white enclave, until a much-touted urban renewal project to the southwest—black community leaders bitterly referred to it as a "Negro removal project"—had uprooted a long-established African-American neighborhood and sent its former residents fleeing like refugees into the Hough District. The ensuing "white flight" from the Hough had left most of the rental units and small businesses in the hands of white owners, usually absentee, serving a populace that was 90 percent African-American and almost 100 percent poor. It was a volatile situation—literally. Just six months earlier, the Hough had erupted into riots and arson and looting when a white bar owner refused to sell a black man a drink, and by the time it was over, four days later, four people were dead—all black—the National Guard was patrolling the streets, and scores of buildings were smoldering, hollowed-out ruins.

Now the fires were long out and the Guard long gone, but the wounds and the anger remained, on buildings and people: plywood, not glass, covered many of the remaining storefronts, burned-out buildings lined the streets like missing teeth, and angry young black men on the street still delivered up an instinctive eye-fucking to anyone who looked like the Man—even if the Man happened to a be a skinny, eager, but still somewhat uncertain young white boy on his first real day on the job.

The immediate task was simple enough: Interview every storeowner, knock on every door, buttonhole every passerby for a radius of several blocks. Identify yourself, flash the creds—the wallet-style credentials holder with your FBI ID card and the small gold badge—state the nature of your business, have your notebook poised for action. Build paper.

"I'm Special Agent Bill Rehder, FBI. I'm investigating a bank robbery that occurred down the street about an hour ago. I'd like to ask a few questions. Did you notice anything out of the ordinary? Someone running? A car traveling at a high rate of speed? Man with a gun? Anything unusual at all? No? Thank you for your time. Can I get your name and address for my report? Strictly routine."

Reactions varied: There was the owner of the mom-and-pop liquor store who went visibly pale the instant I flashed my creds, figuring I'm with alcoholic beverage control or the state sales tax boys, here to find out why he's not sending in his 4 percent for the governor. There was the blowsy, henna-haired middle-aged woman wearing a dirty slip and a tattoo on her arm—bless my soul, I'd never seen a woman with a tattoo before—who answered the door at the rattrap apartment building, looked my fine young form up and down, and told me, no, she didn't see anything, but would I like to come in for a drink? ("No, thank you, ma'am, I'm on duty.") There was the wino warming himself over the toxic black smoke of a garbage fire in a roofless, riot-burned brick building who laughed out loud when, following procedure, I asked him for his address and phone number, and who looked at me like I must be the dumbest slack-jawed cracker who ever came down from the hills.

There was the elderly white woman, an embittered straggler in the "white flight" from the Hough District, who said she wasn't at all surprised that a bank would be robbed, what with all of "them" moving into the neighborhood—and why isn't Mr. J. Edgar Hoover doing something about that? There was the hard-eyed, older black man in the black jacket (I wonder, could this be the suspect?) who told me, I ain't seen shit, and I wouldn't tell you if I had, and what the fuck you need my name for, I ain't done nothing—and even I could figure out that he wasn't our guy; a real bandit would have been more cooperative. And then there were the young boys lobbing around a basketball who stared wide-eyed at the FBI badge and the credentials, then stared at my innocent-looking mug and rendered their ego-deflating judgment: "Aw man, you ain't no Big Law."

And so on. Finally, after a couple of hours, I headed back to the bank. No one I'd spoken with had seen a thing—or, if they had, they hadn't seen fit to confide it to a Special Agent of the FBI. But at least I had accomplished part of my assigned mission: I had upward of thirty names and addresses for file-padding purposes. And I had learned something about how to talk to real people on the real street.

Irv hadn't picked up much, either, except for one citizen who saw a strange man in a black jacket running down the sidewalk three blocks away from the bank—which was good news, because it meant the bandit probably didn't have a getaway car, which meant that he probably lived somewhere in the general vicinity, which meant that as soon as the bank surveillance photos came back we could start flashing the photo over an expanded search area. All of which meant we had a good shot at catching this guy.

But the news was actually even better than that. Because ten blocks away, our bank robber's luck had taken a serious turn for the worse.

A Cleveland P.D. uniformed cop had heard the bank robbery call and the suspect description over the radio, and even though it was outside his patrol area, there's not a cop alive who doesn't want to catch a bank robber if given the chance. So when he sees a small-time pusher and occasional snitch that he knows walking down the sidewalk with a black jacket on, he figures, Hey, it's a long shot, but what the hell. The cop jacks him up, pats him down, and after finding no gun and no money, starts asking him about a bank robbery. Amazingly, the guy allows as how he didn't do no bank robbery, but he just might know who did.

Oh really? Tell me about it.

Well, it just so happens that the small-time pusher was hanging near the corner of 105th and Superior when he sees this guy come out of the bank there and start booking down the street like his behind was on fire. Then a couple minutes later, the cop cars and the G-men sedans come screaming up to the bank, so he knows some kind of shit must have gone down. None of his business, of course, and he's not about to walk up to a bunch of strange cops and starts flapping his lips. But the thing is, he knows the running guy, knows his street name anyway, and since he and Officer Friendly here have what you might call a working relationship, he might just be willing to give that name up.

And without anybody having to say anything more, the deal is done. In return for the name, assuming it checks out, the hype gets one Get-Out-Of-Jail-Free card, good for his next beef, provided his next beef isn't anything really serious. The snitch does the classic, shifty-eyed, left-right-left snitch glance, then leans forward and whispers, so no one else can hear—

"They call him Smitty."

Smitty. The uniform calls in that tidbit to the precinct detectives, and sure enough, one of them knows a player named Smitty; he'd arrested him half a dozen times over the years. Last he heard, he was in the joint.

But when they run his name, they find out that he's on parole, and that he somehow forgot to show up for his subsequent weekly appointments with his parole officer after he peed dirty on a drug test. Which means there's already an arrest warrant out on him for parole violations.

So the local detectives yank his mug shot and bring it down to the bank, holding it up like a gift and naturally taking the opportunity to bust our balls: Here's your bank robbery suspect, Mr. G-man. Always glad to solve your cases for you, Mr. G-man. Don't forget to mention us at your fucking press conference, Mr. G-man. That sort of thing.

It was the usual hard-edged banter between the local cops and the feds, sharpened by the fact that underneath the trash talk lurked some bona fide resentment. It was understandable. FBI agents made more money than local detectives, worked far fewer cases, and, let's face it, enjoyed greater public prestige. Sure, street agents and street cops could work together and respect each other; but too often the FBI brass tended to bigfoot the locals, using the local cops' greater manpower resources and knowledge of the street to catch or identify suspects—as they'd just done with Smitty—and then failing to give them more than a passing nod, if that, when handing out the attaboys. No law enforcement agency in America had a greater love for self-congratulatory press conferences, and less institutional inclination to share the credit, than the Federal Bureau of Investigation. It pissed the local cops off.

But a suspect was a suspect, no matter who came up with him. And we were happy to have one; it was worth a little ball-busting.

Still, we had to have a little more than just an accusing finger from an anonymous street snitch before we started beating the bushes for the aforementioned Smitty. So Bernie Thompson and one of the local detectives went back to the station and put together a six-pack photo array—that is, Smitty's photo mixed in with booking mug shot photos of five other guys—to show to the victim teller to see if she could pick out our suspect from the bunch. A six-pack was like a lineup, except with photos, and putting together a good one was important. You didn't want to use five guys that looked too much like the suspect, because it would confuse the witness; it would be like asking her which one of the Dionne quintuplets had robbed the bank.

On the other hand, if the suspect was, say, a young black guy with a mustache and a knife scar from his chin to his eyebrow, you couldn't surround his mug shot with pictures of a white priest and an old nun and the kid who played Timmy on *Lassie*. If the case ever went to trial, the photo array would be part of the evidence, and if you made it too obvious that you'd salted the thing, a defense attorney would start cranking out motions to suppress that evidence and all the subsequent fruits of the poisonous tree—which if granted would leave your case lying beaten and strangled and dead on the courtroom floor.

As it turned out, that wasn't a problem in this case. The victim teller had already gone home, but when Bernie went over to her house and showed her the six-pack of six black males of similar physical characteristics, she focused on Smitty like a laser beam.

"That's him." You're sure? "Yep. That's him all right."

Bingo. We had a name and a positive witness ID. Now it was just a case of running this guy to ground.

"Think we'll get him?" I asked Ev Hayworth. In my youthful enthusiasm I had forgotten that my role as a fresh-caught kid from the Academy was to listen, and learn, and shut the fuck up. I wasn't supposed to make stupid small talk with veteran agents who'd been chasing bank robbers when I was still scratching my butt in elementary school. But Ev was feeling charitable.

"Sure," he said. "If not this time, then the next time, or the time after that."

Next time? How do you know there'll be a next time?

Ev gave me one of those eye-rolling, long-suffering, "What-in-the-name-of-Jesus-F.-Christ-are-they-teachings-these-guys-in the-Academy?" looks.

"Hey, kid, nobody robs just one bank. You do it once and you're gonna keep robbing banks until you're caught or killed. Even if we catch you the first time, when you get out of the joint you're gonna rob another one sooner or later. It's like an addiction, see? Look, you spend forty-five seconds in a bank and what do you get? A thousand, two thousand, maybe even fifty thousand if you've got the stones and you know what you're doing. It's more money than any of these shitheels has ever seen at one time in his whole miserable fucking life. And when he pisses that money away, what's he gonna do then? Get a job? Bust his ass to pull down ninety fucking cents an hour, before taxes? Shit no. He's gonna rob another fucking bank is what he's gonna do. Nobody robs just one."

Oh. Right.

The fact that our guy was on parole made looking for him a whole lot easier. It was now well past closing time, but the night duty officer at the parole and probation office just happened to be Smitty's P.O. He was surprised when we called, not by the news that one of his boys had gone seriously south on him—to be a parole officer is to live a life fraught with professional failure—but by the fact that Smitty was now suspected of being an armed bank robber. Frankly, the P.O. hadn't thought he had the guts.

Nevertheless, he cheerfully opened up the contents of Smitty's file. No, the P.O. said, he probably wasn't at his residence of record, which was his mother's house. When Smitty stopped making his required appointments, the P.O. had gone looking for him, and Mom had convincingly explained that she had no idea where her beamish boy was, and, truth be told, she didn't want to know. But the P.O. provided us with a long list of prior addresses and known associates: relatives, friends, a girlfriend or two.

You'll find him, the P.O. assured us; the knucklehead doesn't have enough sense to run very far.

We split up, two agents to a car, plus a couple of local detectives, and started running down the list of addresses.

Of course, we couldn't just go up to his sister's house or his girlfriend's house and kick the door. We had an arrest warrant on Smitty for the parole violation, but not search warrants for the various addresses; without probable cause to believe the fugitive was inside, we couldn't force our way in. And with an armed suspect you didn't want to ring the doorbell and say, "Is Smitty at home?"—because Smitty might very well indeed be home, and decide to answer the doorbell with a bullet. So the drill was to knock on the doors near the target address first.

Knock, knock. "FBI, ma'am. We're looking for this man (show the mug shot). We're told he used to live next door. Seen him lately? No, ma'am, there's no danger. We'd just like to talk to him. Has he been around?"

If nobody had seen him, we figured it was safe to knock on the target door and ask some questions. Time after time we got some variation of this:

Cousin Smitty? Naw, man, I ain't seen him. Yeah, he used to hang here, but that was years ago, before he went to Mansfield. Last I heard he was staying over at his sister's house, but I don't know about now. Tell you what, though, I hope you do catch his sorry ass. Last time he was here, that sonofabitch stole my television set!

Then it'd be the same story at the sister's house, and at the other cousin's apartment, and at the half brother's house. He ain't here, try there, and then he wouldn't be there, either.

Our man was an urban will-o'-the-wisp.

Then, at about 2:00 A.M., we finally found the one person who possessed both a knowledge of Smitty's whereabouts and the inclination to share it. Which is to say, we found Smitty's soon-to-be ex-girlfriend, who was working the late shift as a barmaid in a toilet-bowl blind pig bar so dark and vile and lacking in ambition that it didn't even have a sign out front. And she was willing—no, eager!—to talk.

Over the years I would always wonder why criminals weren't nicer to the women in their lives—and, as a law enforcement officer, I would thank God that they weren't. Because seven, maybe eight times out of ten it would be the long-suffering wife or girlfriend, the person who knew best the bad guy's habits and movements and methods, who would give him up. The women were the bad guys' weakest link—and who could blame the women for it? It wasn't as if they had expected all that much from their men, and yet the men had inevitably failed to live up to even the most modest female expectations, leaving their significant others with festering grievances: He put his hand to me. He took my money. He slept with that whore. So when the cops came calling, they'd be ready to even up the accounts.

With Smitty's girlfriend, an angry young woman with a growing heroin habit, it was a money issue. Just two days earlier she had trustingly delivered unto her erstwhile boyfriend some of her hard-earned cash to score some junk for the both of them, and naturally she hadn't seen him since. She was tired of this shit.

You say he robbed a bank? Well, why'd he take my money if he was gonna rob a goddam bank? He musta fired up all my money and then went to the bank to get more. That motherfucker. Go ahead, lock him up. Serve him right. Yeah, you damn right I know where he is. He's got himself a crib in an apartment house over on 85th Street, north of Hough Avenue. No, I don't know no address. But you can find it. It's halfway up the block, next to a burned-out building, with a red door on the front. Second floor, I think. Maybe the third. I can't remember.

Oh, and mister? When you catch him, can you make him give me my money back?

Sure, lady. We'll let you know.

The girlfriend was right. The red-doored apartment house was easy to spot, especially since it was one of the few buildings on the block that hadn't been charred in the riots. It was one of those once grand city row homes that a decade earlier had been carved up into a warren of tiny apartments and hadn't seen an honest building inspector since, a four-story pile of chipping masonry and odd-angled window sashes with garbage scattered over the sideway—garbage that rustled and squished beneath my carefully polished shoes when Bernie Thompson sent me around to check out the back. There was a fire escape on the far end that looked like it could barely support its own weight, but otherwise there was no rear exit. All the ground-floor windows had been boarded up.

Smitty was there, all right. While I was out back, the front door opened and the building super came out on an early morning garbage run, carrying a couple of sacks out to the cans on the sidewalk—although with all the garbage surrounding the building, you wondered why he bothered to make the trip. Bernie buttonholes the guy—it must have scared the hell out of him, seeing a strange white man in a suit come looming up out of the darkness at five o'clock in the morning—and finds out that, yeah, Smitty lives there. He's in No. 304, and yeah, he's pretty sure he's there now; he saw him come in late this afternoon, and he hadn't left. He heard him banging around up there just a few hours ago. And no, he, the super, won't say anything to anybody; none of his business. Besides, he'd just as soon have him out of there. He's an asshole, and always slow to pay.

It took a while to get everybody together: Five FBI agents (three of the Special Agents who'd been at the bank had peeled off early on because they had fugitive warrants to serve this morning), two city detectives, and a city uniformed officer to watch the back alley in case Smitty dove through an upper-story window or ran down the hall to the fire escape and then collapsed in a heap of twisted, sub-code iron. We also called in a parole officer, mostly for legal reasons. The outstanding arrest warrant on Smitty gave us the right, incident to the arrest, to search him and everything within his immediate reach; it was known as the "wingspan rule." But having a parole officer on hand would let us search the entire apartment without going through the hassle of getting another search warrant for the premises, because a parolee is, legally, still in the custody of the state, and therefore doesn't enjoy the usual protections on search and seizure. A P.O. can search a parolee or his place of residence any time he damn well feels like it, and the fruits of that search are admissible in court.

So we waited in our Bureau cars with the engines running and the heaters on, drinking bad take-out coffee from paper cups and wondering which was worse for our health, the coffee or the carbon monoxide seeping up from the battered and leaking exhaust systems. We were all tired, of course—we'd all been up since yesterday morning—and dirty; the industrial carbon that was one of the basic components of Cleveland air had worked its way into our skin and our clothes, turning the whitest FBI shirt an ashen shade of gray. But the veteran agents seemed content. This case was going to go down.

Dawn rolled in as it always did in Cleveland, not with rosy streaks and brilliant shafts of light but with gradually increasing resolutions of gray. Finally at about 6:00 A.M. everyone was in place. We piled out of the cars and after a last-minute consultation on the sidewalk we filed through the red front door, drew our guns, and started up the stairs.

Bernie and the other veteran agents took the lead, with me and the parole officer bringing up the rear. The stairwell was dark, with empty light sockets dangling uselessly overhead at each landing, and it reeked of rot and piss and hotplate cooking. We were trying to be quiet, obviously, but the tired stairs groaned under the weight of eight men, and the thumps of our street shoes echoed up the stairwell. Surely everyone in the building heard the sound, Smitty included, and knew what it meant. We must have sounded like a platoon of God's own avenging angels, come to call.

At the third floor we moved down the hall to 304, half of us on one side of the door, half on the other. Bernie stood closest to the door, leaning in front of it with his ear close, listening. He heard some movement inside, faintly, but it was enough; he nodded to the rest of us. Ev and one of the detectives, the two beefiest—and toughest—guys there, positioned themselves across the hall from the door, the better to build up momentum.

Then Bernie reached over and simultaneously smacked the door with a fist and shouted: "FBI! Open up! You're under arrest!"

Scientists will tell you that one of the shortest denominators of time is the nanosecond, or one millionth of a second. But a nanosecond is an eternity compared with the span of time between the moment when an FBI agent does his legally required "knock and announce" at the door of an armed suspect and the moment that door is smashed open by the onrushing shoulders of a couple of sides of beef wearing badges. The last sibilant syllable of "arrest" had barely made it out of Bernie's mouth when Ev and the detective hit that door like human battering rams, shattering the frame and blowing the door inward. Their momentum carried them through the doorway and into the apartment, and Bernie and the rest of us piled in behind.

Pandemonium: shouts; grunts. A desperate, terrified wail. The only light was a sliver of gray that slipped in under the window shade. I was at the back of the pack, with not much to do, and I instinctively brushed my hand next to the door and hit the light switch, turning on the 40-watt bulb overhead. Light rained down on a tiny apartment, just a room really, now packed with eight men and a howling bank robber. An adjacent bathroom had a backed-up toilet that noxiously announced itself, and on the floor and the industrial-green walls, cockroaches were scattering like quail.

Smitty had apparently heard us coming up the stairs; he knew what we were about. And while he might have been able to summon up sufficient guts to put a gun to a liquor store owner's head, or even to do a bank lick, he wasn't a righteous fighter. So he'd done the only thing that, to him, seemed reasonable under the circumstances: He had turned out the light and crawled under the bed, clutching some sort of childish, brain-dead hope that maybe we wouldn't look under there.

And that was how the light from the 40-watter found him: Lying under the Murphy bed with his legs sticking out, an FBI agent pulling on one foot and a cursing detective pulling the other, trying to drag him out while he clung desperately to the frame underneath and moaned, "Oooooh! Oooooooh!"

The man wasn't exactly endearing himself to anybody in the room.

Finally one of the other agents came up with the simplest solution: He lifted the Murphy bed and swung it up and back into the wall, leaving Smitty lying exposed and ridiculous-looking on the floor, wearing nothing but a pair of dirty underpants. Even Smitty had to acknowledge at that point that the jig was pretty much up; he suddenly seemed to relax as the agents swarmed over him, bending his arms behind him and ratcheting their Peerless-brand handcuffs into place, then jerking him to his feet. He was medium height, and rail-thin, with a defeated, the world-won't-stop-kicking-my-ass set to his face; this was no Dillinger, no Machine Gun Kelly, no gun-wielding cutout figure from Hogan's Alley. This was just a run-of-the-mill shitbird who'd made the mistake of robbing a bank.

Smitty stood there quietly, head lolling down, as we tossed the apartment, kicking through the piles of damp mildewed clothes in the closet and carefully poking at the detritus of ancient fast-food orders piled on the small sink. We quickly found the robbery money stashed under the linoleum; some quick riffs indicated that it probably was all there, except for whatever he'd peeled off to score his shit, the remains of which were sitting on a small bed table, along with his works—the hypo and the spoon and the rubber tubing and the blackened matchbooks he'd used to cook the heroin. We found the gun, a cheap .32 revolver, sandwiched under the pillow when we pulled the Murphy bed back down and stripped it.

Smitty didn't react when we found the money, or the gun. He never protested his innocence, or asked us, "How'd you find me?" It was like he was someplace else. But he mustered up some interest when one of the detectives scooped up his shit and tossed it into an evidence bag. That got to him. In all the whole wide miserable world, with all the trouble that was raining down on his unhappy head, it was the only thing that was really important to him, and now it was gone.

Smitty the bank robber started to cry. I actually felt sorry for him. One of the detectives told him to shut the fuck up.

Finally everything was bagged and tagged, and the agents helped Smitty step into a pair of pants and slip his bare feet into some street shoes. They draped a dirty shirt and his black jacket over his shoulders and then frog-walked him out the door and down the stairs to the back of a Bureau car for the ride down to the police lockup.

It was a slam dunk case, which would only be strengthened when the bank surveillance photos came back and showed enough of Smitty's face tucked down behind the stingy-brim hat to make a positive ID. We had the photos, the stolen money found in his apartment (including the bait bills and their recorded serial numbers that proved the cash came from the bank), we had the gun, we had a positive six-pack ID from the victim teller, which later could be backed up by a lineup ID. The only thing that would make this unassailable case even more unassailable would be a confession. And this Smitty was happy to give.

The *Miranda* decision had already come down from the Supreme Court, which meant Smitty had to be advised of his constitutional rights: right to remain silent, right to have an attorney, and so on. But Smitty was a player, with a street degree in arrest and trial procedures. When Bernie laid out all the evidence, Smitty knew it wasn't a question of if he'd do time, but how much time he'd do. So he formally waived his *Miranda* rights, trading away whatever slight future strategic benefit his silence would gain him in return for the small courtesies that cooperation in the interrogation room would bring: some cigarettes, a cup of coffee, a Coke, a promise from an FBI agent that a good word would be put in to the prosecuting Assistant United States Attorney, and to the federal judge.

Besides, he wanted to get it over with. He was already feeling sick, and he knew that soon he'd be feeling a lot sicker.

"Yes, sir, I want to be honest with you," he told Bernie. "I did it. I robbed that bank."

And that was it. The U.S. Attorney's office approved a federal prosecution for violation of Title 18, United States Code, Section 2113(a) and (d)—to wit, armed robbery of a federally insured financial institution. Smitty eventually pleaded guilty and took a ten-year jolt in federal prison.

I never saw him again. He had been the focal point of my existence for just sixteen hours, and the only time we ever breathed the same air was during those short few minutes in his apartment—and even then he'd never really looked at me.

Still, I never forgot him. I guess it's a little like sex. You always remember your first.

Of course, Smitty hadn't been a particularly challenging or worthy adversary. By bank robbery standards, he'd done everything wrong, and in the end he went down with, literally, a whimper and not a bang. And yet, the case had hinted at a world of possibilities. It had demonstrated all the features of a classic bank robbery investigation: quadrant searches, fingerprints, surveillance photos, field interviews, cooperation with local cops, surveillance, hostile entry, arrest, interrogation—and a healthy dose of plain old luck. I learned more about the actual mechanics of bank robbery investigation in those sixteen hours in Cleveland than I'd learned in fourteen weeks of new agent training.

I also learned something about myself, and what I was looking for in my life.

Sure, a lot of what I'd seen in the pursuit of Smitty had been ugly, and sad. No one with a normally functioning heart could descend into that world and not wish that the world and the people in it were different. Maybe I was soft, but I would never get to the point where I was untouched by violence and poverty and human despair.

But there was something else, too, something that came to me at that moment when we were standing in the hall outside Smitty's crib. For me it had been surreal, unbelievable, something that neither the Academy nor anything else I'd ever encountered in my life had prepared me for. There I was, in a piss-stinking hallway in a rotting brownstone in a god-forsaken section of a crumbling American city, with a badge in my pocket and a loaded gun in my hand, ready to burst through a door and arrest—or, if necessary, even shoot—an armed man I'd never even laid eyes on, a man who had stolen money that wasn't even mine. And what I felt was—

Well, there'd been some fear, I suppose, although at the time I would have put a bullet in my head rather than admit it, especially to those now much-admired veteran agents who had seemed so matter-of-fact, so okay-let's-get-this-thing-done cool about the situation. But there was more to it than that. It may be hard for some people to understand, but what I felt in that hallway, that grimy Cleveland version of the road to Damascus, was an overpowering sense of—exhilaration. Even joy.

It was a physical sensation, a heart-pumping, adrenaline-fired rush—I'm a Special Agent of the F-B-by-God-I, and I'm chasing a bank robber!—that was real as the one Smitty got when he plunged a spike into his arm. Suddenly all the bureaucratic bullshit hadn't seemed so onerous, all the doubts had just faded away. I knew I wanted to experience that feeling again. If, as Ev Hayworth had explained to me, robbing banks was an addiction, then for me chasing the guys who robbed banks would become an addiction that was just as powerful.

That was the feeling I had in that hallway. Yes, the feeling told me, this is what you want to do with your life.

And I did.

✦ ✦ ✦

I spent the next three decades chasing bank robbers for the FBI, almost all of it in Los Angeles, my first and last field office assignment after a year in Cleveland. In fact, as far as I can determine, I spent more years chasing bank robbers, and was involved in more bank robbery cases, than any other agent in Bureau history. In time I became known, if you'll pardon the professional immodesty, as America's foremost authority on the bank robbery genre.

As a street agent with the FBI's L.A. Bank Squad, an elite group of Special Agents whose only job was working bank robberies, I responded to the scene of more than 2,000 bank robberies, and participated in more than 250 felony arrests—some of them of the easy, okay-you-got-me variety, some of them the sort of high pucker factor situations where you've got a white-knuckle grip on a Bureau Remington model 870 12-gauge shotgun and you're screaming: "Drop the gun, drop the gun!" On a few occasions, a case ended with a bandit bleeding out his life on a sidewalk. As a street agent I personally sent more than a hundred bank bandits to prison, and testified in numerous trials; not one bank robber that I built a case on ever beat the rap in court. I also joined the field office's Special Weapons and Tactics (SWAT) Team, undergoing rigorous training back at the Academy in Quantico in special assault weapons, rappeling techniques, hostage rescues, and so on.

Later, as the number of bank robberies expanded exponentially, I developed the position of bank robbery coordinator, a kind of profiling job that required me to track serial bank bandits, to study their methods and habits, and try to predict when and where they would hit next. If you robbed a bank in Los Angeles, or almost anywhere else in America, my job was to try to get inside your head, to figure out what your story was. Although most of them never realized it, thousands upon thousands of bank bandits had me looking over their shoulders.

It was a wild life—and in some ways a strange, almost schizophrenic one. My beautiful wife, Gaye, and I lived in a nice house in a nice neigh-borhood in West L.A., and together we had two fine sons, Erik and Michael; it was about as close to *Ozzie and Harriet* as L.A. had to offer. But every morning I would kiss the wife and kids good-bye, put on a gun and a badge, and wade into a netherworld of surveillances and stakeouts, of car chases and shoot-outs, of men and sometimes women who were bold enough or vicious enough or desperate enough or stupid enough to rob a bank. It was interesting, exciting, sometimes dangerous.

And I never got tired of it. Never.

Sure, at times it could be frustrating, even heartbreaking. But none of that could ever fully take the shine off my job, or make me wish that I'd acted on my earlier doubts about a career in the Bureau and become an accountant or a lawyer instead. The day I worked my last big bank robbery case I still felt the same sense of excitement that I'd felt in that crummy hallway outside Smitty's crib in Cleveland a lifetime before:

I'm a Special Agent of the F-B-by-God-I! And I'm chasing a bank robber!

I never lost my fascination with the people I was chasing, either. They came in every size and description: takeover bandits, one-on-one rob-bers, roof and tunnel men, inside jobbers. Many were junkies and career criminals, but others were businessmen or lawyers or doctors or school-teachers or even cops gone bad, ordinary people driven by desperation or a fluke of fate to rob a bank.

There were some that I hated, guys who would put a cap in a bank security guard's head for no reason except the sheer, nasty hell of it, or pistol-whip a crying, terrified teller because she was too scared to move fast enough. There were a few I respected—not admired, never that; they were, after all, thieves—but guys who impressed me with their determination and ingenuity. There were many that I felt sorry for, and there were a few, a very few, who after I got to know them I actually came to like, even as I sent them to prison.

What I learned from them is that every bank robbery is a tale to tell. These are just some of them.

2

EVERYBODY
LIKES EDDIE

The guy robbing the bank in Brentwood didn't look at all like Eddie.

He was old, for one thing, and gaunt, almost cadaverous, his skin graveyard pale and splotched with sores. He was dressed in a black T-shirt and a wool jacket, with long wisps of ginger-colored hair sticking out from under a black knit watch cap, and his dark sunglasses were perched low on his nose. The green eyes that peered over the glasses were heavy-lidded and rheumy-looking, and his hands were badly swollen. Even in the grainy image of a bank surveillance photo, it was pretty obvious that this guy was seriously sick.

It was 2:45 P.M. on April 9, 1999. Carrying a black leather bag on his right shoulder, and casually eating an apple, the robber walked into the California Federal Bank—a narrow, plush-carpeted branch bank tucked in between the jewelry stores and overpriced restaurants that line San Vicente Boulevard—and quietly took a place in the customer service line. He didn't look like the usual sort of customer in this bank, in this kind of upscale neighborhood, but he didn't set off any mental alarm bells in the other people waiting in line or working behind the teller counters. This was, after all, L.A.; he could have been a bum, or he could have been last year's Academy Award–winning director. Or both. No one paid much attention to him.

The guy stood in line for a few moments, waiting his turn. Finally he went up to a young female bank teller at the counter and started chatting about the weather.

"God, it's windy outside," he said, friendly like, as he set the leather bag on the counter. Sure is, the teller agreed. Then the guy stuck his right hand in the half-opened bag and said, calmly, almost soothingly, "Actually, you know what? I have a gun. Please give me your cash."

At first the teller wasn't sure she'd heard him right. Was this guy serious? But then he nudged the leather bag a little, not especially menacingly, but enough to make the point. It was more strange than frightening, but the teller followed the standard drill, the one they'd taught her in orientation: A guy demands the money, you give him the money—and you also hit the button under the counter that sends out a two-eleven silent alarm (2–11 is the California Penal Code section dealing with robbery) and activates the bank surveillance cameras.

That's exactly what the teller did. Thirty seconds later the robber walked out of the bank with $1,004 in cash, leaving behind no fingerprints, no physical evidence, just his image in the surveillance photos.

The next day, the photographs of him landed on my desk in the FBI bank squad offices on the sixteenth floor of the Westwood Federal Building in L.A. I tacked the best one up on the wall, along with all the others.

This guy was no virgin; the Brentwood job was his sixth bank lick in a little over three months. His debut had come on the day after New Year's, when he'd hit a Bank of America in Beverly Hills for $12,884—a truly excellent score for a "one-on-one" robbery, in which one bandit robs one teller, usually without anyone else in the bank even knowing that a robbery is taking place. That had held him for six weeks, then he hit another Beverly Hills bank for $3,460. Two robberies under his belt made him a certified serial bank bandit, and had earned him—or rather, earned his bank surveillance photos—a spot in my rogues' photo gallery, where I kept surveillance photos of all known serial bandits working in L.A. It had also earned him a nickname.

Nicknaming bank robbers, giving them their criminal "monikers," was part of my job. As the FBI's L.A. Bank Squad coordinator, I had to track serial bank bandits, to analyze their methods of operation (known in law enforcement as their "M.O.'s"), to get inside their heads and try to predict when and where they would strike next. Since at any given moment there might be thirty or forty unidentified serial bank robbers pulling jobs in L.A.—"unsubs" in FBI parlance, short for "unknown subjects"—I always gave them nicknames to keep them straight in my head, names based on some memorable aspect of their appearance or M.O.

That guy who always disguised himself by wrapping surgical gauze around his head? I called him the "Mummy Bandit." The one who for some reason always wore one glove during his robberies? He was the "Michael Jackson Bandit." Two professional armed bank robbers who wore wigs and glasses and fake mustaches were the "Marx Brothers"— when we caught them, we found out they actually were brothers—while the guy who wore a skeleton mask was "Dr. Death." A group of particularly violent and brutal robbers were the "Nasty Boys," while their equally violent female counterparts were the "Nasty Girls."

And so on. "Miss Piggy" was short and weighed about 300 pounds; "Large Marge" was tall and weighed about 300 pounds. The "Miss America Bandit" was an exceptionally attractive note bandit; she also turned out to be a former bank teller. A guy who yelled and waved a butcher knife during his robberies was the "Benihana Bandit," like the Japanese restaurant, while the three-man takeover robbery team who dressed up like a biker, a cop, and a hard-hat construction worker naturally were immortalized as the "Village People." The "Chevy Chase Bandit" was a clumsy robber who tripped over a doormat and fell face-down in the bank lobby—he turned out to be an attorney who needed some quick dough—while guys who bore a marked physical resemblance to celebrities and movie stars took on their names: the Robert De Niro Bandit, the Karl Malden Bandit, the Johnny Cash Bandit.

(I never got any complaints from the celebrities, even after some of the names were publicized in the news media. But there was a beef, and the threat of a lawsuit, from the "Clearasil Bandit," a robber with a bad case of acne. He claimed that the nickname had exposed him to ridicule and humiliation from prison guards and inmates after he went to the joint.)

With the battered-looking old guy who had robbed the banks in Beverly Hills and Brentwood, the nickname had come from the usual process. What captured the essence of this guy?

Well, the first two robberies had been in Beverly Hills. And it was clear from the photos that our boy was on the losing end of a drastic downward personal slide; his shabby clothing and diseased appearance told us that much. He was definitely a down-and-outer, and most likely a hype; no one else steals almost $13,000 and runs through it in six weeks without any noticeable upgrade in his apparel. And a few days earlier I had happened to catch a rerun of an old Nick Nolte movie on cable TV.

Got it: the "Down and Out in Beverly Hills Bandit"—or the Down-and-Outer for short.

Now, with the addition of the Brentwood robbery surveillance photo, there were a half dozen bank surveillance pictures of the Down-and-Outer hanging on my wall.

And he was just starting to get annoying.

You might think that a guy who had robbed six banks would be at the top of everybody's Most Wanted list, that squads of FBI agents and SWAT guys would be jacking up suspects and kicking in doors all the way from Simi Valley to San Clemente to run this bandit to ground. But in L.A., at least, you'd be wrong. Because L.A. is the undisputed bank robbery capital of the world—and if you're going to shine as a bank bandit in that arena, you're going to have to do better than a lousy half dozen bank licks.

Consider the numbers. The hard stats go up and down, but year in, year out, over the past thirty or forty years, roughly one in every four bank robberies in America has taken place in the L.A. area. Let me repeat that: Of all the bank robberies in the nation over the past three or four decades, at least 25 percent of them have gone down within commuting distance of the soaring white spire of L.A. City Hall. In some years the L.A. FBI Bank Squad would handle an astonishing 2,600 bank robberies—which works out to some 10 a day, an average of one bank robbery every forty-five minutes between opening time and closing time.

There are various reasons for it. The easy mobility of the freeway culture, the loose state banking regulations that allow a branch bank or a savings and loan or a credit union on nearly every corner—almost 3,500 of them in the L.A. area by the latest count—the laid-back attitudes that discourage banks from installing bullet-resistant Plexiglas bandit barriers or access control doors.

And then of course there's the sheer, almost unimaginable size of the place. From Ventura County in the northwest to Orange County in the southeast, from the mansions of Bel Air and Malibu to the sea of tract homes in Riverside and San Bernardino counties, the L.A. megalopolis sprawls a hundred miles across and sixty miles deep. The L.A. field office covers seven counties, and encompasses hundreds of cities and towns, of which the City of L.A. is the largest. In that geographical area there are over 1,000 miles of freeways, 100,000 named streets, and people by the millions—some 17 million of them at last count, although it's hard to say for sure, because the city keeps spreading, metastasizing, so fast that it's difficult to draw a line where the megalopolis ends and the rest of the world begins.

Obviously, in any human concentration of that magnitude, there's going to be a lot of crime, of all descriptions. And yet, for all the ubiquity of crime in the L.A. megalopolis, with one exception it's never been a leader among major American cities in any particular crime field. Its crimes may sometimes be more sensational, may be more likely to involve movie stars or ex-football legends, but in crimes-per-thousand-residents, Los Angeles never surpassed the murder body count of, say, Detroit or Washington, D.C., never outperformed New York City in muggings and robberies, or outshone Miami in the pervasiveness of the drug trade.

No, only in bank robberies has Los Angeles consistently led the nation and the world. In 1999, when the Down-and-Outer arrived on the scene, there were more than six hundred bank robberies in the city and environs—way down from some previous years' highs, but still about three every business day, most of them the simple "I have a gun, give me the money" type that didn't rate so much as a line in the next day's newspapers. A guy with just six of those under his belt wasn't going to turn any heads in L.A.—especially since in years past we'd had bandits who had done thirty, forty, even fifty bank jobs before their luck ran out. One particularly prolific bank robber in the early 1980s, a guy I had called the "Yankee Bandit," wasn't caught until his sixty-fourth bank lick—an all-time world record.

By those standards, the Down-and-Outer was a stone rookie.

Of course, a bank squad agent and local police still rolled out on every bank robbery, interviewing witnesses and the victim teller, dusting the counter for liftable prints, ideally flashing the surveillance photo, if we had a good one, on the street and at police roll calls. It was all SOP. But it wasn't like the old days in Cleveland, or even the old days in L.A., when three, four, or five bank squad agents would respond to every bank job and work it until the guy was hooked up. In 1999, there were just too many bank robberies, and too few bodies on the bank squad. So unless there was overt violence involved, or an unusually big score, you did what you could and then moved on to the next bank lick.

That was the reality that governed our search for the Down-and-Outer: If you rob one bank and don't hurt anybody, hey, it's L.A., nobody's going to get too excited. Rob three or four or seven and, yeah, we'll be looking for you a little harder, but we aren't going to toss and turn all night worrying about you. Rob twenty and, well, okay, you're starting to piss us off. But we'll still sleep soundly in the certain knowledge that sooner or later, one way or another, you're going to get caught—if not on this bank robbery then the next, or the one after that.

Sure, anyone with the IQ of a sprinklerhead and a minimum supply of luck can rob a bank or two and stand a good chance of getting away with it. But the more you rob—and you're always going to rob more, because like I said, bank robbery is an addiction—the more likely it is that something's going to go wrong. Maybe a patrol unit just happens to be passing in front of the bank as the two-eleven call comes in and they snag you on your way out. Maybe a bystander gets a plate number from your getaway car, which you have unwisely registered in your own name. It could be that a teller will manage to slip an exploding dye pack into the loot and you'll turn into a human smoke bomb on your way to the getaway car, or maybe some eager young cop just thinks you look hinky, so he dreams up some probable cause to jack you up and then starts to wonder how it is that you've got fresh tracks on your arms and no fixed address and $4,000 in crisp strapped bills stuffed down your pants. Or maybe you've made such an obnoxious pain in the ass of yourself that we in the FBI bank squad have finally gotten fed up, and you walk into one of our stakeouts.

It can be anything. But eventually your number's going to come up.

So no, with just six bank licks to his dubious credit, we weren't too worried about the Down-and-Outer. And he probably would have stayed on the far edges of our radar screens, except that he made a mistake that seriously upped the ante:

He 'jacked a car in L.A.

On April 15, a week after the Brentwood bank robbery, the Down-and-Outer approached a young woman who was about to get into a champagne-colored 1990 Mercedes-Benz parked outside an office building on West Pico Boulevard, just outside Beverly Hills. He told her, gosh, he really hated to do it, but he desperately needed her car to take a sick friend to the hospital—that's right, it was a mercy mission. And just in case she remained unmoved and suggested that he take a bus instead, he displayed the butt end of a gun stuck in his waistband. That was the deal closer. She gave up the keys, he got in the car and, still apologizing through the rolled-down window—I'm really, really sorry to have to do this—he drove off. Forty minutes later the stolen Mercedes was spotted leaving the scene of a $3,000 bank score in Malibu.

It was all very civilized, as carjackings go. The guy had promised the young woman that he'd bring the car back, and had even asked her for a phone number where he could reach her to arrange its return. Amazingly—only in L.A.—she actually wrote down her office phone number and gave it to the guy before he drove off in her car. Even more amazingly, a few days later he called and left a message on her answering machine, once again saying he was sorry, and that he was taking good care of the car, but that he was going to need it for a little while longer. She assumed that "a little while longer" probably meant for all eternity, but as she said later, the Mercedes was insured, and the guy had actually been pretty nice about it, all things considered. Sure, he was kind of weird-looking, and he had these sores on his face and arms—she figured he had AIDS—but he had a soft, soothing, laid-back kind of attitude. Truth be told, she felt sorry for him.

Like I said, it was all very civilized. But when we connected the Malibu bank robbery to the Down-and-Outer, and then connected his getaway Mercedes to the carjacking, the Down-and-Outer was in serious trouble. Because while a bank robbery may be just a bank robbery, in L.A. a carjacking is an actual crime.

Ever since the early nineties, when the Bloods and the Crips street gangs had unleashed a reign of carjack terror across the city, dragging scores of people out of their cars at gunpoint, often as not administering a pistol-whipping in the process, and then using the stolen vehicles for drive-by shootings and as getaway cars in bank robberies, the FBI had taken a serious interest in carjackings, especially if a gun was involved. A bank robber who suddenly starts relieving citizens of their vehicles at gunpoint is dramatically ratcheting up the violence potential, for this simple reason: banks won't fight to save their money, but a lot of people in L.A. will fight like wolverines to save their cars, even in the face of a gun. If this carjacking business kept up, somebody could get hurt.

So with the carjacking and the related Malibu bank robbery—his seventh—the Down-and-Outer had moved himself up to the bigs. And I decided it was about time to put this guy's shit on the street.

Over the years I'd always tried to maintain good relations with the local press, particularly the local TV news guys, so they would help me publicize my bandits. One of the best ways to get an ID on a bank bandit was to get his bank surveillance photos into the news media; five seconds on the local TV news, or a photograph on the front page of the local newspaper, was worth ten thousand FBI Wanted posters turning yellow on Post Office walls. Ideally, someone would see the photo and call the FBI and say, "That guy that was on TV? Yeah, I know him. His name is . . ." And once you got a bona fide ID on an unsub serial bank robber, he was almost as good as caught. You could start interviewing his family members and associates, finding where he hung out, setting up stakeouts. You could also file a federal arrest warrant on him, which meant that if he got pulled over for a traffic violation or simply got jacked up by a suspicious cop on the street, a wants-and-warrants check of the computerized National Crime Information Center (NCIC) would kick back his name, and he'd be hooked and booked.

The problem was getting the press to play along—and that was another reason for the catchy nicknames I'd hang on bank bandits. After all, in a media market with a thousand or two thousand bank licks a year, no editor or news director is going to devote precious newsprint or airtime to some anonymous "Unsub No. 91–8976" just because he'd robbed twenty banks over the past six months. On the other hand, if you can give them something with some zing to it, if you can offer up "Dr. Death" or the "Mummy Bandit" or the "Village People," well, that's something they can work with.

But I had to pick my shots; they weren't going to put a bank robber on the news every day, or even every month. So, in addition to the catchy nickname, I also had to be able to give them a nice, sharp surveillance photo, something that wouldn't show up on the living-room Sony as an amorphous, unrecognizable blob. And finally, I had to give them an angle.

(We had some pretty good shots of the Down-and-Outer from the

Brentwood and Beverly Hills jobs, but they weren't the best bank robbery portraits I'd ever seen in my career. That dubious distinction belonged to an ex-con named John Thomas Harvey—known in FBI legend and lore as "The Invisible Man"—who shortly after I first joined the bank squad had hit a bank on Vernon Avenue in South Central L.A. On his way out of the bank, Mr. Harvey had actually seemed to pause and pose for the surveillance camera, staring straight at it and offering up an enigmatic, *Mona Lisa*–like smile; his face also had this noticeable kind of glow to it, a sort of weird, unearthly-looking sheen that made every feature of his face stand out in dramatic relief. The photos that came back were absolute masterpieces of the genre; I couldn't have gotten a better picture of this guy from a professional portrait studio.

But later, when I found Harvey in Men's Central Jail on a drug possession charge, and I sat him down in an interrogation room and laid those beautiful photos in front of him, the man went berserk, screaming over and over, "They lied to me! The motherfuckers lied to me!" Turns out that some of his erstwhile buddies in the joint had told him that if he rubbed mercury oxide on his skin—available in a widely used over-the-counter topical cream for the treatment of crotch lice—the chemicals would cause certain kinds of light beams to bounce off him, thus rendering him invisible to surveillance cameras. I never found out if the shithouse scientists in the joint were just jerking his chain or if they really believed it, but Harvey, bless his ignorant heart, took it as gospel. He had actually thought that a judicious application of crabs cream would let him rob a bank and then walk out like some sort of Claude Rains character, just an empty suit and a floating hat and some invisible hands clutching big wads of money.

After kicking it around a while, I thought I had come up with a sellable angle on the Down-and-Outer. So I started calling the local TV stations.

Hey, Mr. News Director. How's the news biz treatin' you? Wife and kids okay? Look, I got one you might like. It's a bum robbing banks in Beverly Hills. That's right, a bum in Beverly Hills. It's a guy we call the "Down and Out in Beverly Hills Bandit"—yeah, like the Nick Nolte movie. Thanks, it is kind of catchy, isn't it? And yeah, now that you mention it, it just so happens that I do have some really good photos of this pitiful example of societal inequity making an unauthorized armed cash withdrawal amid the Louis Vuitton opulence and Gucci splendor of the 400 block of North Beverly Boulevard.

It was the class conflict angle that appealed. That night, three local stations broadcast surveillance photos of the Down-and-Outer and asked anyone with information on the unknown suspect to contact the FBI.

And pretty soon, dimes starting dropping on the Down and Out in Beverly Hills Bandit.

In every FBI field office in every major city in America there's a night duty agent whose job it is to sit at a desk and answer after-hours calls. It's not a secret number; anyone who can manage to look up "FBI" in the phone book can call up and sound off. So you get a pretty strange stew: guys who know where Jimmy Hoffa is buried; community mental health center walkaways who are getting Martian radio signals through their dentalwork; lonely little old ladies whose children never call and who get scared at 1:00 A.M. It's like a wee-hours radio call-in show, but without benefit of a screener.

But amid the cavalcade of late-night drunks and all-day lunatics there's an occasional nugget of useful information that will be jotted down, typed up, and forwarded to the relevant case agent. The night the Down-and-Outer surveillance photos were broadcast, two tipsters—one anonymous, one not—called the duty agent to offer up a name ID on the Down and Out in Beverly Hills Bandit. The duty agent wrote up the tips and passed the information to FBI Special Agent Andy Chambers, the case agent on the Down-and-Outer robberies.

Shortly thereafter, Andy stopped by my office in the bank robbery squadroom. Andy's a tall, good-looking, always impeccably dressed Virginian, a guy who could model for FBI recruiting posters. He was smiling.

Hey, Bill, I got an ID on the Down-and-Outer. Somebody called it in after the TV news.

Yeah? Beautiful. Who is he?

Andy glanced at his notebook.

Guy named Dodson. D-O-D-S-O-N. First name—

What? No. It can't be.

Not *Eddie* Dodson? I said.

Andy shrugged. He was a veteran agent, but he wasn't on the bank squad back in the early eighties. There was no reason he should have recognized the name.

Could be Eddie, Andy said. First name's Edwin, middle name Chambers. Apparently he did some bank jobs back in the eighties. And get this: until a few months ago he was living up at Jack Nicholson's place in Malibu. He's like some old pal of his.

Andy must have noticed the look on my face.

Hey, you know this guy?

Yeah, I knew him. And I couldn't have been more surprised if Andy had told me that the Down-and-Outer Bandit was J. Edgar Hoover, risen from the dead.

After Andy left, I took the Down-and-Outer surveillance photos off my wall and studied them again. Even though I now knew who he was, his face had changed so much in the fifteen years since I'd last seen him that I still couldn't recognize him. Certainly the sick old junkie in the surveillance photos no longer even marginally resembled the Eddie Dodson I'd known: the charming, sophisticated young-man-about-town who once had been a successful and respected Los Angeles art collector and businessman. The guy who had dated a string of beautiful Hollywood models and actresses and partied with Mick and Bianca and Belushi and Nicholson. The guy whom the wealthy and powerful and glamorous people of Hollywood had happily invited into their homes. And the guy who also had single-handedly robbed more banks than anyone else in the history of the world, in the process prompting one of the most frustrating manhunts of my FBI career.

I wished it wasn't so, for a lot of reasons, not least of which was that it was sad to see a worthy adversary of long ago suddenly brought so low. It was the sort of thing that makes you feel old.

But Andy's ID on the suspect was solid, the facts undeniable.

Eddie Dodson—aka the Yankee Bandit, and now also aka the Down-and-Outer—was back in the bank robbery business.

✦ ✦ ✦

Everybody liked Eddie.

Cops, movie stars, FBI agents, convicts, judges, probation officers, parking valets, lawyers, certainly women of every age and form and configuration—they all liked him. There was just something about the guy, a gentleness that made people want to help him, to protect him, to forgive him his trespasses, which in the eyes of the law would be many. Much later, in letters to a judge, people would describe him this way: "A gentle, charming, intelligent man" . . . "A sweet, sweet person" . . . "One of the kindest, most loving people in the world."

"He was very polished, very well-mannered, very funny," a female friend later told a newspaper reporter. "You couldn't help but like him."

He was born in Shelby, North Carolina, in 1948, the son of an insurance company executive who died when Eddie was a baby. He had left his wife and son relatively well off, though, and Eddie had a happy, small-town Southern childhood. An intelligent, sensitive, even delicate boy, he was extremely close to his mother and grandmother, genteel Southern ladies who taught him appreciation for the arts, for music, for the finer things in life. There was a lot of love in the house. It wasn't exactly your typical breeding ground of crime.

It might have all turned out differently if Eddie hadn't bumped into the 1960s. After high school he enrolled as an art major at the University of North Carolina in Charlotte, grew his hair long, started smoking marijuana—which eventually led to his first brush with the law. A cop stopped him while he was driving to the beach, tossed the car, and found a small amount of weed, which in that time and place was considered a serious crime, a felony in fact, potential chain gang stuff. Rather than take the chance, Eddie skipped bail and hit the road with his girlfriend, living under a phony name, hanging out in New York and Boston and later traveling through Europe. In 1972 he blew into L.A., where he eventually learned from a friend from back home that his lawyer had somehow managed to make the outstanding drug possession charge disappear. The fugitive warrant had been quashed. That's how it was with Eddie; he was one of those guys who always seemed to just float out of trouble, without any effort on his part.

He had a buddy who owned an antique store on Crescent Heights Boulevard in the Melrose District, a neighborhood of funky little cottages on narrow, tree-lined streets, with a commercial section along Melrose Avenue of low-rent, single-story shops, cafés, and small art galleries. It was a place where artists, musicians, struggling actors, and others of the demimonde lived and hung out—hip but not yet trendy. Eddie helped out in the friend's antique store, which specialized in stained glass. It was popular among top interior decorators and the people they served—Warren Beatty would stop by sometimes; Julie Christie, too.

Watching his friend at work, Eddie learned valuable lessons about the beauty of the quadruple markup and the importance of a celebrity clientele. Celebrities made a lot of easy money, they had a lot of time on their hands for shopping, and they didn't particularly care what things cost. And if somebody famous was seen coming into your shop, six dozen other people would want to come in, too, just to breathe the same air as a movie star—and they'd pay the same inflated prices as the stars did. It was crazy, insane, but it worked.

Eventually, Eddie decided to set up his own shop. He leased a storefront in the 7400 block of Melrose and started stocking it with items he'd find at auctions and garage sales, particularly Art Deco–style pieces from the 1920s and 1930s: chandeliers, ceramic objets d'art, etched mirrors yanked out of old L.A. movie palaces, chairs and tables made from the "new materials" of the post–World War I era, aluminum and plastic. He called the place, simply, Dodson's, and although on his city business license the shop was listed as a "second-hand furniture store," Eddie always thought of it as more of an art gallery.

And after a year or so, it actually started to click. He had good stuff, in a cool atmosphere, and soon people were lining up to buy things or sell things, or just to hang out. Some days he'd gross in the five figures, an amazing amount of cash for a low-rent-district storefront that specialized in what a lot of people would consider glorified junk. Meanwhile, the Melrose District was changing from funky-hip to certifiably trendy, with prices to match, and Eddie was riding the wave. Celebrities were becoming a big part of the Melrose scene, and a big part of Eddie's business. Steve Martin, Jack Nicholson, Lily Tomlin, Liberace, Joan Collins, Tony Perkins, John Lennon and Yoko Ono—the stars were rolling through the door.

But Eddie wasn't just some shop-owner, some small businessman; he was part of the celebrity scene. In Hollywood—the concept, not the geographical place—status is everything, but class is unimportant; if he's sufficiently hip, a tradesman can easily rub shoulders socially with the biggest stars in the Hollywood universe. So Eddie the small-town boy turned antiques dealer became part of that select group of hairstylists, decorators, real estate agents, designers, personal trainers, restaurateurs, and other purveyors-to-the-famous who glowed with reflected star power and swam in star money. The general public couldn't have picked them out of a lineup, but they were always at the right parties, ate at the right restaurants, were seen at the right nightclubs. They were known to everybody who mattered.

It was quite a leap for a guy who just a few years earlier had blown into town with dust on his shoes and hair down to his ass and a warrant out for his arrest. Eddie had a beautifully furnished—naturally—town house in upscale Hancock Park, not far from the shop. He wore Italian suits, except when leather was more appropriate, and he drove around town in a restored 1965 Lincoln, black-on-black, with "suicide" rear doors; it was a true land yacht, and one that he later would use as a somewhat incongruous getaway car.

And he always, always had beautiful girlfriends—models, aspiring actresses, sometimes actresses who no longer were just aspiring, including Marisa Berenson, Tony Perkins's sister-in-law, a dark-haired wealthy socialite turned fashion model turned actress who later starred in Stanley Kubrick's *Barry Lyndon*. They were together for about six months. It wasn't that Eddie was particularly handsome, at least not in the movie star sense. He certainly wasn't a big, rugged, macho type. On the contrary, he was slender, even delicate-looking, with soft green eyes and a sensitive, soft-spoken, kind of dreamy personality. But women loved the guy.

In short, Eddie was more than just an antiques dealer, and Dodson's was much more than just a furniture store. In his book *Wired: The Short Life and Fast Times of John Belushi*, *Washington Post* reporter Bob Woodward described how Belushi had once picked up a *Playboy* Playmate of the Month at Hugh Hefner's mansion in Holmby Hills and told her he was taking her to an after-hours party at this furniture store on Melrose, a place called Dodson's. And the Playmate, more or less fresh off the farm, had wondered why anybody would want to go to a party at a furniture store—as if it were a Levitz showroom or something. She didn't understand that Dodson's wasn't a store; it was a hipster salon.

Of course, drugs were a part of it. They were as much a part of the L.A. scene in the late 1970s as too-long sideburns and unprotected sex—with cocaine being the drug of choice, at least among those who could afford to pay a hundred bucks a gram for it. It seems a quaint notion now, but the prevailing attitude at the time was that cocaine was the perfect drug: personally empowering, artistically stimulating, nonviolence-inducing and, oh yes, completely non-addictive. Cocaine use was so open and uninhibited that it hardly even seemed illegal. This was a time when bowls of the stuff were being passed around at parties in Malibu, when celebrities wore tiny coke spoons on gold chains around their necks, when producers and directors were cutting hundred-million-dollar movie deals across desks graced with heaping double rail-road tracks of white powder. Doctors, lawyers, politicians, stars—everybody was doing it.

And for some, the shift from one form of white powder to another white powder didn't seem like any big deal.

Eddie had been using cocaine steadily for years, but he'd never tried any heroin. Although he'd seen it passed around and snorted at parties, usually in a "speedball" combination of heroin and cocaine, it still had a lingering sense of the taboo about it, an aura of spaced-out junkies nodding off in dark alleys and filthy tenement houses. Then one night in 1979 he was at a Rastafarian music club in Hollywood with a friend, a part-time male model and part-time drug dealer, who had a speedball mix: cocaine and China white heroin. Eddie figured, What the hell. He snorted up.

It was a nice feeling, the coke acting as the gas pedal, the heroin the brake. Better yet, there were no thunderclaps, no Greek chorus in the background prophesying doom; there was no clue at all that this would turn out to be a defining moment in his life. The friend and part-time drug dealer even made a little joke about it, using the old stereotypical drug pusher line: "The first one's always free." And they both laughed, because everyone knew that just snorting a little wasn't going to get you strung out.

And it didn't—not immediately, anyway. For a year or so after that, Eddie would be at a party some place and he'd do a little if it was available. It was like a group activity, a tribal practice; you'd do it partly because it felt good, but also because it was the new thing. It set you and your friends apart from the lesser hipsters who still thought coke was the ultimate drug. It was fun. And if from once a month or so it started evolving into every weekend, then during the week, then three nights in a row, well, so what? There were never any needles around—that was still considered low status, and thus taboo—and everybody you were doing it with was young and good-looking and wealthy and successful. So how bad could it be? It wasn't like they were junkies or anything.

But there were signs. Eddie started noticing that if he didn't do any heroin for a while he'd start feeling bad, sick and listless and depressed, and he'd wonder why. It took him the longest time to finally make the connection, to say to himself, Gee, do I maybe have, like, a habit?

No one ever sets out to become a junkie. It's a lot more subtle than that.

Still, Eddie thought he could handle it. He detoxed on his own for a week, a hard week of lying in bed, not working, not eating, thinking he'd have to get better just to die. He managed to stay off it another few weeks after that—which in the long run may have been a bad thing. His thinking now was, Okay, I can do it, I can kick it if I need to. No problem. So I'll just do a little tonight and then no more for, say, a month. Okay, maybe a week. And of course he'd be right back on it, full time.

It would have been bad enough if he'd just kept on doing it in blow form. But then he ratcheted up the stakes. No more China white snorted up the nose. Eddie found a Persian connection.

Beginning in 1979, when the Shah of Iran was toppling and wealthy Iranians were fleeing the mullahs and flooding into L.A., various supply lines opened up for almost completely pure "Persian brown" heroin from Iran. Eddie's connection was an Iranian guy who lived "over the hill" in the San Fernando Valley. Persian brown was sandy-looking in texture and brown in color, and could be cooked and injected, or—the preferred method for people who could afford it—smoked in a process called "chasing the dragon." You put a little of the powder in a metal bowl or piece of tinfoil, then hold a flame under it; the powder starts to liquefy and boil, sending up wisps of sinewy, seductive smoke that you "chase" and inhale with a straw. It gives you an incredible feeling of warmth and happiness, well-being and power. Any Persian brown dragon-chaser would tell you: It was better than the best sex you ever had in your life.

But it wasn't cheap. At the time, Persian brown was retailing for about $700 a gram, which translates to about $20,000 an ounce. A junkie who was "tying off," using a needle, could get by on one or two or three tenths of a gram a day, maybe $25 to $100 worth, depending on the size of the habit. But smoking it was far more wasteful. Pretty soon Eddie was dropping an average of $200 a day, then $300, then $400 or more. However much heroin he had was how much heroin he used—and the more he used the more he had to have.

He tried to kick from time to time. He went to an acupuncturist, a hypnotist, even some Narc-Anon meetings, but treating heroin addiction was way beyond their capabilities. As soon as the sickness started, Eddie couldn't stand it; he had to have some heroin. And as long as he had some, he was able to function more or less normally. Mix in a little cocaine for energy, and some marijuana for appetite, and he could get by, assuming the money lasted.

Which, of course, it didn't.

By the early eighties, the Melrose scene was changing. Punk rock was coming in, and the Melrose District was starting to get crowded with hard-looking kids with purple mohawks, spiked dog collars around their necks, and safety pins in their cheeks. It was the sort of crowd that frightened people who actually had money. And even if the old clientele had come around, they increasingly would have found Dodson's closed for business in the daytime, but open for parties at night. It was still a popular party spot with some of the faster elements of the Hollywood and rock-'n'-roll crowd. John Belushi was there one night just weeks before he died from a "speedball" injection at the Chateau Marmont Hotel in the spring of 1982. But partying wasn't conducive to dragging yourself out of bed in the morning—assuming you had made it to bed at all—and running a business. Parties didn't pay the bills.

"You wondered how he could stay in business with the doors closed all the time," a neighboring shop owner later told a newspaper reporter. The answer was, he couldn't.

So, by the summer of 1983, this was the condition of Eddie Dodson's life: He was thirty-five years old, and he still had a nice town house, nice clothes, nice car, a beautiful girlfriend, and a lot of important, or at least famous, friends. He also had an empty bank account, a failing business, large outstanding debts that he couldn't make good, and a heroin habit that was now pushing $500 a day.

Clearly, something had to be done. He had to get his hands on some money.

Of course, some guys might have tried a little harder to kick, or abandoned the dragon chasing and started using a needle, cutting the heroin bill down to a more manageable $50 or $100 a day. Or they might have sold the Lincoln, or cleaned out the town house, selling those Queen Anne rugs and the J. Robert Scott fabrics. They might have unloaded the Piaget watch before they risked a fifteen-year jolt in federal prison to get some fast cash. Unfortunately, that wasn't Eddie's style.

Eddie can't even remember when the idea first came to him. Most likely it was just one of those fleeting fantasies, something that might creep unbidden into the thoughts of anyone who finds himself in deep financial crisis, some vague, silly notion: "Well, I could always rob a bank."

Most of us would dismiss it out of hand. But Eddie was a junkie who needed to keep the sickness away; there is no stronger incentive to do anything—anything—to fix the problem. And Eddie had that dreamy, romantic streak in him. He saw bank robbers—and this was backed up by generations of Hollywood pop culture—as glamorous types, latter-day Robin Hoods. Jesse James, John Dillinger, Bonnie and Clyde! They made movies about people like that. Never mind that every one of them was a murderer and that they all wound up being shot down like dogs. The fantasy was much more fun.

Besides, if you massaged it around enough, if you looked at it from every rationalizing angle, you could eventually work your way around to the point where robbing a bank hardly even seemed like stealing. It wasn't like grabbing some old lady's purse, or pistol-whipping some Korean liquor store owner and grabbing a couple of twenties and a roll of dimes out of the till. They, the banks, were all just huge corporations; they wouldn't miss the money. And nobody would ever get hurt. Eddie Dodson would never hurt another human being. Hell, he was a vegetarian.

He fantasized about it, and dismissed it, and then fantasized about it again. He even went out and bought himself a gun. Not a real gun, of course. Eddie had never fired a gun, never even held a real gun, but he figured he would need at least a pretend gun to carry out the fantasy. So he bought a cheap little track-and-field-style starter pistol. He didn't bother to buy any blanks for it to make it go bang; that seemed too violent.

He tried to remember everything he knew about bank robbery, things he'd heard about or read about or seen in movies, but it frankly wasn't much. He'd spent a lot of time in banks, depositing the daily store receipts at the commercial teller windows, so he knew a little about how they operated. He had read somewhere that tellers usually just handed over the money, and that there were silent alarm buttons, and cameras that you had to somehow hide your face from, with a hat or a mask or something. Beyond that, he didn't have much of a clue. But that was okay, because it was mostly just a fantasy, a junkie's idea of planning for the future: I can always rob a bank.

But the habit didn't go away, and neither did the fantasy. The day soon came when Eddie was down to his last dime, his credit all dried up, not another dollar to be borrowed or earned. The sickness had to be kept at bay. He had to do it.

That day was July 5, 1983.

He woke up early, as usual—early afternoon, that is—and put on a white shirt, an expensive white shirt, some black slacks, and a pair of Puma running shoes, just in case running became necessary. To hide his face as much as possible, he wore extremely dark sunglasses; wearing sunglasses indoors wouldn't arouse any suspicion in L.A. He put the starter pistol and a New York Yankees baseball cap, his favorite team, inside a soft Italian leather briefcase, checked himself in the mirror, and headed out the door.

There was a bank on Larchmont Avenue, not far from his town house, that he'd passed by many times. He figured it probably was as good as any. Eddie parked the Lincoln around the corner, then walked into the bank and stood in the lobby for a moment, taking it in. It was a typical L.A. branch bank: slightly threadbare carpet, plastic potted plants, a branch manager and a couple of loan officers sitting behind cheap mahogany laminate desks, a few customers waiting resignedly in line beside the imitation velvet ropes for the next available teller. There were of course no bars separating the tellers from the customers—L.A. banks liked to seem "customer friendly"—and no guard, guards being, in the L.A. banking community's opinion, more trouble and expense than they were worth. All Eddie had to do was stand in line, go up to a teller, say the words he'd practiced, and then he'd be out of there with the life-saving cash in hand.

But he couldn't do it. He had to, but he couldn't. He was afraid. He walked over and sat down in a chair next to a plastic ficus tree, his heart pounding, his breathing shallow, trying to get his courage up. This is insane, he thought. I can't do this—but I have to. It was like one of those cartoons where a guy has a little angel on his right shoulder and a little devil on his left shoulder and they're both whispering into his ears: "Do it, don't do it, do it." But the devil carried the bigger stick: "If you don't do it, if you walk out of here without money, in a few hours you're going to wish you were dead."

Finally Eddie stood up and got in the line, trying to go Zen-like, seeing himself from outside his own body, willing himself to be just another customer waiting to make a withdrawal. When his turn came he took a deep breath, walked up to the teller window, smiled, put the briefcase on the counter, unzipped it to show the "gun," and then calmly said the words that would change his life forever:

"You know what? This is a robbery."

✦ ✦ ✦

By the fall of 1983 the Yankee Bandit was driving us crazy.

It wasn't the size of his scores that was so frustrating; he was only averaging a couple of thousand dollars per bank robbery, which was more or less standard for a one-on-one bandit. And it wasn't that he posed any great physical threat; although he showed a gun during his robberies, he never waved it around or pointed it at anyone. On the contrary, he went out of his way to be as non-threatening as possible under the circumstances, speaking to the targeted teller in a soft voice, using the minimum necessary level of coercion—telling her he had a gun and to hand over the money—but never calling her a "bitch" or a "motherfucker" or threatening her with immediate physical harm the way so many bank robbers did. In fact, he was one of that group I called "apology bandits." As a teller handed over the cash, he would often say things like, "I wouldn't do this if I didn't have to," or, "I'm sorry to have to do this." He was always clean and nicely dressed. As bank robbers go, he was a pretty nice guy.

But his numbers were getting seriously out of hand.

He had come out of nowhere on July 5, 1983, walking into a Crocker National Bank in the Larchmont District of L.A. with a zippered leather briefcase, waiting in line for a teller, then putting the briefcase on the counter and demanding cash; a gun was visible inside the briefcase. As he walked away from the counter with $991, he put a New York Yankees baseball cap on his head to help hide his face from the surveillance cameras. He was smiling. He hit again soon thereafter, once again wearing the Yankees cap and the smile. With the second robbery, it was time to put him in the serial bandit pantheon and give him a name.

If I'd known how large this guy was going to loom on our horizon, I probably would have given the name a little more thought, come up with something really special. But we were pretty busy just then—that year we would have a total of 1,800 bank licks in the L.A. area—and I didn't have time to agonize over it. I went with the baseball cap, and dubbed him the "New York Yankees Bandit"—the Yankee for short.

Of course, at first the Yankee was just another face in a very crowded field. But within three months after his first robbery, the Yankee had hit fifteen banks, and his surveillance photos were hanging in a long string on my wall. He was starting to get our attention.

FBI Special Agent Bernard "Biff" Flanigan had been assigned the first Yankee Bandit robbery in July, which meant that all the subsequent Yankee robberies were his, too. Flanigan was—well, take five centuries of Irish cops, then squeeze them into a 200-pound slab of raw corned beef, and pack it into a suit, not necessarily an expensive suit. Then sprinkle the tie with some of last week's spicy beef noodle soup at Hu's Chinese, stick an old-fashioned Smith & Wesson Model 10 .38 revolver in a Bureau belt holster, and crank the bullshit tolerance level down to zero: that was Biff. He was also, hands down, one of the best bank robbery guys we ever had.

But as the Yankee's numbers started going up, with nothing for us to go on and not a clue as to who this guy was, I couldn't help needling Biff a little. I'd sidle over to his desk in the bank squad bull pen, drop the latest Yankee Bandit surveillance photos in front of him, and then lean over and coo in his ear:

Say, uh, Biff? This guy's turning into a pretty accomplished bandit. Think maybe you oughta try to catch him or something?

And Biff would give me one of those "fuck you" looks and say, Shit, I don't even start worrying about them until they get to twenty.

But within a few days after that, even Biff was, by definition, getting worried about the Yankee Bandit.

The Yankee's motive was easy enough to figure out. Like most serial one-on-one bandits, he almost certainly was a drug user; no other category of humanity needs to rob banks with such frequency and consistency. They would steal enough to feed their habit, and when it was gone, they'd steal some more. If they didn't get enough with one robbery, they'd do another the same day. And you could almost always depend on them to keep robbing and robbing and robbing until they got caught; it was what they had to do.

Most of them got caught before their numbers got to be too embarrassing. But the Yankee was having an amazingly good run. By early November, he was up to thirty bank robberies; by the end of that month, forty. And we still had nothing. No getaway car plate, no passing cop, no luck. We didn't have any worthwhile prints, and even if we had, in those pre-computer fingerprint databank days, having a print really didn't help you unless you already had a suspect to match it with. For a political assassination or a particularly gruesome string of serial murders, the boys back at the FBI Identification Division in D.C. might be willing to laboriously examine, by hand, thousands upon thousands of prints on file to possibly find a set with the right configuration of arches or whorls or ulnar loops to make a match with the crime scene prints. But they weren't going to do it for a bank robber. The Yankee would have had to put a slug in the mayor, or better yet, a senator, before prints would have done us much good for identification purposes.

The short form was that we had no idea who this guy was. All we had was a wall full of pictures of a white guy, twenty-five to thirty-five, slim build, with half his face hidden behind sunglasses and a baseball cap—and that smile mocking us.

Then came November 29, 1983—to paraphrase FDR, a date that will live in bank robbery infamy.

At 1:30 P.M. that Friday afternoon, a bandit hit a Bank of America in the Melrose District for $1,740. As usual, the two-eleven call to the bank squad office was fielded by Linda Webster, an FBI civilian communications specialist. (Years later, CBS's *48 Hours* TV newsmagazine would describe me as "the FBI's secret weapon in the war against bank robbers"—thus ensuring a never-ending ration of shit from my pals on the bank squad. But the news guys had it wrong. If there was a secret weapon, Linda was it. She knew as much or more about working bank licks as any Special Agent on the bank squad.)

With every two-eleven call that came in, Linda would contact the bank by phone and confirm that there actually had been a robbery.

(About half of the two-eleven silent alarms turned out to be false alarms, caused by tellers accidentally hitting the buttons, shorts in the electrical system, or whatever.) If it was a bona fide two-eleven, Linda would get a physical description of the bank robber—height, weight, race, clothing, make and model of getaway car, if known—to put out over the Bureau radio to local police and FBI agents in the area.

Then she'd ask a series of questions about the robber or robbers' methods: Did he have a gun? What kind—revolver, semiautomatic, sawed-off shotgun? What words did he say, or write on a demand note, when he announced the robbery? Was he nervous, calm, angry, polite? Did he address the teller as "Miss" or "motherfucker"? Did he put the money in his pockets, a paper bag, an attaché case? Did he hit both teller drawers or just one? Did he tell her not to push the alarm, to step away from the counter, to count to a hundred? If it was a takeover robbery, did the bandits jump the counter, put everyone on the floor? Were there shots fired, customers or employees injured or robbed personally? (Later, I developed my own computer program that would store that kind of data on every bank robbery.)

Every one of those factors was like part of a signature; the overall M.O. of their first bank robbery most likely will be the M.O. on their last bank robbery, and all the ones in between. And after two minutes on the phone with the manager of the Melrose bank, Linda knew exactly who our bandit was.

Bill, she tells me, it's the Yankee.

Thirty minutes later and sixteen blocks due west he hits a City National Bank in the Fairfax District for $2,349. Linda goes through the same drill.

Bill, it's the Yankee again.

Forty-five minutes after that, still heading west, he hits a Security Pacific National Bank in Century City, but when he tells the teller to hand over the cash she gets scared and backs away from the counter, and the Yankee gives it up and runs out. He gets zero on that one, but he walks a block over to Century Park East and hits a First Interstate for $2,505.

Bill, it's the Yankee. Twice. Back to back.

Forty-five minutes later he's four miles west, hitting an Imperial Bank on Wilshire Boulevard in Westwood for $4,190—which is particularly galling, because the Imperial Bank is just six blocks west of the FBI headquarters in Westwood. The cocky bastard probably drove right past my office on his way to the bank.

Believe it or not, Bill, Linda says, it's the Yankee again. He probably waved at us as he went by.

Then the Yankee jumps on the 405 Freeway and heads north, into the San Fernando Valley, where he exits on Ventura Boulevard and hits another First Interstate Bank in Encino for $2,413 before calling it a day at 5:30 P.M.

Four hours. Six banks. It was unheard of. Pulling off two bank robberies in one day was common enough; the Yankee had done that before. Three in a day was less common, but I had certainly seen it in my career. I'd even had one guy who had hit four in a day. But nobody had ever done six in a day. It was a new world's record, still unbroken. It was also insulting as hell. This guy hits a bank, and then another, and he has to know that his description is crackling across every police and FBI radio in the entire city; but he still has the nerve to hit another, and then another and another and another.

For me it was one of those *Butch Cassidy and the Sundance Kid* moments: Who *is* this guy?

The six-in-one-day spree suddenly made the Yankee Bandit the hottest ticket in town. It also convinced the brass to free up the resources for a series of bank stakeouts to try to nab this guy in the act. My job was to try to figure out where he would hit next, and make sure we were waiting for him.

It wasn't going to be easy. There were something like three thousand banks in the L.A. area at the time—almost literally one on every corner—and only twenty-five FBI agents on the bank squad. Obviously, all-day stakeouts on every target would be impossible. But I could narrow it down a little.

Serial bank bandits like the Yankee are creatures of habit. Once they find an M.O. that works, they'll usually stick with it, hitting the same kinds of banks, sometimes even the exact same bank, at roughly the same time of day and generally in the same area, generally wearing the same kinds of clothes and using almost the same exact words every time. I've had bandits who were like baseball players on game day: They wouldn't rob a bank unless they were wearing their lucky socks. And with bank bandits who were hypes, it was pretty easy to predict when they'd hit next: Simply divide the dollars taken by the number of days between robberies and you'd get a pretty good idea of the size of their daily habit, and thus when they would be out of money and have to make another cash withdrawal at a bank.

By that calculation, the Yankee Bandit had a monster habit, upward of $1,000 a day, which put him in a different league from your average hype. The junkie never lived who could fire a thousand bucks a day worth of heroin into his arm without nodding off for all eternity, so I figured the Yankee probably was free-basing cocaine or heroin, which was a lot more wasteful—and expensive—than spiking it. It was also more in keeping with his upscale appearance and educated demeanor. And his habit obviously was growing, because the time between robberies was steadily getting shorter.

Another key part of his M.O. was that he liked banks in the tonier sections of town, in Beverly Hills and West L.A., although occasionally he would roll up to the middle-class San Fernando Valley. On his multiple-robbery days, he would always start at the far eastern edge of his territory, no further east than the Mid-Wilshire District, then move west. He usually robbed in the afternoons, and although he would rob on any business day of the week, he particularly liked Fridays—for obvious reasons. In those days not many banks were open on Saturdays, so he had to lay up enough cash on Friday to nurse his habit through the weekend. And when he had a good score at a bank, he liked to come back a few weeks later and hit it again. The Yankee wasn't shy about re-robbing: for example, he had hit the same First Interstate Bank in L.A.'s Mid-Wilshire District four times in four months.

So I set up a series of rolling stakeouts of twenty banks in West L.A. and the Valley, all of which the Yankee had hit before. Eight teams of FBI agents, joined by LAPD Robbery-Homicide detectives (in L.A. the FBI and the LAPD shared joint jurisdiction on bank robbery cases), would drive around near two or three of the targeted banks, hoping to spot the Yankee going into the bank or catch him on the way out after the two-eleven silent alarm came over the dispatch radio. The surveillance photos hadn't given us much of his face, but they gave us a pretty good idea of his physical shape and style, the way he dressed, the way he moved; we figured there was a good chance we could spot him on the street if our timing was right, and if I had picked the right banks. It was all a question of getting inside the bandit's head.

That was always more art than science. Sometimes the bandits would confound my predictions. But sometimes I could hit the thing squarely on the head. For example, we had a takeover bandit who'd hit sixteen banks on the West Side over the course of a year, a guy I called the "Squaw Man Bandit" because he wore a waist-length wig of silky black hair during his robberies; except for the fact that he was six two, weighed upward of 250 pounds, and had a bushy black mustache, in the wig he looked a lot like Cher. He also spoke English with a heavy foreign accent, which caused him problems on his seventeenth bank lick, when a teller he was trying to rob couldn't understand his directions; she just stood there while he got more and more frustrated. Fortunately, instead of shooting her he ran out of the bank empty-handed.

The two-eleven call came in a few minutes later, and as soon as I heard the description, I knew it was the Squaw Man. Having tracked his robberies for so long, I also had a pretty good idea of what he'd do next. After an earlier aborted robbery he had gone out and successfully hit another bank within an hour, so I figured he would do the same thing this time. Also, all of his robberies had gone down near the West L.A. area, and he tended to hit some banks more than once; if he got a good score at a certain bank, he'd go back and rob it again two or three months later.

With that information, and a little intuition, I pinpointed a First Federal Savings Bank on West Pico as his probable target—and I predicted he would hit it within the hour. So we sent a joint FBI-LAPD Robbery Homicide team to stake it out, and sure enough, our guy walked right into it. He turned out to be a South African criminal fugitive named Johannes Albertus Beukes, who was robbing banks to finance a deep-sea diving business he was trying to set up. Beukes got a long prison sentence with a deportation order at the end of it. And I got a reputation as a bank robbery clairvoyant.

But the Yankee's psychic aura turned out to be harder to read. Day after day that fall, whenever we could spare time from other cases, we would stake out the targeted banks: Flanigan and Powers on the First Interstate in Brentwood, Stewart and Shelby on the First L.A. Bank in Century City, Chavez on the Bank of America in Studio City, me on a

Security Pacific and an First Interstate in the Mid-Wilshire District, and so on.

There was only one problem: Wherever we were was exactly where the Yankee Bandit wasn't. I'd spend hours hassling through bumper-to-bumper traffic in a crap-brown Bureau Chevrolet, checking out people on the sidewalks, eyeballing drivers and passengers in other cars, looking for that now familiar figure. I was itching to spot him coming out of a bank with the briefcase in his hand and the smile on his face, at which point I'd stick my .357 Magnum behind his ear and slam some cuffs around his wrists and watch that smirky little smile fade off into the ether.

It was a pleasant reverie, one that filled many an hour, but at the end of a long day I'd still have nothing—and neither would any of the other guys. Then, of course, the very next day the Yankee would hit one of the banks we'd been watching the day before. Or maybe one day the Yankee would make a good score at a bank we weren't watching, say, $4,000 or $5,000. As soon as we heard about that hit we'd blow off the surveillances, figuring he was done for the next several days—only to have him break pattern and hit one of our targeted banks the same day.

It was maddening. In the bank squad, the Yankee was starting to assume mythical proportions. How could this guy slip by two dozen FBI agents and police detectives? It was unbelievable! By rights he should have been hooked up long ago. Our collective professional assessment, which we muttered into our beers at the Scotch & Sirloin on Sepulveda after another day of fruitlessly chasing this slippery bastard, was that the little bank-robbing sonofabitch was simply the luckiest bandit who had ever trod the earth.

Which was part truth, part ego massage. I couldn't say I admired this guy. After all, I had spent my entire career trying to put some teeth in the Seventh Commandment, insofar as it related to robberies of federally insured financial institutions. And the Yankee Bandit hadn't merely violated that commandment; he'd beaten and strangled it.

Still, in my more reflective moments I could manage to summon up a little professional admiration for a guy who had the audacity to rob—how many was it now?—fifty banks, six of them in one day. Lucky he surely was, but he also had a certain roguish style, an élan that harkened back to an earlier, perhaps mythical time when it had seemed that bank robbers constituted a better class of crook. Compared with the general run of violent psychopaths and coked-up brain-deads who were starting to crowd into the bank robbery field, the Yankee stood out like a diamond in a coal bin. Even some of the victim tellers, particularly the young and pretty ones, noticed it. A lot of times in other cases, bank tellers would still be trembling hours after a bank holdup, even though the bank bandit hadn't committed any overtly violent acts; just the idea of being robbed by an armed man scared the hell out of them. But the Yankee's victim tellers were calmly describing this guy as being "gentlemanly," even "nice." And he always said "please" and "thank you."

It's those small courtesies that can mean so much.

Of course, I never breathed a word of these Scarlet Pimpernel musings to the other guys on the bank squad, for obvious reasons. Just using a word like "élan" around those guys would get you the fisheye. Apply it to a bank robber and they'd probably draw their guns on you. The bank squad syllogism was simple and direct: Bank robbers are assholes and lowlifes. The Yankee Bandit is a bank robber. Ergo . . .

Maybe they were right. Nevertheless, the low-life asshole was getting the better of us.

In mid-December, the Yankee hit four banks in one day for a total take of about $12,000. And then the robberies suddenly stopped—which, ironically, worried the hell out of me. I wondered if maybe he had moved to another city, but I studied the FD-430s, the reports from other FBI field offices, and couldn't find anyone else in the country who matched his description and M.O. Junkie bank robbers don't take vacations—or at least I'd never known one who did. A better bet was that he'd OD'd, or had been picked up on a drug possession or parole violation beef and was sitting in jail or in some sort of lockdown drug treatment facility.

Either way, it was bad news for us—and it forced us into what I call the Lawman's Paradox. Sure, as citizens we could be glad that the Yankee wasn't robbing more banks. But as FBI agents we desperately needed him to rob more banks. If he was dead or otherwise out of circulation he would never get caught, and we might never find out who he was—which would leave us with an embarrassing number of unsolved cases on our books. And it was getting real personal with us. We wanted to find him.

Weeks went by without a Yankee hit, and we were no closer to identifying him than we'd ever been. I managed to get the local newspapers to run one of the surveillance photos, with a "Have you seen this man?" story, but the results were disappointing. If anyone recognized the guy in the somewhat fuzzy newspaper photo—and as I found out much later, at least a few people did—they chose not to discuss the matter with the FBI.

It was unbelievably frustrating. There were times when, I have to admit, I found myself muttering a silent little prayer, one that only a lawman who's looking at having to eat fifty-plus unsolved crimes can truly understand: "Please God, don't let Mr. Yankee be dead. Please don't let him be in jail or kicking his habit at Betty Ford or Impact House. In your infinite wisdom, please bestow your favor on your friends in the L.A. FBI Bank Squad and make that little sonofabitch rob another goddam bank! Amen."

Well, sometimes our most heartfelt prayers are answered. In late January 1984, after a five-week hiatus, the Yankee was back in business. There was a $538 score at a Sherman Oaks bank on January 23, a $730 hit the same day in Van Nuys. They were both chump-change licks, but the last one represented another milestone in the Yankee Bandit saga: It was his fifty-fifth bank robbery, which made him the all-time world record holder, surpassing the previous champ, a guy known as the "Brown Bag Bandit." The Yankee's total take over the previous six months was more than a quarter of a million dollars. A half dozen robberies later, on February 1, the Yankee snagged a whopping $14,881 at a First L.A. Bank in Century City, his single biggest score ever.

And then finally the Yankee's luck ran out.

♦ ♦ ♦

By February of '84 Eddie had lost track of how many banks he'd robbed and how much money he'd stolen. He knew it had been a lot.

He vaguely understood that people were probably looking for him—cops, or the FBI, or somebody. All these robberies couldn't just be taking place unnoticed. There were times when he'd be walking along a sidewalk, heading for a bank, and in his head he would hear ticking, a palpable *tick, tick, tick,* like a time bomb. And he would understand, rationally, with momentary clarity, that if he kept doing it, he surely was going to get caught.

And then he'd rob the bank anyway. The alternative was just too horrible: No money, and thus no heroin, and then the withdrawal sickness that would start out like a really, really bad case of the flu, with hot and cold sweats and aching bones, and then get indescribably worse. Compared with that, robbing a bank was nothing.

Besides, except during those brief, shocking moments of clarity, he knew he was invincible. The drugs told him so.

He never cased the banks beforehand; his only concession to planning involved his wardrobe. If he was going to hit in Westwood, near UCLA, he'd drape a sweater over his shoulders to try to look like a student. In the glass-and-steel towers of Century City, he'd wear a tie; in West Hollywood, he'd wear a leather jacket. The idea was to blend in, inside the bank and out. On robbery days he would pose in front of a mirror in his Hancock Park town house, an actor playing the Bank Robber, pumping himself up for the role. Then he'd get in his black Lincoln and head out, with the music roiling out of the tape player: heavy metal, Puccini, Chuck Berry—whatever seemed to be the appropriate sound track for today's movie. He'd drive around the selected area until he spotted a bank that looked okay. He wasn't scientific or analytical about it; almost any bank would do. He'd park the car a block or so away, tuck his Italian leather bag under his arm with the starter pistol and the cap inside it, then stroll the sidewalk and into the lobby.

Confidence was the thing, Eddie knew. Confidence. Don't let your eyes dart around, even behind the shades; don't let your hands shake; don't look hurried or tentative or unsure. Wait there for a moment, feeling the vibes, and if they're good, do it. Stand in the teller line, perhaps chatting casually with the person in front of you. What's to be nervous about? You're a customer waiting to make a withdrawal. When your turn comes, walk up to the counter, not too fast, smile at the teller, exchange a customer-like pleasantry—"How are you today?"—put the leather bag on the counter, unzip it. Then explain to her in your soft Opie–of–Mayberry, North Carolina, accent, "Gosh, gee, I really hate to do this, but, uh, I have a gun. Please give me all your large bills."

Keep smiling. The last thing you want to do is scare her, make her flip out and cause a scene. Don't swivel your head around as she puts the cash on the counter. Don't look furtive. Just stand there, calmly, calmly, stuffing the money into the bag. When you think the bag is full enough, say thank you and ask the teller, politely, of course, to take a step back from the counter and away from that alarm button. As you leave the counter, take the Yankee cap out of the bag, put it on, the bill down low over your face in case the camera's watching, and walk—don't run!—toward the door, secure in the knowledge that no one else in the bank even knows that a robbery has taken place. Even if the teller has pushed a silent alarm button, you'll be on the street before anyone can react. Get back to the car, pull slowly into traffic, stick your hand in the bag, and give the cash a quick riff.

If it's enough, head over the hill to the Persian's place and then wrap yourself in the warmth. If it's not enough, no problem. Just find another bank.

It was easy—maybe too easy. It was also—might as well admit it—exciting. After the first one, back in July, when he'd finally worked up the courage, he'd been scared, sure, but he'd also felt . . . exhilarated! As he walked out of that bank, he couldn't help smiling. And even now, after so many, it was still a kick. It was like a drug rush, an upper, to be standing outside a bank, with normal people all around you not suspecting a thing, and you know you're just going to walk right in and take the money. If they could take that feeling and bottle it, it would sell for more money than any drug. It was better than any drug.

Well, almost any drug.

Yeah, there were a few close calls, some unexpected turns. There was the time the female teller chased him out of the bank—she wasn't even the one he had robbed—and he just barely managed to clamber over a wall and get away. There was the time he hit a bank right at closing time, and as he walked away from the counter with the money in the bag, a bank employee was already locking the front door. He thought he was a goner, but he kept his cool—confidence, confidence—and the bank clerk, not even realizing that a teller had been robbed, had cheerfully unlocked the door and let him out, telling him to "Have a nice day."

Another time he got back to his car after a bank lick and discovered that he had a flat tire. A flat tire on the getaway car—John Dillinger meets Woody Allen! But there was a service station right there and he drove the car in, standing in the shadow of the work bay while they changed the tire, the clatter of the impact wrench mixing with the wailing of sirens as he watched the cop cars screaming by on their way to the scene of a fresh bank robbery—his bank robbery.

And then there was that time he hit a bank on Sunset Boulevard and was walking east toward the car when he heard someone shout, "Eddie! Eddie!" When he turned, he saw this young (and now famous) actress he knew pull up next to him in a purple convertible Volkswagen. She wanted to chat, catch up on old friends, while he's standing there on the sidewalk with a fake gun and a fistful of bank loot in his briefcase, just a block away from the bank, and expecting any minute for the cops to show up. Finally he asked her to give him a lift to his car, and he piled into the VW and they drove off. But he noticed that a couple of attendants in a parking garage across the street had been looking at him, or at least looking at the beautiful, vaguely familiar girl in the purple Volks. Much later he found out that the FBI had started looking for a young, very good-looking, VW-driving female accomplice to the infamous Yankee Bandit. Fortunately, the parking attendants obviously hadn't gotten a plate number.

And once, he got robbed of his robbery money. That was when he got an exploding dye pack—the only time, in fact—from this old biddy of a teller who clearly didn't understand the gentle, non-violent, who-am-I-really-hurting-here spirit that he was trying to bring to the thing. She glared at him as if it were her own money she was handing over. She was so slow and grudging about it that, frankly, he started getting annoyed, and finally he hissed at her to hurry it up. When he got outside, he heard this strange, muffled crackling sound coming from the bag—it sounded a little like eggshells breaking. For some reason he didn't even bother to check it until he was at Persian's place, and then he opened the bag and found that every bill was stained bright red. The starter pistol, too. He was angry about it—justifiably, he thought at the time. The Persian wouldn't take the stained money, of course, so he cleaned off the fake gun as best he could and did what he had to do. He went out and robbed another bank.

The whole thing had this kind of weird, Jekyll and Hyde quality to it, and yet, in the context of his world, it seemed almost normal to him. Somehow it didn't even seem wrong—or at least, he would say later, "Not wrong in capital letters." He wasn't hurting anybody, not really; even some of the tellers he robbed seemed to understand that, particularly the young pretty ones, like that teller at that bank on Santa Monica Boulevard that he'd hit a couple of months before. When he went back to hit it again, he walked up to the next available teller and it was her, the same teller he got the last time he hit that bank. She recognized him immediately, but instead of throwing up her hands and running away or something, she put on this exaggerated, mock-exasperated look, said, "You again?" and started emptying the drawer before he even said a word. She wasn't scared or anything. None of them were. So how bad a guy could he be?

And when he wasn't robbing banks he was a normal person, doing normal things: He paid his rent, took his girlfriend, Jennifer, to dinner at nice restaurants, made love, went to parties, sometimes opened the shop—although now that was more the exception than the rule. The banks were his real job, his secret job, and if there was something special that he needed or wanted, in addition to the drugs, he simply had to work a little harder. The six banks in one day was like that: The rent was coming due, it was a Friday, and of course the Persian had to be fed. Then there was that day in December, when he and Jennifer were planning a trip to England, and he needed cash and a big stash of Persian comfort for the trip, so he had to hit four banks the same day. It was a lot of work, but still, you know, normal.

And yet, every now and then there was still that *tick, tick, tick*—the time bomb. This couldn't go on forever.

Some of Eddie's friends had figured out what he was doing. His friend Charlie Fine, a local artist who had known Eddie since the seventies, had watched Eddie's slide into serious addiction in the months before the bank robberies began, watched as the store clearly started to fail, and as time went on he wondered how Eddie was keeping body and soul together financially. And there were these strange little things he did. Like, for example, months earlier Charlie had loaned Eddie five hundred bucks, which he frankly never expected to see again. But then one day in November 1983, Eddie called him and said to come on over to the town house, he wanted to pay him back. Eddie took Charlie upstairs and started pulling cash out of a silver champagne bucket—all ones and fives, hundreds of them, all wadded up in the bottom of the champagne bucket. Eddie started counting out the five hundred in these small bills, but he kept telling Charlie to be sure not to deposit the cash in a bank account. He said it two or three times. Don't take it to a bank. Weird.

Charlie didn't know that the ones and fives were the "trash cash" from a bank robbery, the small bills that tellers often hand over along with the fifties and the hundreds to make the bank robber think he's getting more cash than he really is. But later, when Eddie and Jennifer were in England visiting Jennifer's parents, Charlie saw a photo in the newspaper of a bank robber called the Yankee Bandit, a guy wearing sunglasses and a Yankees cap. Charlie remembered a photo he'd seen of Eddie and Marisa Berenson standing on the porch of a cabin in Big Bear, and Eddie was wearing—yes, the same kind of sunglasses and a Yankees cap. The more Charlie looked at the newspaper photo, and the more he thought about that wad of cash in the champagne bucket, the more convinced he was that his pal Eddie was getting into some serious shit.

So Charlie decided to call Eddie at Jennifer's parents' house in London. Trying to be discreet, because he didn't know if anybody else was listening, Charlie told him, "Look, Eddie, I saw your picture in the paper, and if you're doing what I think you're doing, you'd better stay over there." Eddie didn't confess or anything, but from the way he reacted—or rather, didn't react—it was pretty obvious that he knew exactly what Charlie was talking about.

And Charlie wasn't the only one who knew. Other friends and acquaintances had started putting it together, too; hell, Eddie had even bragged to some of them that he was a bank robber, although they weren't certain he was serious. Still, nobody had gone so far as to drop a dime on him.

After five weeks in England—he'd been able to maintain his habit through some London dealers he knew—Eddie came back to L.A. He was running out of money, and what was he going to do, rob banks in London? At home in L.A., he thought about trying to stop altogether, get in a program or something. Of course, even as he said it he could hear a sneering little voice in his head saying, Yeah, right.

Later, Charlie Fine described Eddie's state of mind this way: "You want to know what was going on with Eddie? Two words: Total denial."

So he hit a few in the Valley, and a couple in Hollywood, and then he had a tremendous score, almost $15,000 from a bank in Century City, his best ever. In a little over a week it was all gone.

Fifteen grand, pissed away in a week. Even Eddie realized it. This was really getting out of control.

Then came February 10, 1984.

He got up early that afternoon. He was running late; there was the weekend to prepare for. He'd have to hurry. The Lincoln was in the shop, so he climbed into Jennifer's MG and headed for Hollywood, to the corner of Sunset and Vine.

It was further east than he usually liked, further east than he'd ever hit before, and seedier; despite what the tourists liked to think, no bona fide movie stars ever trod those Hollywood sidewalks. But there were always a lot of people around, hustlers, hookers, mohawked street kids, and, of course, yokels by the busload, which was good; it made it easier for him to get lost in the crowd. The plan was to hit a bank there and then start moving west, to a better part of town, and hit another one. He parked the MG at a meter on Selma and then walked a block south to the First Interstate Bank on Sunset Boulevard.

Later he decided that it was the expression on the teller's face that gave it away. That and the fact that this other teller, this Mormon-looking guy—short hair, white shirt, dark tie—must have been smitten by her, because he kept tossing these moony-eyed looks her way. In the intensity of the bank robbery experience you pick up on these things.

The teller was pretty in a girl-next-door way, but she wouldn't cooperate. In fact, she was utterly uncharmed by Eddie, the Gentleman Bank Robber. He asked for large bills, but she said she didn't have any. He asked her, very politely he thought, to give him whatever she had, but she got this pissed-off look on her face as she handed over the money. At the other end of the teller counter, Mr. Mormon noticed the look. Eddie could almost see the light bulb going on over the guy's head: Robbery! By the time he hit the door, Mr. Mormon was out from behind the counter, coming toward him.

Confidence, confidence. Eddie was out on the sidewalk now, walking, not running, but when he looked behind him, there was Mr. Mormon, bent over at the passenger window of a car sitting idling at the curb in the front of the bank. He said something to the driver and then started heading down the sidewalk, the car rolling slowly beside him along the curb; Mr. Mormon and the car were both trailing him. He walked a little faster, still not running, but Mr. Mormon and the car kept pace, not trying to catch up to him, not yelling or anything, but not falling back, either. They were dogged, but they weren't heroes. It was obvious to Eddie that they assumed his gun was fully operational.

He turned the corner, north onto Argyle, but they were still following him. He didn't want to lead them back to the parked MG, so he kept heading north, all the way up the hill to Franklin. They were still on him. Eddie thought that maybe they just wanted the money back, so he reached into the briefcase and threw some of the cash onto the ground, like a hiker tossing a sandwich to distract a pursuing bear. They stopped and picked up the money, all right, but then they were back on his trail, both of them in the car now, just hanging back and following him as he walked. It was the slowest kind of slow-speed chase. He walked by a knot of young Hispanic guys loitering at the corner of Franklin and Vine, and behind him he heard Mr. Mormon shout from the car window: "Stop that man! He robbed a bank!" Eddie had to smile when he heard the Hispanic kids tell Mr. Mormon to fuck off. This was, after all, Hollywood.

Next Eddie headed down Vine, trying to mix in with the crowds of tourists gawking at the bronze stars imbedded in the sidewalk on the Hollywood Walk of Fame—Charlton Heston, Paulette Goddard, John Ford—and for a minute he thought that he had lost them. But when he looked back again, there they were, relentless. That was Eddie's *Butch Cassidy and Sundance* moment: Who *are* those guys?

There was a big traffic and tourist crunch at the corner of Hollywood and Vine—it was five-thirty on a Friday evening—but Eddie threaded his way between the backed-up cars and continued down Vine. Looking back, he saw that the Mormon car couldn't get through the intersection. Eddie figured that he was safe; he didn't see Mr. Mormon flagging down the motorcycle cop. Now Eddie was desperate to get back to the car, because every bank in town closed at six, and the thin roll of bills left in the briefcase would never get him through the weekend.

He knew it was insane even to think about it after this close a call. But he had to rob another bank.

Eddie sensed the cop's presence before he saw him. It was as if the blue-and-red flashing lights from the police motorcycle had actual weight; he could almost feel them bouncing off his back. He ducked down behind a parked car, hoping the cop would pass him by, but the cop was already off his motorcycle, gun in hand, shouting at him. Eddie dropped the briefcase and stood up and put his hands behind his head. In seconds black-and-whites were screaming toward him and he was surrounded by cops, their guns pointing at him, all of them screaming and angry-looking. Eddie couldn't understand why they were being so rough; it was as if they thought that he was some sort of violent, dangerous criminal.

The cops ordered him to turn around. The next thing he knew, he was facedown on one of the grimiest stretches of sidewalk in North America, surrounded by sirens and flashing lights and gawkers, with a cop's knee in the small of his back and a pair of handcuffs rasping shut on his wrists.

It wasn't the way this movie was supposed to end.

✦ ✦ ✦

There were high-fives in the bank robbery squadroom when the call came in. I'd been following the chase on the Bureau radio, and it was pretty clear that it was the Yankee who'd been tagged on the Hollywood sidewalk, but we couldn't be absolutely certain until Biff Flanigan got down to LAPD headquarters at Parker Center to take a look at him. The cops had him in an interrogation room in the Robbery-Homicide Division, looking a little worse for wear; his hair a mess, his clothes disheveled, looking smaller than he did out on the street, kind of shrunken within his clothes. Getting arrested can do that to you. Biff Mirandized Eddie and he copped to the Sunset Boulevard robbery, although he wanted to see a lawyer before he said anything else about his other robberies. He was friendly in the interrogation room; he apologized to Biff for all the trouble he caused. He wouldn't have done it, he said, except for the heroin.

"It's him," Biff tells me over the phone. "It's the Yankee."

"Beautiful. Who is he?"

"Dodson, Edwin C. He owns some sort of artsy-fartsy antique store on Melrose."

Antique dealer? From trendy Melrose? That was a new one.

"Business must have been bad, huh?"

"Yeah," Biff says. "That, and a thousand-a-day heroin habit."

"So I figured. Was he cooperative?"

"Oh yeah," Biff says. "In fact, he's actually a pretty nice guy."

And that was that. After months of teeth-grinding, desk-pounding frustration, the Yankee Bandit was on ice. Of course, it would have been nice, a point of personal and bank squad unit pride, if we had tagged him ourselves, but that's not the way it works in the bank robbery business. Besides, an arrest is an arrest; a bargeful of bank robberies were tagged and bagged, and our stats were up accordingly.

In his seven-month bank robbery career the Yankee had robbed sixty-four banks—ten more than the all-time previous record holder. He had stolen in excess of $280,000, but except for the $600 or so he took in the last abortive bank job, none of that money was ever recovered. Most of it had, literally, gone up in smoke.

There was a flurry of news media interest as reporters found out who the Yankee Bandit was—or rather, who he had been. "Yankee Bandit Suspect a Mild-Mannered Antique Dealer," a headline in the *L.A. Herald Examiner* said. The tabloids signed on, too: "Celebrity Antique Dealer Led an Incredible Double Life as America's Greatest Bank Robber!" the *National Star* proclaimed, describing Eddie as a "debonair playboy."

Eddie's friends and acquaintances, at least the ones who hadn't been in on his secret, could hardly believe it. A *Herald Examiner* reporter who'd gotten a jump on the story started calling around before the news broke. He heard the same response again and again. He'd explain that Edwin Dodson had been arrested as the Yankee Bandit, history's most prolific bank robber, and he, the reporter, was calling to get some comments from people who knew him. Every single time there'd be a long silence, and then the person on the other end would say, "Is this some kind of a joke?" The friends who'd known about it were the ones who weren't talking.

Meanwhile, the mild-mannered antiques dealer and debonair playboy was spending a hard weekend in the Parker Center lockup, going through the coldest of cold turkey withdrawals. It was a weekend of wishing he could die.

Monday afternoon, Biff Flanigan picked him up at the lockup and took him, handcuffed and sick, over to the U.S. District Courthouse for his arraignment before a federal magistrate. If a jury had been in the courtroom, Eddie would have been allowed to put on a suit in the basement holding cell, but for routine court appearances, prisoners wore regular jail garb, blue jumpsuits and slippers.

The high-ceilinged, wood-paneled courtroom was crowded with

spectators: reporters, Assistant U.S. Attorneys, U.S. marshals, court-house secretaries, railbirds—that is, the old guys who made a hobby out of watching trials and other courtroom proceedings, the more sensational the better. The Assistant U.S. Attorney handling the arraignment laid it out: The defendant was a flight risk, a serious heroin user who had the "dubious distinction of having robbed more banks than anyone in American history." He requested high bail.

Eddie stood in front of the judge, head down, sweaty and pale, looking miserable. After robbing banks of more than a quarter of a million dollars, he had to tell the judge that he was a pauper, didn't have dime. The judge said he'd appoint an attorney, and ordered that Eddie receive medical treatment for his heroin withdrawal. Eddie thanked him.

When Biff got him back on the elevator for the ride down to the marshals' lockup, Eddie was trembling and moaning softly. Standing up in front of all those people, dressed the way he was, looking the way he did, had been mortifying, and the sickness was getting worse. As the elevator doors closed, Eddie kind of slumped over and laid his cheek on Biff's shoulder.

Now, the average bank-robbing asshole who'd had the temerity to touch Biff Flanigan would have been bounced off the elevator walls like a racquetball. But this guy was sick, and he'd been cooperative, even friendly; he'd never hurt anybody; he wasn't your usual asshole. Somehow Biff couldn't bring himself to jack the guy up. So they stood together as the elevator descended, the beefy Irish cop–FBI agent providing a there-there shoulder for "America's Greatest Bank Robber."

Biff was embarrassed when he told the story later. He wasn't even sure why he'd done it. There was just something about this guy that made you want to help him out.

Like I said: Everybody liked Eddie.

Edwin Chambers Dodson was indicted by a federal grand jury on twenty-five counts of bank robbery. Any more counts would have been useless for sentencing purposes, and would have compounded the paperwork. His lawyer eventually worked out a plea bargain with the U.S. Attorney: Plead guilty to eight counts and take a dime and a half—fifteen years in federal prison. Eddie took the deal, and disappeared into the prison system. For me and the other guys on the FBI bank squad, he became just another bit of bank robbery lore and legend, a story to tell at the bar or the retirement party. We never expected to see him again.

Eddie started serving his time at Terminal Island, a grim, windswept and aptly named conglomeration of concrete and razor wire situated on a man-made spit of ground in San Pedro, south of L.A. Eddie was fortunate in doing federal time, as opposed to being in the state prison system. There, a gentle guy like him would have been raw meat, but at the time the federal system generally had a better, more professional class of cons: a few truly bad guys, sure, but mostly counterfeiters and high-level drug dealers and federal-level con men—and of course, bank robbers. As the bank bandit with the highest numbers ever, Eddie was something of a celebrity in the joint. One day another bank bandit, a black guy from South Central L.A., came up to him and said, "Yankee, you is a bank-robbing motha-fucka!" It was a big compliment.

Another time this big, kind of goofy-looking white guy sidled up to him in the chow hall and asked, "You the Yankee Bandit?"

"Yeah," Eddie said.

The guy stuck out his hand, "I'm the Plaid Shirt Bandit." Michael Mason Wolke, a career criminal with fifty bank jobs, was the third-place record holder in the bank robbery Hall of Fame. "It's a real honor to meet you."

Everybody is wrong. There is honor among thieves.

Eddie stayed in touch by phone and letter with some of his friends from the old days. His girlfriend, Jennifer, hung on for about six months, visiting him at Terminal Island every week, until, inevitably, she slipped away. In time all of his beautiful things—the Queen Anne rugs, the Lincoln, the artwork, the things he had robbed banks rather than sell—disappeared, sold off or lost. Eddie worked in the prison kitchen as the "vegetable man," chopping carrots and onions, and ran a sewing machine in the prison uniform factory. He found refuge in dreaming—he called it "scuba diving"—discovering that for him the detail and vividness of prison dreams about women, food, and freedom were much more intense than on the outside. It was as if the brilliance of his dreams was compensating for the grimness of the surroundings. He read, he wrote, he waited; he declined periodic news media requests for interviews.

Eddie had been lucky, as always: he'd been sentenced prior to passage of the 1987 Federal Uniform Sentencing Guidelines, which require that every federal prisoner serve 85 percent of his time before he's even considered for release. Under that rule he would have had to serve almost thirteen years on a fifteen-year sentence; but Eddie's sentencing required a parole board hearing every two years. He was turned down the first time, which he more or less expected, and then again the second time, which was harder to take, and then the third, which sent him into despair. His problem was that he was a high-profile prisoner at a time when the public's tough-on-crime attitudes were at their peak. No appointee to the federal parole board wanted to see his own name anywhere near a newspaper story headlined: "Parole Board Frees America's Most Prolific Bank Robber."

After six years at Terminal Island, the Bureau of Prisons sent him up to Boron, in the California high desert, and later to Oregon and Arizona. Finally in 1993, at age forty-five, and after ten years inside, Eddie made parole on his fourth try. He moved into a halfway house for addict ex-cons in the Silverlake District of L.A.

Jack Nicholson, one of his friends from the old days, whom Eddie described as "a very kind-hearted, generous man," eventually gave him a job as caretaker at his ranch in Malibu, high up in the hills overlooking the ocean, a weekend retreat where Jack would spend time away from his compound on Mulholland Drive in Beverly Hills. It wasn't a high-paying gig, but room and board were included, and the view from the caretaker's cottage was spectacular. Eddie stayed clean, attending AA or Narc-Anon meetings at least once a day.

Shortly after his parole, Eddie called Biff Flanigan at the FBI office to say hello. It was friendly, cordial, sort of like one of those World War II reunions where bald former Luftwaffe pilots toss back beers with potbellied veterans of the Eighth Air Force and talk about ancient air battles over France. No hard feelings on either side; it was just war.

I just want to say that you were always straight with me, and I appreciated it, Eddie tells Biff.

Don't mention it, Biff says, a little amused.

And I want you to know that I'm clean now, and I'm going to stay that way. I'm out of the bank robbery business forever.

That's good, Eddie. Glad to hear it. Good luck to you.

That should have been the end of Eddie's relationship with the FBI Bank Squad. And for the next six years it was.

Eddie was back in the periphery of the Hollywood scene which, when it came to drugs, was a much different place than it had been in the old days. The violence-ridden crack epidemic of the 1980s, the drug-related public disintegration of careers, the overdose deaths of such figures as John Belushi and producer Don Simpson—those and other grim stories had given hard drug use a certain low-rent image. That's not to say that no one used them—of course they did—but no one was being too open about it. Going to AA meetings was more fashionable than passing around a bowlful of coke at a party.

Eddie wasn't shy about talking about his past, and as a consequence he enjoyed a certain notoriety in Hollywood circles. People who produced, directed, or starred in movies that fantasized about crime and criminals would stand in awe of Eddie's real-life tales of bank robberies and time in the joint. He was colorful. And although he was in his late forties, his attractiveness to women hadn't diminished; he had a string of young, beautiful girlfriends.

Then Eddie fucked up.

Although I spent much of my career dealing with dope users, I can't say that I really know much about drugs—unless you want to call Scotch a drug. In my entire life I've never so much as smoked a joint, much less used heroin. But I'm told by people who've been addicted to heroin that the desire never, ever really goes away. Years can pass, decades even, and not a day goes by that they don't think about it, that they don't remember how good it felt. It must be a terrible battle, going through life with all the usual ups and downs, and thinking in the down times that you're only a needle and a half a tenth of a gram away from making your troubles disappear. I'm not sure I could do it. Eddie certainly couldn't.

He met a girl, a woman he cared about. Unfortunately for Eddie, she was also a cocaine user. You can fill in the blanks from there. It was cocaine first, just a little, and then, of course, heroin again—relatively cheap Mexican brown this time; the days of chasing the dragon with expensive Persian were long gone. For the first time in his life, Eddie started "tying off," using a needle.

The slide was exponentially faster this time. He was losing weight, his face took on that sickly, junkie pallor, his hair even started falling out. The heroin—or rather, the times between heroin—made his skin itch and crawl, and he'd wind up scratching his face and arms raw. There was no hiding it. The word got back to Jack, who was understandably concerned about having his ranch house, with its art collection and fine furnishings, being watched over by a heroin addict. Nicholson, through his management agency, told Eddie his services would no longer be required. Eddie was out.

He stayed with friends for a while, bouncing from one address to another. When he applied for unemployment benefits and had to tell the clerk he had no fixed address, she listed him on the form as "homeless," which pretty much summed up the situation. He was a homeless, broke, unemployed, needle-using junkie, and help was not on the way. The solution, or at least the next step, was probably inevitable.

On the day after New Year's, 1999, Eddie found himself standing outside a Bank of America in Beverly Hills with a briefcase and a replica handgun he'd bought at a Hollywood toy store.

He knew from experience how it had to end, knew that eventually he'd be killed or caught, which essentially would be the same thing: This time he'd die in prison.

But he did it anyway. He walked in and held up the bank.

Suicide doesn't have to be quick.

From the moment the tipster phone rang on the night duty agent's desk after the TV news reports on the Down-and-Outer, Eddie Dodson was as good as in the bag. It wasn't the same as the first time he robbed banks, when we'd had to chase all over town looking for a bank bandit whose identity was unknown, who could have been anybody. Knowing who he was, we could start tracking him down, questioning his friends and associates, find out where he was hanging his hat.

Actually, Eddie made it easy for us.

He wasn't nearly the bank robber he'd been in the old days. For one thing, his failing health and appearance made him feel self-conscious, particularly in Beverly Hills. A couple of times he went into banks and imagined that the tellers were eyeballing him as he stood in line, with their fingers hovering over the two-eleven button, wondering who is this derelict, and what the hell is he doing in a bank in the City of Beautiful

Rich People? He had to give it up and walk away empty-handed. He probably was wrong; in the Brentwood job and others, no one had paid any particular attention to him. But the feeling had robbed him of his confidence. And confidence was everything.

Technology had changed, too. In the fifteen years since Eddie had last been in the bank robbery business, surveillance cameras had improved; some were now mounted behind the tellers' positions so they could get a nice clear shot of the bandit as he was committing the robbery, not just as he was booking it out the door. The images were sharper, clearer—and even more recognizable on TV.

Exploding dye packs had improved as well. First invented in the early 1960s, they originally were crude mechanical devices that exploded a .410 shotgun shell charge hidden in a stack of bogus cash; the idea was to frighten the bandit into dropping the money. But by the late 1990s, they were extremely sophisticated. Modern dye packs look like a regular strapped stack of twenties or fifties, but except for a few bills on the top and bottom they're actually worthless retired bills with the centers cut out. Inside that hollowed-out space there's a 9-volt battery, an electronic receiver, and a small, pressurized CO_2 canister containing about a half ounce of an extremely fine-grained powder dye—methyl aminoanthraquinone, if you want to get technical. (Some dye packs also contain a small dose of tear gas.)

The phony cash stack containing the dye pack is kept in a teller's cash drawer on top of a magnetic safety plate that keeps the pack in an "off" position; but when the pack is lifted off the plate during a robbery, the broken connection pre-activates the pack. It doesn't go off immediately; the last thing banks want is a cloud of noxious, indelible red dye exploding in a lobby full of people who might have lawyers. Instead, as the bandit moves toward the exit door, he enters an electromagnetic field generated by a transmitter hidden near the door. Sometimes it's in a phony Muzak speaker, sometimes in a phony philodendron planter; you can put them almost anywhere. The signal from the speaker or the plant fully activates the dye pack—sort of like cocking a gun. Twenty or thirty or forty seconds later, depending on how it's set, the dye pack explodes in a billowing red cloud that permanently stains everything it touches—skin, clothes, money. Usually the bandit will drop the money, and even if he doesn't, it's still a discouragement: the bandit can't spend the stained cash.

(It's a pretty reliable device, although not foolproof. I had a guy once who robbed a bank in Boulder, Colorado, and got a dye pack, but somehow the activating signal didn't work, and the pack didn't go off as he walked out of the bank. A week later, this guy and his girlfriend walk into a bank in West Hollywood, not to rob it but to buy a money order with some of the cash from the Boulder job. The girlfriend still has the dye-pack cash in her purse, and this bank has the same dye-pack electronic-activating system as the one in Boulder. As they walk in, the transmitter at the door activates the pack—after all, it doesn't know whether a bandit is walking into the bank or out of it—and *boom!* the thing goes off while they're standing in line. It was an attention-getter. We made the guy for the Boulder job, and he went to the joint for eight years.)

So, the dye packs can get you. And by the time Eddie got back into the bank robbery business, there were more dye packs around than ever before. The security companies that market the packs—the system runs about $4,000 to install, and each pack costs about $500—were offering bank tellers a $200 or $300 bonus if they slipped the pack into the money during a robbery, which was significant money for notoriously underpaid bank employees. They were handing over the packs every chance they got.

Eddie's numbers tell the story: In his first string of sixty-four robberies, he had gotten only one dye pack; the second time around, he got two in eight bank hits. After the first one, he specifically told the next teller not to give him any dye packs—and then, to his astonishment and dismay, she went and did it anyway. On both occasions, it rendered the money useless.

It was a grim fact, but Eddie had to face it: It was getting harder and harder to be a bank robber.

Eddie also assumed that this time we knew who he was. He knew that the banks must be getting surveillance shots, and he had even seen his picture on the TV news after the carjacking on West Pico. He was surprised at the quality of the shot, and although he didn't look like the Eddie of old, he knew that anyone who'd seen him recently would recognize him. He figured someone was bound to drop a dime on him. Of course, he should have blown town, but his only concession to his new notoriety was to drive the stolen Mercedes a hundred miles north to hit his next bank, a Wells Fargo in the beach community of Santa Barbara. Despite the reassuring phone message to the young woman, he hadn't quite gotten around to returning her car. Santa Barbara was a nice score: $12,000. It was also the last bank he would ever rob.

Charlie Fine, Eddie's artist friend from the old days, ran into him at a coffee shop in the Fairfax District the day after the Santa Barbara hit; he hardly recognized him. His hair, what was left of it, was long and stringy, his arms were badly swollen, he had sores on his face. Eddie was obviously drugged up on something; he looked like death. Sure, in some ways he was the same old Eddie, bantering with the waitress and talking easily about the old days, but when the check came, Eddie pulled a thick roll of bills out of his jacket pocket. When Charlie saw it he thought, Uh-oh. Charlie hadn't seen the TV report with Eddie's picture, but he figured something was up.

Meanwhile, acting on the tips that had been called in, Special Agent Andy Chambers had started running Eddie to ground. He learned from one of Eddie's acquaintances that Eddie might be hanging out near the Farmer's Market, a vast, semi-open-air collection of fruit stands, gift shops, and ethnic food joints in the heart of the city's Fairfax District. Andy had gotten a recent photo of Eddie from the DMV—Eddie had had to renew his license a few months before—and he started making the rounds. On the afternoon of April 27, 1999, three days after the robbery in Santa Barbara, Andy checked out the parking lot at the Farmer's Daughter, a mid-scale, $65-a-night motel on Fairfax Avenue. Sure enough, there was the stolen Mercedes. Andy walked into the motel office, badged the deskman, and showed him Eddie's photo.

Yeah, he's here, the deskman told him.

You mean he stays here?

I mean he's here right now. In the back, second floor. Room 117. I saw him go in a while ago.

He ever give you any trouble?

Well, he looks like maybe he's using drugs. But he seems like a nice guy. I guess he's in some kind of hassle, huh?

Yeah, you might say that.

Andy walked outside and eyeballed the outside of the room. It was an end unit; the shades were drawn. He already had an arrest warrant with Eddie's name on it in his pocket, and if he'd seen Eddie coming out of the room he would have taken him right there. But in this situation, where you may have to kick in a door, procedure called for backup.

Within forty-five minutes the Farmer's Daughter was surrounded by FBI agents, LAPD Robbery-Homicide detectives, and uniformed cops, and the few other guests in the motel were quietly evacuated. By now Andy was familiar with Eddie's record, and knew that in the past he was never violent, that he never used a real gun. Still, things can change. If they kicked the door and it turned out Eddie had a working firearm, and a newfound propensity to use it, somebody could get hurt. Since the area was fully secured, and Eddie wasn't going anywhere, they decided to try to bullhorn him out.

Andy and the RHD guys took up position in the parking lot, watching the door. The RHD guys had their 9-millimeter handguns drawn; Andy was carrying an MP-5, a 10-mm submachine gun that he kept in the trunk of his Bureau car.

An RHD detective called out through the bullhorn: "*Eddie! Eddie Dodson!*" It sounded like the very voice of God. "*We have a warrant for your arrest! Come out with your hands up!*"

The drapes on the window parted. Eddie peeked out. Yep, he was in there.

EDDIE! YOU'RE SURROUNDED. COME OUT NOW!

The door to Eddie's room cracked open.

"I'll come out in a minute!" he yelled out, and then the door slammed shut.

Andy and the RHD guys are looking at each other. He'll be out in a minute? What is this guy thinking? That we're his date, that we're picking him up to go to the movies? Their reaction was, Christ, now what are we gonna do?

Minutes went by. Andy figured they'd have to use SWAT to flash-bang him—that is, toss in a disorienting but non-lethal sound-and-light grenade through the window and then kick the door and grab him before he could come to his senses. This was turning out to be a huge pain in the ass.

Inside the room, Eddie called an old friend, a woman, and left a message on her machine: "The cops are here. I'm surrounded. It doesn't look like I'm going to make it. Good-bye."

After he hung up, he assessed the situation: There he was, in a dark, crummy motel room, needles lying around all over, old fast-food containers stinking up the scarred dresser, bed unmade, dirty clothes strewn about. He was sick, bad sick, and the only two options waiting for him on the other side of that door were death or a long prison sentence. He was fifty-one years old. It was the end.

Eddie picked up his works, tied off, and fired up what was left of his shit; he was disappointed that it wasn't enough to kill him. Then he got dressed, putting on some jeans, an old suede jacket, and a brown fedora. He still had $6,000 or so left over from the Santa Barbara job, but he didn't even bother with it. He picked up the replica handgun, took a deep breath, opened the door—and, gun in hand, stepped out on the balcony.

Suicide doesn't have to be quick. And you don't necessarily have to do it yourself.

Outside, watching, Andy could hardly believe it. The door opens and this guy in a fedora—a fedora, for Christ's sake—comes strolling out on the balcony with a gun in his hand, like some kind of Indiana Jones. A dozen cops are screaming at him, along with the RHD guy on the bullhorn—"Drop the gun! *Drop the gun!*"—but he won't, he just stands there, waving the gun around. It's obviously a case of attempted suicide by cop—and it's damn close to being successful. As far as they know, that's a real gun in his hand; legally, under policy, they can ace him right there and nobody would say a word. Andy is close to letting one go, drawn down on him with the MP-5, about a pound of trigger pressure away from punching this guy's ticket.

But miraculously, nobody fires. Instead, they keep shouting—"Drop the gun!"—but the guy is acting as if he doesn't even hear them. Then he suddenly walks down the balcony and steps into the elevator, like he's taking a stroll down to the pool or something.

What the hell?

The elevator door opens on the ground floor and the guy walks out into the parking lot. He's heading for the Mercedes, still holding the gun. It's insane; this guy has to know that a couple dozen cops and FBI agents aren't going to let him just drive away into the sunset. They'll have to take him out; they'll have to.

And they would have done just that, except that just as Eddie got next to the car, a young uniformed cop bravely—foolishly, too—bolted out and delivered a flying tackle, knocking Eddie so hard into the side of the Mercedes that his head left a dent in the door, right through the hat. Then everybody was swarming him, while he struggled and screamed:

"Kill me! Kill me! Kill me! Kill me! Kill me!"

Finally they got him subdued and hooked him up, hog-tied, wrists and ankles, and put him in the back of a police black-and-white. He was bleeding from a gash on his head.

It wasn't exactly a textbook arrest, not something that's ever going to be taught at the Academy. But at least nobody got killed—not even the guy who wanted to be.

And for the second time—the last time—the Yankee Bandit was down.

They took Eddie to the jail ward at County–USC Medical Center, which is just like any other hospital ward except that all the doors are locked, and patients are sometimes shackled to the beds, and sheriff's deputies make the rounds with the doctors. They treated him for his head wounds and his withdrawal pains, and a week later he was in good enough shape to be interviewed by Andy Chambers and Robbery-Homicide Detective Dennis English.

Eddie was Eddie—the old Eddie—cooperative, friendly, a nice guy. No, he didn't want a lawyer. Yes, he wanted to cooperate in every way he could, regardless of the outcome, with no deals beforehand. Andy took him through all eight of the recent robberies, and Eddie copped to every one—which gave him a lifetime total of seventy-two bank robberies, seventy of them successful. No one else has ever come close to that record, nor do I expect anyone to.

Eddie kept saying how sorry he was, how ashamed of himself he was for getting back on drugs, for falling so low. He was utterly mortified by the carjacking—"Would you please tell her again how sorry I am?"—and by what he called "the dreadful, embarrassing scene" he'd caused at the motel.

And he was grateful to the guy who was putting him back in prison.

"I want to thank you, Mr. Chambers," he said, "for finding me. You saved my life."

"No problem, Eddie," Andy reassured him. "Hope it works out for you."

Amazingly, it did. As a two-time loser, Eddie should have been look-ing at another fifteen years, minimum, and under the new Federal Sen-tencing Guidelines he would have had to do 85 percent of that before he'd even be eligible for parole. But the young woman who interviewed him for the presentencing report to the judge saw something in him—young women had always seen something in him—and she gave him a good write-up. "This," she told the judge in her report, "is someone who's salvageable."

There were other considerations as well. At the jail ward they tested him for AIDS, which came back negative, but he was positive for hepa-titis C and advanced cirrhosis of the liver. The prognosis was gloomy—terminal, in fact. In the medical report to the court, the doctors pre-dicted that Eddie would require extensive hospitalization and treatment, and that he'd probably die before he ever finished a long prison term—or maybe even a short one. The Bureau of Prisons' attitude toward cases like this was pragmatic: Hey, keeping healthy people locked up is expen-sive enough; why not let this guy die on somebody else's budget?

U.S. District Judge Edward Rafeedie took it all in, and in October 1999, Eddie pleaded guilty to one count of bank robbery and was sen-tenced to just forty-six months in prison, followed by five years 'close probation. It was a miraculously lenient sentence.

As I write this, Eddie is serving his time at the Federal Correction Facility in Victorville, California, a new, medium-security prison about a hundred miles outside of L.A.

And he and I have become—well, friends.

I'd always been curious about Eddie Dodson, and how it was that a guy like him had taken up the bank robbery business. In my FBI career I had dealt with literally thousands of bank robbers, and although some of them had pretty interesting tales to tell, I'd never encountered anyone quite like him.

So, after I retired from the Bureau, while Eddie was doing his stretch in the joint, I wrote him a letter. And he wrote back.

> . . . *You FBI boys were always cool with me. You're decent human beings, and I respect that. I must tell you that I never*

> *perceived myself as a career criminal. I've only broken the*
> *law twice now in my life—well, two rather large times, with*
> *a King Kong drug habit as the motivating reason. I accept*
> *responsibility, of course; there's mortification and shame still*
> *in my game. I lost so much . . . so quickly. And here I am.*
> *However, I have less than two years remaining to serve,*
> *and plenty to look forward to. I stay as positive and clear as*
> *I can, and I trudge on. . . .*

Since then we've exchanged letters, and spent hours on the phone together—two retirees talking about old times. He told me his story; I told him mine. His health is better—he plans to confound the doctors' mortal prognoses—and he's looking forward to getting out of prison.

We've even talked about going on the road together after he gets out.

Since my retirement I've often been asked to talk about bank robberies to various groups of bankers, security officials, and law enforcement officers. They bill me, flatteringly, as "America's foremost authority on bank robberies." I think it would be interesting to put Eddie up there on the podium with me to talk about bank robberies as seen from the other side of the counter.

But Eddie's a little worried about the reception he might get.

"Bill," he asked me one day, "do you really think there's any chance of forgiveness, any chance for redemption on my part after what I did—not just once, but twice?"

Actually, I do. I don't think any of those bankers and cops and security guys would hold it against him that he robbed more banks than anyone else in the history of the world.

After all, everybody likes Eddie.

3

CASPER

They weren't much more than boys, most of them, the sort of hard-eyed, menacing-looking young men you can see hanging on street corners or lounging on stoops in every ghetto in America—guys with street names like Li'l Brim, Baby Insane, S-Bone, Baby Gumby, Tiny Hog, Li'l Scoobie, Suicide, Li'l No Sense.

Some were the sons of crack addicts or criminals, or of foolish, hopeless young girls who should have been in the eighth grade instead of giving birth in the county maternity ward. Others were from families that did their best, hardworking, churchgoing people who tried to protect their kids from the crime and drug dealing and gangs that saturated their neighborhoods, but somehow couldn't keep those inner-city wolves from the door. Sure, some of the corner boys were near morons and right-out-of-the-cradle sociopaths, stone criminals almost from the day they were born, but others were quick-witted, bright young men who could have done well in school, in the world, in life. Only they chose the streets instead.

Their entire world was the 'hood, a world measured in city blocks, the borders marked by gang tags on walls that defined the territory. Each of those territories was a subset of the larger 'hood known as South Central L.A. Once home to the thousands of defense industry workers, black and white, who flocked to the city during World War II, it was now largely a tired, forlorn swath of urban real estate, its commercial centers crammed with check-cashing outfits and Korean-owned liquor stores and blind pig bars and storefront churches, its gridlike residential streets lined with unpainted bungalows and two-story box apartment buildings that had started springing seams and growing roaches the moment the building inspector had been paid off.

Outwardly, at least, South Central couldn't match the desperation of East Coast slums: even in the toughest, grimiest sections there were trees and shrubbery and sunshine, and here and there, sandwiched between crackhouses with their weed yards and drawn blinds and steel front doors, there were bungalows with fresh paint and flowerpots on the porch, signs of hope for a better, safer life. But hope was one thing, reality another; every window in every building in the 'hood, on crackhouse and family house alike, was equipped with heavy iron bars. Because of those boys on the corner.

It was a hard place to grow up in, but few of the young men realized it; they had nothing to compare it to. Later, after we caught them, we'd be astonished at how unsophisticated they were about what lay beyond 60th Street or Crenshaw Boulevard. At age fifteen or sixteen or seventeen, they'd grown up ten miles from the beach but had never seen the ocean; some didn't even know that ocean's name. They lived within sight, smog permitting, of the towering San Gabriel Mountains, but they'd never drawn a breath of mountain air. Malibu, Orange County, the Valley, Beverly Hills—they had heard of those places, seen them on TV, but to the boys on the corner they were distant, forbidding lands, full of strange white people and suspicious cops and certain trouble. Except for brief stays at the juvenile detention centers scattered through the far corners of L.A. County, most of them had never been out of the 'hood.

And yet, they had their ambitions—limited ambitions, by most standards, but essentially the same ambitions all young men have. Girls, of course, constituted their primary hormonal imperative, but they also aspired to money and possessions and, even more important, to power and prestige. They were boys who wanted to be men, as they understood the term.

And what better way to shine as a man than to hold up a bank?

Bank robbery wasn't a notion that would come to them on their own. No, that would require the intervention of an older, wiser, more experienced hand, someone who would take these young boys and arm them, train them, and send them out on "missions" far beyond the limits of the 'hood—"rollin' deep," they called it—to rob and pillage and bring the loot back to the bandits' lair. Their leader and mentor would become a sort of modern-day Fagin, transported in time from the Dickensian slums of London to the hip-hop slums of South Central L.A.

His name on the street was "Casper." And under Casper's advice and counsel, these young men, these boys, these "Baby Bandits," would unleash a reign of bank robbery terror unlike anything L.A., or America, had ever seen.

But that was in the future. The opening chapter in the Casper story started with a hapless, broken-down crackhead named Rock, who had a strange tale to tell.

✦ ✦ ✦

It began in early 1990, when FBI Special Agent Notah Ben Tahy stopped by my office next to the bank squad bull pen. Ben was a Navaho Indian—he was, I'm pretty sure, the only special agent in the Bureau who could speak the Navaho language—a quiet, reserved kind of guy who generally didn't let his emotions make the trip from his heart to his face. But this time I could see that something was bothering him.

Ben had a guy named David Lee Clark, aka Rock, aka the "Money or Die Bandit," a career small-time criminal and chronic smokehead—crack cocaine user—who had been arrested after robbing a couple dozen banks between November 1988 and January 1989. They'd all been note jobs—that is, the bandit wrote the robbery demand on a piece of paper and handed it to a teller—and all of the notes had contained some version of the phrase "Give me the money or die." A thin, ropey-muscled thirty-nine-year-old with a bushy mustache and the furtive, wary eyes of a bottom feeder, Clark had several earlier arrests for robberies on his record—none of them involving banks—and had served time in state prison before getting out and turning to bank jobs.

I'll give the guy his due: at least he wrote his demand notes in a clear hand, with some respect for the English language. A lot of note men don't. In the extensive collection of bank robbery demand notes I've assembled over the years, there are any number of linguistic travesties. One note job robber wrote—I swear to God—"This is a stippup" on a bank deposit slip and handed it to a teller. Another genius wrote, "This is a robery, don't make it a muder," while another handed over a note that said, "Give me the mony, bicth." The list of spelling and grammatical howlers is almost endless. By those standards, the Money or Die Bandit was William Safire.

He also had the added attraction of being succinct. I'd had guys who would hand over typewritten demand notes that ran a page, even a page and a half, starting with something like "I don't want to do this, but my mother is sick," and ending with "Merry Christmas, and God bless." The Money or Die Bandit at least got to the point.

But other than that, he wasn't an exceptional bank robber. The man lacked consistency, and finesse. His scores had ranged from $8,520 taken from a First Interstate Bank in downtown L.A.—an excellent haul for a note job—to a lousy $40 he got at a Wells Fargo on Sepulveda Boulevard in West L.A. Forty bucks, for a crime that could earn fifteen years in the joint.

And it was a particularly stupid forty bucks at that. In that job he made the mistake of trying to rob a bank with thick Plexiglas "bandit barriers" separating tellers and customers, which deprive a bank robber of his primary weapon—the fear he engenders in bank employees. A more accomplished bank bandit would have taken one look at the bandit barriers and found another bank.

But not Clark. He waited his turn in line, then walked up to a teller, and showed her the "money or die" note. But he didn't show a gun—he never did in any of his bank jobs—and the "money or die" threat had considerably less impact on someone standing safely behind an inch and a half of bullet-resistant Plexiglas than it would have on someone looking at a bank robber eyeball to eyeball. The teller grabbed two twenties out of her drawer, pushed them out through the slot, and then dropped down behind the counter, pushing the alarm buttons and yelling: "Robbery!"

A better bandit would have realized immediately that the twenties were bait money—bills with recorded serial numbers that could be tied to the bank robbery if he was caught with them. Why else would the teller bother to hand over the two bills if she was going to drop behind the counter and start yelling her head off? But to a guy like Clark, forty bucks is forty bucks. He grabbed the two twenties and ran out of the bank.

Like I said: No finesse.

Still, Clark was lucky that time: the police response time on the two-eleven silent alarm was too slow, and he got away. Later that same day he did better, hitting a Great Western Savings in Culver City for $2,800. But we could always count on guys like Clark to make more mistakes— and he did. A week later he hit a Great Western Savings bank in El Segundo for $521, but this time he left the "money or die" note behind, with his fingerprints all over it. We ran the prints through Cal ID, the California law enforcement fingerprint data base, and a month later— they were pretty backed up on print search requests—we got a good print hit: Clark, David Lee, DOB 3/15/51, a small-time career crook with a long rap sheet.

Special Agent Tahy pulled Clark's booking mug from an earlier arrest and compared it to the surveillance photos of the Money or Die Bandit. Yep, that was our guy, all right. Tahy showed one of the victim tellers a photo six-pack, and she picked Clark out immediately—which, with the fingerprints, gave us more than enough evidence to get a federal judge to issue an arrest warrant. Now all we had to do was find Clark and pick him up.

Problem was, we were a little backed up ourselves. In the previous twelve months we'd had 1,350 bank robberies in the L.A. field office area, and the bank squad was down to just fifteen agents; you can do the caseload arithmetic yourself. For a big case, sure, we'd put bodies in the field, but we really didn't have time to chase all over the city looking for a brain-dead smokehead bank bandit who didn't even carry a gun. So, since several of the bank robberies had occurred in the South Bay area of L.A. County, our resident agent in the South Bay, FBI Special Agent Lane DeSilva, asked the West Regional Burglary Team to see if they could find this shitheel.

The burglary team consisted of a half dozen young, aggressive street cops from the L.A. County Sheriff's office and some smaller city police departments: Manhattan Beach, Torrance, Redondo Beach. We loved those burglary team guys, because they just loved working bank robbery cases; in a lot of ways, they reminded me of me when I was their age. Their reaction to Agent DeSilva's request was: No problem! What's the shitheel's name?

Clark's last known address was an apartment on Crenshaw Boulevard in the Hyde Park neighborhood of South Central L.A., which he shared with his loyal but long-suffering wife when he wasn't in jail or laid up in a crackhouse. So the burglary team members sat on the apartment house for a few days, on and off, waiting for Clark to show, but he never did.

Finally, they decided to tail Clark's wife, Toni, as she came out of the apartment—he had her name tattooed on his chest—and then see what they could see. That day she came out and drove to Harbor General Hospital in Torrance, the team members discreetly keeping apace, and when she entered the hospital, one of them followed her. He watched as she went into a patient ward and then he backed off. After she left, the deputy came in with the warrant and the ID photo and there was Clark, lying in a hospital bed with a festering bullet wound in his right shoulder. The deputy arrested him.

It turned out that Clark had checked himself into the hospital earlier that day under a phony name, complaining that a wound he'd suffered in a street shooting a month earlier wasn't healing properly, which it wasn't, since he'd been trying to treat it himself with Band-Aids and monkey-blood (mercurochrome). Hospital workers are required to report all bullet wounds to the cops, which they had in Clark's case; eventually the local police would have sent someone out to check on it. But a month-old bullet wound wasn't going to fire the imagination of any police agency, at least not in L.A.; there were too many fresh bullet wounds to attend to. So the West Regional Burglary Team got to him first.

Harbor-UCLA didn't have a jail ward, so Clark was transported and booked into the jail ward at County-USC Hospital in downtown L.A. Clark's parole officer was contacted, and since Clark hadn't reported to him in weeks, the P.O. cordially violated him on his parole, which automatically put a no-bail hold on him. The next day Special Agent Tahy went to the jail ward to interview him—and to try to get a confession out of him.

A confession is always a nice thing to have. No matter how much physical evidence and witness IDs you have on a suspect, nothing wraps a case up with a pretty bow more effectively than to have the guy say, "Yeah, I did it." And as you'll probably notice in this book, when confronted with the evidence against them, many, maybe even most, suspects eventually sign on the dotted line.

Which always seems to amaze law-abiding civilians. Often they're skeptical that anyone would willingly offer up a confession that's going to earn him a ten- or fifteen-year dump in federal prison. After all, what kind of moron rolls over on himself without giving a lawyer even the chance to spring him on some technicality—especially after he's been told, per *Miranda*, that he has the right to an attorney, on the taxpayer dime if necessary, and that he doesn't have to say a damn thing if he doesn't want to, and if he does, we're going to use it to put his sorry ass in jail? Civilians figure we must have beaten the confession out of him.

But no, we don't beat suspects with fists or rubber hoses to get confessions. I'm not saying that never in the history of the world has some smirking, loud-mouthed suspect smacked a G-man's hand with his jaw, or taken an unfortunate backward flip over his chair in an interrogation room. And any suspect who has the temerity to take a swing at an agent is invariably going to undergo some pretty intensive physical counseling.

But beat a confession out of a guy? Why bother? Why risk my career? Or even my freedom? Besides, as I said, most of the time a confession is just insurance. If I've got enough evidence to have the guy under arrest in an interrogation room, there's a good chance I've already got enough to convict him in court—especially since, for most suspects, the lawyer who's going to be standing up for him in court isn't going to be Johnnie Cochran or Alan Dershowitz, but some overworked and inexperienced young public defender.

No, the reason criminals confess is because they understand the system. They know that cooperation up front is rewarded at charging and sentencing time, and that the longer you delay coming clean, the worse deal you're going to get.

With Clark, the Money or Die Bandit, getting him to see the wisdom of an early confession was even easier than most. Special Agent Tahy Mirandized him and then laid it all out: the surveillance photos, the teller ID, and that mother-of-all-damning-evidence, the prints that his fear-sweat–oozing fingers had left on the demand note. Clark knew it was over.

"I did it," he told Tahy. "I robbed those banks. But I was all cracked up."

Clark told Tahy that he'd gotten the bullet wound in his shoulder a month or so earlier, when some gang-bangers had tried to rip him off; no, he didn't know who they were. The gunshot wound had nothing to do with the bank robberies, he said, and Tahy figured it was true, or at least irrelevant; there'd been no shots fired in any of the robberies.

So Tahy took him through each one of the bank robberies, trying to confirm details. Clark could provide some of them, but he said he couldn't remember others. He didn't remember how many banks he'd robbed, he said, because most of the time he was high on rock cocaine—"cracked up." But it didn't really matter whether he remembered all the details or not: the Money or Die Bandit was on ice. Clark later pleaded guilty to nine of the robberies in a let's-make-a-deal, and was looking at a negotiated sentence of fourteen years in federal prison.

And that was it. It was, it seemed, a pretty standard bank robbery case. But then a couple of months after the arrest, the "Money or Die Bandit" case took an unusual turn.

Because unbeknown to Clark, he'd been talking to a snitch.

Every prison and large county jail in America has an intelligence unit, a group of guards or deputies whose job it is to gather information about the inmates and the crimes they've committed, both in and out of jail. Some of the intelligence comes from full-time snitches, some from guys wanting to settle a score, some from gossip overheard by guards in the messhalls and the cellblocks, some from monitored phone calls. Firsthand, secondhand, thirdhand—it doesn't matter, the information is collected and reviewed by the intelligence guys. If it relates to a crime committed outside the prison or jail, the information is forwarded to the investigating officer who's handling that criminal case.

That's what happened in Clark's case. He was sitting in L.A. County Jail awaiting sentencing for the bank jobs—at the time there was not a separate federal lockup in L.A.—and he started talking about his bank robberies with another inmate. What Clark didn't realize was that the other inmate was a snitch, a guy who built up deposits in the favor bank by passing along tidbits to the jailhouse intelligence unit. The snitch passed on Clark's story to the intelligence guys, and they passed it on to Special Agent Tahy.

According to the story from the snitch, Clark had admitted during a jailhouse bullshit session that he'd done the bank robberies. But he said he hadn't done them alone. In fact, he claimed he'd never wanted to be a bank robber, that somebody *made* him do it.

He said it started when he was standing outside a crackhouse in South Central, empty-pocketed and desperate for drugs, and some guys, local gang-bangers, drove up and asked him if he wanted to make some money. Clark said he surely did. So he got in the car with the three guys, one of whom he knew as "Peanut," a member of the Rollin' Sixties

Crips street gang. He didn't know the other two, but Peanut called them "Cas" and "C-Dog." They were both big guys, buffed out. C-Dog was sullen, mean-looking, while Cas was quiet, cool, sort of laid back. Peanut was doing all the talking, but Clark had the impression that Cas was the shot-caller.

Clark asked the gang-bangers what the job was. No big deal, they said; they were going to do a bank lick. Or rather, he, Clark, was going to do a bank lick.

Whoa, Clark says. I dunno. I never robbed no bank. Shit, man, it's easy, they say. You just walk up to a teller and hand her a note, and she'll hand over the money. And they told him exactly what to write on the note: "Give me the money or die."

Clark wasn't so sure, but he needed money. Okay, he'd do it. So they drove him to this bank, he didn't remember where—actually it was a First Interstate Bank on Airport Boulevard in L.A.—and Clark wrote, "Give me the money or die" on a piece of paper. The gang-bangers waited in the car around the corner while Clark went inside. He was a little nervous, but it turned out to be as easy as they'd said. He showed the teller the note, she handed over $1,200, and he grabbed it and ran back to the waiting car. The gang-bangers took the cash and then drove him back to the crackhouse. When he got out of the car, they gave him $100 from the stolen cash.

That was it. A lousy hundred bucks.

Well, even a smokehead could figure out that a hundred-dollar pay-off on a $1,200 score that he'd taken all the risks on was a stone rip-off. But what was he gonna do? These were big, mean guys. He took the money and kept his mouth shut.

And then a couple days later the gang-bangers stop him on the street again and tell him they want him to do another bank lick. Well, okay, he says, but this time he wants more money. Sure, no problem, Rock, they tell him. So he robs another bank and this time they give him a lousy $150. Shit. Still, he does a few more bank jobs for the guys, hoping the compensation package will improve, but it's the same thing again and again: He'd steal thousands and they'd shine him on with $100 or $150 or sometimes just a few rocks of cocaine. Finally he told the gang-bangers to forget it, he didn't want to rob no more mother-fucking banks.

So they shot him.

That's right, they shot him in the shoulder with a small-caliber pistol, Clark told the snitch, and they told him if he didn't continue to rob banks for them, the next bullet would be in his motherfucking head. Clark believed them; they were bad dudes. So he patched up his shoulder wound as best he could—obviously, he'd done a poor job of it—and for the next month he was a bank robbery work-a-daddy. Every few days or so the gang members would pick him up in the morning and drive him around to banks all over L.A., he said, sometimes two or three on the same day, and wait outside in the car while he went in and flashed the "money or die" note and brought the money out of the bank. The gang-bangers never went into the bank. At the end of the day, from a total take of $5,000 or $6,000, they'd give him a couple hundred, tops. And then a few days later they'd spot him on the street and make him do some more licks.

But then his shoulder started to hurt real bad, oozing shit, you know, and his wife made him check into the hospital. And that's where the cops found him, he didn't know how.

No, Clark told the jailhouse snitch, he never told the cops or the FBI about the gang-bangers putting him up to the robberies. He was no snitch, he told the snitch, and besides, he was still afraid of those guys. They could kill him just as easy in prison as on the outside; easier, even. And the thing is, he'd heard that he wasn't the only one the gang-bangers were using to rob banks; they had a bunch of other guys they were making rob banks for them, too.

Well, that was the story the snitch passed on to the jail intelligence guys, which they passed on to Ben Tahy. Ben was a veteran FBI agent, he knew his way around, but he was still new to the bank squad—and he'd never heard anything like this.

So he walked over to my desk that day and laid out the whole story and asked me what I thought.

My first response, frankly, was that it sounded like total bullshit to me.

You have to understand something: Criminals never tell the whole truth. On any given occasion they may tell half the truth, or a tenth of the truth, or even 90 percent of the truth, whichever suits their immediate purposes, but they never tell the whole, unvarnished truth; it's simply beyond their capabilities. They lie to the cops, they lie to each other, they lie to themselves. In an interrogation room or in court or in jail, they may lie to diminish their culpability for their crimes, to make themselves seem the victim; other times they may lie to enhance their culpability, to pump up their image as a bad guy, as someone to be feared. The short rule is that every hour of every day of every year, in every jail and prison in America, bullshit reigns. And if you can't independently corroborate the information a criminal gives you, it's virtually worthless.

Besides, Clark's story, as related by the snitch, just didn't sound right. At the time I'd been chasing bank robbers for more than twenty years, and I'd never heard anything like it. Sure, there'd been cases of, say, a guy robbing a bank and claiming his drinking buddy or his wife or the devil made him do it. In the Patty Hearst case, the kidnapped heiress's unsuccessful defense was that she'd been coerced into robbing that bank where she was photographed holding a machine gun.

But a guy claiming he'd been forced to rob dozens of banks over a six-week period? And getting a lousy couple hundred bucks for each one? And walking around free and easy between the bank licks, perfectly able to flee the neighborhood or, less likely, tell the cops? It didn't add up. The only thing that sounded half right was Clark's claim that he hadn't been able to keep the money from the robberies. He'd stolen a total of about $70,000 in his robberies, which is a lot of dough for a crackhead to run through in six weeks; he couldn't possibly have smoked that much rock. But maybe he'd given some of the stolen cash to his wife, or his mama, or his buddies. You never knew.

And even if the snitch's story was accurate—snitches lie, too—it wouldn't make much if any difference in Clark's case. He was already down for his first, and admittedly voluntary, robberies. Even if he wanted to put on a coercion defense for the subsequent robberies, the ones committed after the gang-bangers supposedly shot him, that wouldn't reduce his sentence. And he'd have to rat openly on the gang-bangers, which would put a snitch jacket on him when he went to prison—and no experienced con wants that shithouse shiv of Damocles hanging over his head in the joint.

So, no, the jailhouse snitch's report wasn't going to change the Money or Die Bandit's immediate circumstances. And we couldn't even go back and ask Clark about it, since he might be able to figure out where we'd gotten the story, which would burn the jailhouse snitch.

But it was something to think about. So I put out the word to the bank squad guys and throughout the L.A. field office to let me know if they heard any reports of gang-bangers moving into bank robberies. Meanwhile, I checked the gang activity files for the street names Clark had mentioned.

Yep, there was "Peanut," a twenty-year-old parolee from the California Youth Authority and a hard-core gang-banger. And there was "C-Dog," true name Donzell Lamar Thompson, another hardcore. And yes, there was "Casper," aka Cas, aka Baby Cas, true name Robert Sheldon Brown, the guy Clark had described as the shot-caller on the bank licks.

There was nothing solid, no definite way to connect these guys to Clark's bank robberies, nothing we could build a case on; all we had was the secondhand jailhouse ramblings of an admitted smokehead. Still, as I reviewed their files and looked at their mug shot photos from prior arrests, I couldn't shake a bad feeling.

Peanut and C-Dog didn't particularly stand out; they offered up to the camera only the blank, soulless look of a million other jailhouse portraits, communicating nothing.

But there was something about Casper, the quiet shot-caller. He was a big guy, six two, over 200 pounds, with a strong, handsome face that by itself didn't look at all dangerous or threatening, an open, even friendly-looking face. But it was his eyes that revealed him. If you looked deep into that 3 by 5 color glossy, you could see the ruthlessness in those brown eyes, ruthlessness made all the more sinister by the intelligence that lurked there with it. Like a Mafia Don, Casper exuded menace rather than advertising it with hard looks or posturing. Just looking at him I could tell that this guy was no ordinary gang-banger, no common street thug. This guy was different.

So who are you, Casper? I wondered as I studied his mug shot. What's your story?

✦ ✦ ✦

He had been in trouble with the law since he was nine—stealing, tagging, skipping school, running away from home, an urban feral boy roaming wild on some of America's most lawless streets.

Like so many other boys of his time and place, he had a young mother who loved him but couldn't control him, and a father who couldn't be found. He was a smart boy, a good boy in many ways, loving and kind to his mother and younger brother, and his mother tried her best to save him, taking him to counselors and county psychiatrists and youth programs. But nothing ever worked. Always there was the call of the wild streets echoing in his head—and the wolves that were calling him were the Rollin' Sixties Crips.

Street gangs had always been a factor of life in L.A. The oldest gangs were the pachuco gangsters in East L.A. who had sprung up in the 1930s and had fought each other—initially with fists or chains or knives, later with guns—from generation to generation ever since. The African-American gangs of South Central were a much newer phenomenon. There had been black social clubs in South Central in the fifties and early sixties, with names like the Gladiators and the Black Cobras, but the violence generally was low-level and personal; it was more *West Side Story* than *Boyz N the Hood*. It wasn't until the late 1960s that the black ghetto gangs starting taking on their modern form, when some young men in Watts formed a gang known as the Crips—so called, legend has it, because one of their members was a cripple, a "crip," who walked with a cane. Out of admiration, or for protection, other gangs started forming throughout South Central, some aligned with the original Crips, others part of a new gang group called "Bloods," after the term black GIs used for themselves in Vietnam.

Eventually, there was a dizzying array of gang sets scattered throughout South Central: the Playboy Gangster Crips, the Bounty Hunters Bloods, the Grape Street Crips, the Six-Deuce Brims Bloods, the Eight-Trey Gangster Crips, the Sirkle Sity Piru Bloods, and so on. (Out of disrespect for the Crips, Blood sets refused to use any "Cs" in their names; hence Circle City became Sirkle Sity.) Although Bloods and Crips were mortal enemies, with different "colors"—Crips were blue, Bloods were red—both Bloods and Crips also carried on never-ending internecine wars with other Blood or Crip sets. The wars were as childish and petty as they were bloody, an endless cycle of attacks and paybacks that started over nothing—a chance remark, an overture to the wrong girl—and then took on a life of their own. By the late 1980s, L.A. was home to some five hundred warring street gangs, with a combined strength of perhaps forty thousand hard-core members and tens of thousands of associates and wannabes. The body count from gang-related drive-by shootings and street twists (robberies) and assorted acts of violence numbered more than seven hundred a year; too often, it was innocent bystanders who bled.

Even by the tough standards of L.A. gangsterism, the Rollin' Sixties Crips were among the worst of the worst. The gang had been founded in the early 1970s by some guys who had attended Horace Mann Junior High School together, guys named Big Rick and Lunatic Frank and Stagger Lee and Doe Eyes and Skull. They were the OGs, the "Original Gangsters," a term that later would be applied to any long-standing and well-respected—or well-feared—member of the gang. The gang's name derived from the streets where they lived—60th through 69th streets, between Van Ness and Crenshaw boulevards, in the Hyde Park neighborhood of South Central L.A.—and from their boasts that they were "rollers," that is, rolling in cash. (Later, as the Rollin' Sixties turf expanded out of Hyde Park and into a more affluent, middle-class black section of Baldwin Hills, the Sixties split into two affiliated groups, the Rollin' Sixties Neighborhood Crips and the Rollin' Sixties Overhill Crips.)

The cash the Sixties were rollin' in came from street jacks and burglaries and selling dope, mostly marijuana in those early days, and later crack cocaine. On his worst day, the devil couldn't have come up with a more soul-killing, community-destroying drug than crack. Producing a much more intense, and more addictive, high than the powdered form, crack came in the form of small "rocks" that were easily available to anyone who could put together five or ten bucks from petty thefts or car boosts or street prostitution. Like the other street gangs, the Sixties ruthlessly controlled the crack business on their own turf, and used part of the proceeds to arm themselves for their disrespect wars with the Inglewood Family Bloods and the 74 Hoover Bloods, or for internecine conflict with the Eight Trey Gangster Crips, the gang that later would help touch off the Rodney King riots at the corner of Florence and Normandie.

The Sixties were stone killers, all right, and were involved in some of the most violent carnage in L.A. history. For example, in 1984 three members of the Sixties walked into a South Central home and brutally murdered two children and a woman in a wheelchair; it turned out they'd been hired to do the hit in retaliation for a business deal gone bad, but they had gone to the wrong house. One of the people they murdered, the woman in the wheelchair, was the mother of L.A. Rams player Kermit Alexander.

These were the guys that young Robert Sheldon Brown admired and looked up to and wanted to be a part of.

At age fourteen he was "jumped in" to the gang, a process that involved the older, bigger gang members beating the shit out of him to see if he was man enough to take it, if he was "down" for the gang, or if he was a "buster," a coward who'd go runnin' home to mama. He was known as "Baby Casper" or "Baby Cas" on the street—Casper because of his quiet, almost ghostlike ways, the "baby" indicating his rank as a junior member of the gang—and he was definitely no buster, no mama's boy. At about the same time he was jumped in he ran away from home for good, this to his mother's heartache and guilty relief. He slept in cars and on friends' couches, making his eating money with petty thefts; school was just an unpleasant memory. Shortly after he was jumped into the Crips, a carload of rival gang members drove by his mother's house on Madden Avenue in Hyde Park, thinking Casper still lived there, and riddled it with bullets; his mother caught a bullet in the leg. Terrified, she moved out, taking Brown's younger brother with her.

Although he occasionally visited her, he didn't talk about his gang activities. Still, whenever she drove through the old Hyde Park neighborhood, she was able to track her son's increasing status in the Rollin' Sixties by the gang graffiti on the walls. When she saw OG CAS RSC spray-painted on a building, she knew the translation: Her son was a "Baby" no longer; he was now an original gangster in the Rollin' Sixties, one of the shot-callers who controlled the gang, a stone-banger who had devoted his life to street gangsterism.

Like so many other mothers in South Central, she knew that the most she could hope for now was that her boy would wind up in prison. Because the only alternative was that he would wind up dead.

By the time he was twenty, Robert Sheldon Brown had the proverbial sheet as long as your arm: he'd been arrested for drug dealing, carrying a concealed weapon, burglary, robbery, grand theft auto—and he had undoubtedly done a hundred other things he never got caught for. The law never did much to him; this was before voters in the early nineties started passing ballot measures to bring the hammer down on repeat offenders. Casper would disappear for weeks or months at a time as he shuffled in and out of Juvenile Hall and the California Youth Authority (CYA) and the county jail, and then he'd be on the street again, on probation or parole, and get right back into the life. As a Sixties OG he was big man in the Hyde Park 'hood, a good-looking, charismatic guy who was admired by the young gang wannabes who hung around.

There was something about him, a certain coolness, a quiet confidence, that made him a natural leader. Although he'd never been charged with murder, the word on the street was that he'd killed some guys from rival gangs—and in Casper's world, being known, rightly or wrongly, as a killer didn't hurt his reputation. He was also actively admired by women; at any given time he had a half dozen girlfriends that he supported to one extent or another—this despite the fact that in his whole life he had never held a real job.

At first the money came from burglaries and robberies and crack dealing, but Brown was too smart not to figure out the down side of those criminal endeavors. Take crack, for example. There was a popular misconception that the street gangsters who controlled the crack business in South Central were like Colombian drug lords, awash in millions of dollars of cash. But the economics of the drug trade didn't work that way, at least not at the retail or mid-level wholesale side of it, which is where most gang-bangers came in. Think about it: How many ten-dollar rocks would you have to sell to how many smokeheads even to gross a million dollars, much less net? Sure, you could make a living at it, a few hundred here, a couple thousand there, maybe ten or twenty thousand if you were dealing in kilo weight. But damn it, when you came right down to it, dope dealing was hard and dangerous work.

So were burglaries and robberies. Steal a stereo out of a guy's house and you're gonna have to fence it off for pennies on the dollar; even if you did a high-end twist, like a jewelry store robbery, which a lot of the Sixties were into, you had the same problem in moving the merchandise. And finding cash to steal wasn't easy: no sane small businessman within ten miles of South Central ever kept more than a couple hundred bucks in a cash register, and the bigger businesses always had security on hand, which complicated things.

No, the thing to do, Casper realized, was to eliminate the middlemen and go straight for the big cash. The thing to do was to start hitting banks.

"I've robbed, I've done burglaries, I've done a little bit of everything," Casper said later. "But the money couldn't compare to the banks. You could go into a bank and in two minutes get what on the streets would take you six or seven weeks to get."

Exactly. And in retrospect, I'm surprised it took the street gangsters as long as it did to figure that out.

It's a little uncertain whether Casper ever personally robbed a bank. Later he would claim to have done a couple of bank licks himself in his younger days, but I went back over every unsolved bank robbery in L.A. from the time Casper was thirteen years old and never found one that I could link him to. I suspect that he learned about bank robbery secondhand, from more experienced guys in Men's Central Jail or CYA, guys who filled him in on two-eleven buttons and dye packs and other details of the bank robbery art.

But Casper took the lessons a step further. Casper's genius—and remember, this kid's not even old enough to buy a beer yet—was to figure out a way to eliminate the personal risk of doing a bank job. Instead of putting himself in jeopardy, he would be the planner, the organizer, setting up the bank lick and getting other people to actually do the robbing. Meanwhile, he'd wait safely far away, and then he'd take the lion's share of the stolen cash. He would never, ever set foot in the bank.

Yes, it sounds unbelievable. I mean, where could you possibly find guys who would be stupid enough to rob a bank for you and then give you the money?

Actually, finding such henchmen was a lot easier than you might think. There were two powerful recruiting tools. One was crack. The other was fear.

Casper put together a crew to manage the thing, starting with his best pal, the aforementioned C-Dog, another Rollin' Sixties OG who had been tight with Casper since they were in Horace Mann Junior High together. They were physically similar, big and buffed out—some people thought they actually were brothers—but C-Dog didn't have Casper's brains. He was the lieutenant, the number two man, and often the muscle. Other gang members, such as Peanut, also helped round up potential robbers.

They started out using crackheads like Clark, or sometimes winos, guys for whom the pressing needs of today outweighed the risks of prison tomorrow. There were plenty of them in South Central, hanging out on corners or stumbling out of crackhouses after they'd smoked up what little money they had. Casper and C-Dog would cruise up and offer them a chance at some quick cash, the guy would get in the car, and they'd take off, looking for a likely target. They'd tell the crackhead exactly what to do, how to behave in the bank, what to write on the demand note. They never wrote or handled the notes themselves, since that could leave their prints or handwriting samples. They'd tell him how easy it was, and if the guy didn't want to do it they'd give him an eye-fucking and suggest that his only options were to rob the bank or suffer an asskicking, or worse. Sometimes they'd give a guy ten or twenty bucks—for food, they'd say—and then the next day they'd come back and tell him that by accepting the money he'd signed a "contract" and had to pay off by robbing a bank for them.

They'd drop the guy outside the bank, watch to make sure he went in, and then wait a block or so away at a prearranged rendezvous point, someplace where they could keep the bank in sight. If the guy made it out with the money, great, they'd take it and then drive him to another bank for the same drill; sometimes they would hit three or four banks in the same day before taking the robber back to the 'hood and kicking him loose with a few hundred bucks or so, while they kept thousands. If the guy didn't like the split, fuck him, that was the way it was.

And if anything went wrong, if the robber got caught as he was leaving the bank, or if they saw some bank employee chasing the guy down the sidewalk, Brown and his crew would drive away and leave him to rot. Brown knew that even if the guy got caught and ratted them out—and most, like Clark, would be too afraid to do that—the cops and the FBI wouldn't be able to prove anything with just the word of a wino or some addle-headed crack addict. Hell, most of the time the smokehead wouldn't even know their names.

It was a pretty amazing concept: Gang members driving around with crack addicts and bums and ordering them to rob banks. The only drawback was that too often the press-ganged henchmen just didn't shine as bank bandits—for obvious reasons. Sleeping on sidewalks or getting high on crack usually doesn't leave you with a clear head and a sharp sense of purpose; sometimes these poor bastards could barely tie their own shoes, let alone rob a bank. And often they just didn't have the heart to be bank robbers; they'd come out of the bank and back to the waiting car with no money and some lame dog-ate-my-homework excuse: A teller recognized me, the security guard wouldn't let me in, I saw the bank manager hit an alarm while I was in line—whatever.

But there were as many successes as failures. Later I figured that Casper and C-Dog and their addle-headed henchmen had pulled off at least eighty-five note job robberies over a year and a half, for a total take of about $350,000. It was a lot of money, more than Casper and his crew could ever have made in the retail dope trade or doing street twists, but it didn't last long. Casper liked nice clothes and nice cars, and as you might expect, his many girlfriends were a significant drain on his finances.

Still, he might have been able to string the bank licks out indefinitely if he had stuck to his original program of sponsoring note job robberies. None of his coerced note job robbers had ever fingered him after they were caught, at least not to the cops or the FBI, and the comparative volume of his bank robbery business wasn't enough to put him at the center of our radar screens, even if we'd known what he was doing. Besides, note jobs ranked at the low end of bank squad priorities.

But in the fall of 1991, Casper took his bank robbery business to another, more serious level. His inspiration for the move, strangely enough, was a couple of weird, middle-aged white religious fanatics I called the "West Hills Bandits."

✦ ✦ ✦

Except for their shared penchant for robbing banks, it would be hard to think of two guys more different from Casper and C-Dog than Gilbert Michaels and James McGrath.

They had grown up together in the San Fernando Valley in the 1950s, Michaels the stepson of a wealthy businessman, McGrath a more or less normal suburban kid. McGrath was an avid competitive swimmer at North Hollywood High, and although Michaels was widely considered a geek and a weirdo, his parents had a large pool that Michaels let McGrath practice in; the two boys grew close. Later McGrath attended Valley College, where he became a national junior college freestyle swimming champion. That earned him a swimming scholarship to USC and a slot on the team that swept the national championships in 1964. An injury kept him out of the 1964 Olympic trials, but after a hitch in the Air Force he started coaching. He taught Olympic pole vaulter Bob Seagren how to swim, this in preparation for the "Superstars Competition" TV show, and helped coach Olympic swimming hopefuls in Greece. He also worked for a while as a deputy probation officer for L.A. County.

Michaels, meanwhile, had gone to UCLA as a premed student, but dropped out to pursue an acting and music career. Always a strange kid, he had grown into an even stranger adult; by the 1970s, he was wading off into the deep end of the mental health pool. Eventually he answered what he described as a call from God, and went on to develop an obsessive interest in a religion of his own devising, a belief system based on the conflict between "Luciferians," the evil ones who walk among us, and the Prophets of God—of whom Michaels was, naturally, the leader. Unfortunately for Michaels, Prophets were few; his only followers were his wife, Rose Ann, and McGrath, who had renewed his friendship with Michaels in the early 1970s and had fallen under his harebrained spell. In addition to honing their religious theories, Michaels and McGrath started a small candy business, marketing a product called Rose Ann's Old Style Fudge, which Michaels's wife cooked up in the family kitchen.

They were a weird pair, all right, but no weirder than a lot of other half-baked religious nuts in L.A. What put them over the edge was that Michaels had inherited a substantial fortune after his parents died— over a million dollars, according to some estimates—but the money was tied up in a trust, and the trustees refused to hand it over in a lump sum to capitalize an expansion of Michaels's fudge business. In Michaels's eyes this made them, by definition, Luciferians, and eventually he told McGrath that God had ordered him to "repossess" the disputed money from the banks in which it was being held. That was good enough for McGrath, who later described himself as Michaels's "right-hand man, Tonto to his Lone Ranger."

So Tonto and his Kemo Sabe started robbing the banks that Michaels claimed were illegally holding his inheritance. But while they may have been crazy, they weren't stupid. Their takeover bank robberies—that is, robberies in which the bandits take control of the entire bank and clean out all the tellers' drawers and, if possible, the vault—were planned and executed with astonishing skill and precision. Heavily armed with military-style assault weapons, including AR-15s and Thompson sub-machine guns, and wearing a variety of disguises—wigs, ski masks, false beards and mustaches—the pair would burst into a bank, herd employees and customers into a corner, and then force the operations manager to open the vault, where they would load stacks of cash into duffel bags and then take off, ditching the getaway car at a preselected location and switching to a "cold car," a legally registered vehicle that would arouse no suspicion. Once they dressed as Postal Service employees and used a surplus postal truck as the initial getaway vehicle.

They were invariably polite, telling customers and employees to remain calm and "Watch the show," and as they left the bank they yelled out: "Thanks, everybody!" They were also enormously successful, taking in more than a million dollars in nine robberies between March 1991 and February 1992. They used part of the money to buy more weapons and ammunition—most of them legal purchases from gun dealers—and to build a large underground bunker, complete with an indoor shooting range, beneath a house they'd rented in the upscale West Hills section of the San Fernando Valley. Their plan was to use the bunker as a redoubt in the battle of Armageddon when the Luciferians unleashed their tribes of heathen followers to destroy the world.

Meanwhile, the West Hills Bandits, as I named them—not because I knew where they lived, but because their first bank job had been in the West Hills area—were driving us nuts. The break finally came when Special Agent Randy Aiden, who worked on one of the L.A. FBI anti-terrorism squads, mentioned to me that an informant had told him about two white guys who were buying unusual quantities of assault weapons, handguns, and ammunition at various gun dealerships, tens of thousands of dollars' worth at a time, and always paying in cash. Randy wanted to know if I'd seen anybody using assault rifles or other unusual weaponry in bank robberies.

You bet I had. I pulled the surveillance photos of the West Hills Bandits and Randy showed them to his informant, who despite the disguises thought they looked like the same guys who'd been stocking up on guns. It wasn't enough for an arrest warrant, but we got their names from the gun purchase records and put the two men under surveillance, watching as they cased various banks and bought getaway cars for cash under assumed names. In February 1992, we nabbed them as they robbed a bank in Woodland Hills of $150,000; as our FBI SWAT team guys drew down on them, they shouted out: "We are messengers from God!" but other than that they didn't resist. When we searched the underground bunker we found 119 weapons, including assault rifles with laser sights, .50-caliber sniper rifles, drum-fed semiautomatic shotguns, and 27,000 rounds of ammo for heathen-killing purposes.

McGrath wound up taking a fifteen-year jolt in prison. But Michaels, a certifiable nutcake, was ruled mentally incapable of assisting in his own defense and was eventually released from federal custody under close and continuing medical supervision.

So what did these two affluent white bank-robbing lunatics have to do with Casper and C-Dog? Nothing except this: On their fifth bank robbery, the West Hills Bandits had made an enormous score, taking $437,000 from the vault at a Wells Fargo in Tarzana. At the time it was the biggest haul from a bank robbery in L.A. history—and ideally, no one in the general public would have ever found that out. You may have noticed that whenever you read about a bank robbery in the newspaper, the amount that was stolen is almost never revealed; the loss is usually described by FBI agents or bank officials as an "undetermined amount" of cash. Which is bullshit. Banks keep close track of how much cash is in a vault or in tellers' drawers, and within hours of a robbery they know exactly how much is missing. But banks don't want to advertise their losses—it upsets the customers—and cops don't want people to know how much money you can get from robbing a bank, especially if it's in the neighborhood of half a million dollars.

Unfortunately, in the Wells Fargo robbery somebody shot his mouth off. The *Los Angeles Times* printed a story about the record-breaking heist, with all the details of how they'd done it, and with the $437,000-loss figure included; the TV stations picked up on it, and for a couple of days it was all over the news.

And, of course, they have TVs in South Central.

Casper and C-Dog saw the news and realized they were being chumps. Why drive a bunch of guys all over town to do note jobs for a thousand or two thousand or even ten thousand when you could send some guys in to take over the whole goddam bank and steal maybe a half a million? Takeovers were where the real money was.

Obviously, if they were going to move into takeover robberies, they'd have to make some changes; they couldn't use winos and crackheads like Clark anymore. Half the time those guys fucked up or pussied out even on a simple note job; they'd be worthless as hard-core takeover bandits. No, takeovers required guys with heart, guys who were wild enough or brave enough or stupid enough to burst into a bank and stick a gun in somebody's face and tell the motherfucker to hit the floor and then hop over the counter and clean out a vault.

Casper knew just where to find guys like that. They were all around him, inside and outside the Rollin' Sixties.

At any given time the Rollin' Sixties gang might number only twenty or thirty OGs on the street, the rest being locked up in CYA or prison— or dead. But there were scores of "li'ls" and "babys," usually younger gang members who were committed to the gang but hadn't yet achieved senior status; for them, doing bank licks would be an instant status ticket, not to mention a moneymaker. Casper knew that a lot of them would jump at the chance to work for him, and that unlike his fellow OGs they wouldn't bitch about an uneven split on the loot. The 'hood also had deep reservoirs of young wannabes, the hangers-on who associated with the gangsters, who admired and envied them their power and their money, but who for one reason or another—fear, family influence, a natural aversion to a life of crime, whatever—were not active, jumped-in members of the gang. They, too, could be challenged or cajoled or coerced into doing bank licks. And in a world of poverty, there were always other people, older guys and women, who were willing to play the smaller, less dangerous roles in return for a quick payoff, people who would serve as chauffeurs and getaway drivers and providers of guns and getaway cars.

The recruiting process was simple enough. On the street, in a park, on a basketball court, or even on a schoolyard (one young robber was recruited right out of "nutrition period" at Crenshaw High School), Casper or C-Dog or both would approach some young guy, usually some kid with a connection to the Sixties, and sound him out: Hey, man, you wanna make some money, you wanna get paid?—"getting paid" being a 'hood euphemism for doing a robbery. Most would eagerly sign on. Casper was, after all, admired, respected and envied. Shining as a man in Casper's eyes was important to these young guys. If the guy backed up, if he said no, they'd taunt him, call him a pussy and a buster, a do-good mama's boy; it was a challenge to manhood that, in the code of the 'hood, was hard to back down from. And if the kid still backed up, they might beat the shit out of him, especially if he was an official junior member of the gang. Gang rules required that the babies and the littles work for the gang, and the OGs called the shots.

Before it was over, Casper and C-Dog would enlist scores of young men to rob banks for them. Some were older, in their twenties, and some were impossibly young; one of them was just thirteen. But most of the actual robbers ranged from sixteen to nineteen—maybe old enough to know better, but too young and wild to care.

And when in the fall of 1991 I first started seeing these "Baby Bandits" in action, I could hardly believe my eyes.

In the entire decade of the 1980s, I'd seen less than a dozen bank robberies committed by juveniles, and most of those were wobbler juveniles, kids on the cusp of age eighteen and legal adulthood. Before, bank robbery had always been a man's game. Now, suddenly, I was seeing younger teenagers holding up banks by the dozens.

The names and faces changed constantly as Casper rotated personnel. But usually there were at least three robbers for every job, with one designated as the triggerman and the others as bagmen, plus a getaway driver. Casper would brief them on the street or in a motel room on Crenshaw Boulevard that he and other gang members hung out in, coaching them on the fine points of takeover bank robberies, as he understood them, and assigning each one a specific task within the bank. Then they'd set out in a caravan of three cars for a preselected bank. Casper, in the lead, would be in a "cold car," a legitimate car with valid registration and good plates, so he'd avoid being pulled over by cops; another cold car driven by a getaway driver would follow, with the three robbers bringing up the rear in a "gangster ride" or "G-ride," a recently stolen or carjacked vehicle.

The actual robbers often had no idea where they were or where they were going. Whenever gang members ventured out of their territory, they'd call it "rollin' deep," and Casper had them rollin' deeper than many of them had been in their lives, taking them twenty, thirty, forty miles away from the 'hood, south into Orange County or north into the San Fernando Valley or east into the San Gabriel Valley. Casper would always tell them that the target bank had been "peeped out" (cased) beforehand, and sometimes it was true; other times, Casper had simply picked a likely-looking bank at random, and never even bothered to check it out. Often he'd also tell the robbers that it was an inside job, that the bank employees or security guard were expecting the robbery and would readily cooperate—which was the purest bullshit, but which served to put a little heart into the robbers. After pointing out the bank, Casper would park nearby and watch to make sure the robbers didn't chicken out. As soon as they went inside the bank he'd drive away and head back to Hyde Park.

The young bandits' bank robbery technique, as taught by Casper, was called "goin' kamikaze." The robbers would burst into the bank in an explosion of hooded sweatshirts and baggy pants and Nikes, screaming and shouting motherfucker this and motherfucker that, waving guns, often squeezing off a shot or two into the ceiling to demonstrate the seriousness of the situation. They would order everyone to the floor, kicking or pistol-whipping those who didn't move fast enough. Sometimes they'd wrench gold wedding bands off women's fingers, or steal purses, or make male customers hand over their wallets.

Once the bank was under control, and customers and employees were cowering on the floor, the bagmen would leap over the counter and start scooping money into pillowcases. Casper had told them to be sure to hit the commercial teller's station, which would have larger amounts of cash, and the vault if it was open. He told them how to avoid tracking devices and dye packs inserted into the currency bundles—"If it don't bend it don't spend," was the way Casper explained it, meaning that the robbers should avoid the rigid currency bundles that indicated a security device hidden inside. It was advice that a lot of these young, inexperienced bandits would fail to heed.

Then the robbers would run out of the bank, pile into the "G-ride," and drive to a rendezvous point where the cold car and getaway driver would be waiting; often the second getaway driver would be a well-dressed woman or a Latino male whom Casper had hired, someone who didn't fit the "young black male" description of the bank robbers. The bandits would abandon the G-ride, climb into the cold car, and hunker down in the backseat, hidden from view, as the wheelman or -woman drove off. They'd meet up with Casper, usually at a motel room, to split the cash. Out of $20,000, $40,000, or $50,000, the actual robbers might get $500 to $1,500 apiece, the getaway driver the same; Casper and C-Dog kept the rest. If Casper thought the robbers were holding back some of the loot, he'd make them strip and then search their clothes. And if the take wasn't big enough, he'd send them out to do another bank lick—and another, and another.

The sheer number of takeover robberies these young bandits were pulling off was astonishing. In the first nine months of 1991, there were only about forty takeover robberies in L.A., most of them involving professional robbery crews. But in the last three months of the year, after Casper & Co. got into the takeover business, there were more than a hundred bank takeovers in L.A., the vast majority of them involving young African-American gang members. Whereas takeovers had once constituted only a small percentage of bank robberies—about 4 percent—they now accounted for almost 30 percent, with a corresponding increase in violence.

Pretty soon the surveillance photos papered the walls of my office, and put faces to the fear: women employees kneeling behind desks, clutching each other in terror; a bank manager looking shell-shocked as a baby-faced young bandit points a sawed-off shotgun at his head; customers scattered across the floor, their faces pressed into the thin green carpet, wondering if they're going to survive. You could almost see them trembling. And with good reason. These young gangsters, these Baby Bandits, were the most gratuitously violent bank bandits I'd ever seen.

"He grabbed Jennifer by the hair and then hit her on the head with his gun," a female bank employee said of one robbery. "She was bleeding and screaming; everyone was screaming. There were three of them, all very young-looking. They had come into the bank, it was about five P.M., and started shouting, 'This is a holdup, get on the floor, get on the fucking floor!' and firing shots into the ceiling and the walls. Two of them jumped over the counter, and Jennifer was still standing there, like she was in shock, and one of them said, 'I told you to get down, bitch!' and that's when he hit her. He kept yelling, 'Don't fucking move, don't fucking move!' The other one started taking the money from the tellers' drawers and putting it into a white bag, a pillowcase. The other one, the third one, was in the lobby and he was shooting more shots and yelling to the others, 'Get the vault, 'cuz! Get the vault!' One of them grabbed Daniele and started dragging her toward the vault, and she was crying, 'Oh no! Oh no!' She thought he was going to rape her, or kill her. He screamed at her to open the locked vault gate, but she was pleading with him and saying that she didn't have the key. He fired his gun into the wall and said, 'I'll kill you, bitch! I'll fucking kill you!' Finally I guess they got scared, because suddenly they all ran out of the bank, but everybody stayed on the floor for what seemed like a long time, crying and shaking. We all thought we were going to die. I never want to go through anything like that again."

The whole thing was scary—and for me, depressing, an indication that the bank robbery world had fundamentally changed, and not for the better. It wasn't at all like the old days, when your usual takeover bandits were cool, calm professionals—guys like the Marx Brothers, for example.

Between 1984 and 1986, the Marx Brothers—I gave them the name because in one of their early robberies they wore Harpo-style wigs and Groucho-style fake mustaches and glasses—pulled off eleven bank robberies in the L.A. area, for a total take of about $400,000. These guys knew what they were doing. They'd walk into a bank, pull out semiautomatic pistols, and announce the robbery in a firm but polite manner; no motherfucker this or motherfucker that, no rough stuff. One would keep the customers and employees under control while the other hit the vault and loaded the money into a briefcase. They were careful: one of them would always wear an earpiece connected to a police scanner clipped to his belt, so they could hear if the cops were being dispatched to the bank, and they both frequently checked their watches to make sure they got out of the bank in under two minutes—the usual minimum police response time to a two-eleven silent alarm. That was important, because it reduced the chances of a violent encounter with the cops. And they were disciplined about it. When they hit the two-minute mark they were out of there, no matter how much money was left to steal. That was the mark of true professionals.

Don't misunderstand. I'm not saying I admired these guys as human beings. The Marx Brothers were armed bank robbers, and therefore my sworn enemies. I never doubted that they'd be willing to kill me or any other law enforcement officer who got in their way; in fact, we later found out that during a robbery in the 1960s the Marx Brothers had shot and wounded a sheriff's deputy in a running gun battle. But the Marx Brothers would never pistol-whip a teller just to make a point, or stoop to stealing a ring off some old lady's finger. They had standards, and style, and for me it was almost a pleasure to chase guys who had respect for the rules of their chosen profession.

(We finally caught the Marx Brothers after I got their surveillance photos on the TV news. Despite the disguises, someone recognized them and ratted them out; the Marx Brothers, both middle-aged ex-cons, turned out indeed to be brothers. They enjoyed the high life in Vegas, gambling especially, and they financed their lifestyle the old-fashioned way: with quick, clean, competent bank robberies.)

But the Baby Bandits were no Marx Brothers. They were turning takeover bank robberies into indoor muggings. In addition to being unnecessarily violent, they were also rank amateurs, and dangerously incompetent. Which wasn't surprising. Remember, these were ghetto kids, uneducated, unsophisticated teenagers; for many, maybe most of them, the first time they'd ever even been in a bank was when they robbed one. And they had a habit of screwing up—with bloody results.

For example, in August 1992, Casper set up a robbery with three teenagers as the entry team and an older guy as the getaway driver. The three boys burst into a Wells Fargo in Downey, screaming and terrorizing; one of the Baby Bandits tried to shoot into the ceiling but couldn't figure out how to release the safety on his gun, so he pistol-whipped a female customer and left her bleeding on the floor. The bank robber finally released the safety and started cranking rounds into the ceiling, apparently for the hell of it, while the others vaulted the counter. One of them, dressed in the baggy-pants style of gang-bangers—and eventually of suburban kids as well—wasn't wearing a belt, and the victims later said he seemed to be having trouble keeping his pants up; he kept holding his waistband with one hand, and waving the gun in the other.

As they were scooping up the money, the cops roared up outside, responding to the two-eleven silent alarm. The robbers had foolishly stayed in the bank way too long. None of them carried watches, and like a lot of teenagers, I doubt that they had much concept of time in the first place. The bandits broke a window in the rear of the bank and bailed out, carrying $56,000 in cash; two were quickly caught and the money recovered, but the third jumped a fence to try to get to the getaway car. A Downey cop caught up with and drew down on him with a shotgun, ordering him to surrender, but the bandit fired a shot at him and the cop let go a round with the shotgun. The young bandit collapsed across the hood of the getaway car, with one hand holding a Colt .45 semiautomatic, the other clutching at his waistband, still trying to hold his pants up. He was fifteen years old.

In another robbery, Casper put together one young gunman, two young bagmen, and an older getaway car driver with a carjacked Ford Escort to hit a Hancock Savings in the Fairfax District. Casper waited at the rendezvous spot—a motel in Hyde Park—while C-Dog escorted the robbery crew to the bank. The three robbers charged into the bank, one of them waving a .357 Magnum, and the bagmen cleaned out the tellers' drawers. But as they ran out of the bank, an explosive dye pack hidden in the cash went off, spraying the robbers with tear gas and red dye. C-Dog saw this go down and took off, leaving the robbers behind. They abandoned the money and the stolen car and managed to get away, later linking up with Casper at the motel. Casper was furious at the screwup and ordered them out again, equipped with yet another stolen G-ride. This time he personally led them to a Cerritos Valley Bank in Norwalk and watched from a distance as they burst in.

But again the bandits screwed up, spending too much time in the bank. Waiting in his car at a rendezvous point a few blocks away, Casper saw a phalanx of sheriff's deputies' black-and-whites screaming toward the bank. Naturally, he took off. Meanwhile, the robbers piled into the getaway car, a stolen Chevy, and drove to the cold car, a red Firebird. But as they were leaving the area in the Firebird, a police chopper caught up with them; despite Casper's warnings about "If it don't bend it don't spend," the bandits had taken a currency bundle with a tracking device inside, and the helicopter was picking up the signal. A high-speed chase ensued, captured on live television by TV news choppers. The robbers blew a tire, bailed out, and carjacked a passing car, pulling the female driver out and pushing her to the ground. Finally they crashed the carjacked vehicle into another car and were captured after they holed up in a nearby apartment.

In another case, Casper sent a three-man—or rather, three-boy—robbery crew into a Southern California Bank in Downey. One of the robbers, a fifteen-year-old whose street name was Li'l Scoobie, was armed with a .38 revolver; the others, Rollin' Sixties gang members with the monikers Ice Man and Li'l Gilbone, were the bagmen. But they didn't get a chance to bag any cash. As soon as Scoobie shouted "Freeze" and everyone in the bank dropped to the floor, an armed security guard in the bank opened up with his .45. Li'l Scoobie dropped the gun and started running—he really didn't have the heart to be a bank bandit—but he tripped on a rug near the bank door, and as he fell a bullet caught him in the side. The guard kept firing—eight rounds in all. Ice Man caught one in the foot and Li'l Gilbone got a through-and-through wound in the fleshy part of his calf. The three bandits bailed out of the bank and, trailing blood, ran to a getaway car where a female accomplice, a friend of Casper's, was waiting.

As the young robbers screamed and bled and cried about their wounds, the woman drove them back to Hyde Park, where they split up and, in best gang-banger tradition, tried to self-treat their injuries. But Li'l Scoobie was in serious shape, with internal injuries; his mother called an ambulance, and the cops also showed up. Scoobie told them he'd been shot in a drive-by, but the cops weren't buying it, especially since he matched the description of one of the bandits in the Downey shoot-out. After doctors yanked the bullet out of Li'l Scoobie's body, it was matched to the bank security guard's gun. All three young robbers eventually were charged with bank robbery.

Sometimes the screwups were almost comical. In one robbery, a Baby Bandit climbing back over a teller counter dropped the money all over the bank floor and got so rattled as he was trying to pick it up that he accidentally shot one of his partners in the ass. In another, a baggy-clothed bandit jumped up on the teller counter and his pants promptly fell down; witnesses couldn't give much of a description of the bandit's face, but they all clearly remembered his striped boxer shorts. In a third, three young robbers forced the bank manager to open what they thought was the vault, but which turned out to be a storage closet; the young bandits had never been in a bank before and had no idea what a vault even looked like.

And so on. Casper's young henchmen were being caught with amazing regularity. Casper, of course, couldn't have cared less. His system of bank robberies was a little like drug smuggling: Sure, you're going to lose a shipment every now and then, along with the mules who were bringing it in. That was simply the cost of doing business. But the successes more than made up for the failures, and there were always more mules where they came from.

And the violence wasn't limited to banks. Casper's system consumed a lot of getaway vehicles—at least one per bank robbery—and the usual procurement method for G-rides was carjacking. Although few people in the civilian world realized it, a high percentage of the carjackings that terrorized L.A. in the early 1990s were directly related to bank robberies. People were dragged from their cars, pistol-whipped, sometimes even shot—and a few hours later the car would be found abandoned in an alley after being used in a bank lick.

Casper's crews accounted for dozens of such carjackings; at times he'd have a virtual motor pool of stolen G-rides stashed in alleys and apartment building parking lots.

But sometimes Casper showed more restraint—and even some real innovation—in the procurement of getaway vehicles. On at least two jobs, in Long Beach and West Covina, Casper "borrowed" a yellow school bus from an acquaintance who worked for a private school bus company and gave it to his bandits to use as a getaway vehicle. As far as I know, these were the first, and only, examples in history of a "getaway school bus" in a bank robbery. On other occasions, Casper prevailed upon an acquaintance who worked for the Post Office to lend him a red, white, and blue postal delivery truck, which he then gave to one of his crews for use as a switch-off getaway vehicle in several bank robberies. And believe it or not, once Casper rented a neighborhood ice-cream truck for use as a cold car.

Boy bandits, wild shoot-outs, getaway school buses, postal trucks, ice-cream trucks, high-speed chases, pistol-whippings, carjackings, blood and bodies on the streets—there was a Wild West feel to it, a sense that things were getting out of control in the bank robbery world.

And in fact they were. In 1992, with Casper & Co. in full swing, there were 448 takeover robberies in L.A.—three times more than the previous year—the vast majority of them committed by young gang members from South Central L.A. More alarmingly, in 1991 shots had been fired in only four takeover bank robberies in L.A.—just four. But in 1992, there were forty-eight bank robberies in which shots were fired. Meanwhile, bank robberies of all types in 1992 had soared to a new record: 2,641 of them in the L.A. area, about one every forty minutes of every business day.

It was a reign of terror, all right. But strangely enough, the general public—or at least the predominately white, suburban portion of the general public—never really understood what was happening. Every day they'd pick up the paper or turn on the TV news and see stories of violent carjacks and shoot-outs and police chases in their previously safe neighborhoods, and they thought it was all about gang wars and crack. The news media thought so, too, despite my best efforts to persuade them otherwise. They didn't understand that bank robberies were the primary reason these young gangsters were invading Woodland Hills and Simi Valley, Downey and Mission Viejo, and other bastions of middle-class white America. It was bank robberies that took gang crime out of the ghettos and into suburbia; bank robberies that led to the lion's share of street carjackings that had so terrified the city; bank robberies that were being played out live on television as news choppers filmed cops chasing getaway cars through the streets.

Yes, there was a crack epidemic in South Central L.A. But the violent takeover bank robbery epidemic had spread all across Southern California. And no one was paying attention.

Casper wasn't responsible for all of the takeovers. As word of Casper's techniques got around, other Rollin' Sixties started getting into bank licks on their own, and then other gangs as well. But Casper was the innovator, and the single biggest player. Eventually I would connect Casper's crews to at least ninety takeover robberies in the L.A. area, with a total take of over $1 million, not to mention the associated carjackings and assaults. Casper's guys fired shots in twenty of the robberies, physically assaulted dozens of bank employees and customers, and ripped off watches, wallets, or jewelry from dozens of terrified victims.

It was an enormous criminal undertaking, not unlike a Mafia family enterprise, and Casper was the Don. He showed amazing organizational skills for a guy who was only twenty-three years old and had dropped out of school when he was fourteen. All day, every day, he was recruiting personnel, procuring guns and getaway cars, setting up licks. Before it was over, hundreds of people had worked for Casper, as robbers or getaway drivers or stolen-car procurers or bank peepers who would check out a bank before a job. Others, usually Casper's girlfriends, stashed the huge amounts of cash he was bringing in: $10,000 here, $20,000 there; obviously, he couldn't deposit the money in a bank.

Casper was never ostentatious about his newfound wealth, never drove a Rolls-Royce or bought a big house. His one affectation was a collection of Detroit classic cars from the fifties and sixties, T-Birds and Chevys and Pontiacs, each beautifully restored and waxed to a deep, lustrous shine. But even without the external trappings of wealth, everyone in the 'hood knew what he was doing. They knew that OG Cas was the South Central Godfather of Bank Licks.

The FBI knew it, too. But we were having a hell of a time doing anything about it.

✦ ✦ ✦

The explosion of Baby Bandit robberies had caught our attention in a way that Casper's earlier note jobs never could have. Once again, this was L.A., and we on the bank squad could almost forgive you your trespasses if you stuck to non-violent note job robberies. But when you start pistol-whipping employees and jacking cars and tearing rings off little old ladies' fingers and getting people killed, you've gone too far. We're going to make a project out of you.

We had several agents on Casper's case. Special Agent George Schroder of our West Covina office was one, since a number of Casper's robberies had taken place in his area. Another was Special Agent Tracy Hanlon of the FBI gang task force, a young female agent who before joining the Bureau had been a West Point graduate and an Army helicopter pilot.

Hanlon was then part of the South Central Task Force, a joint FBI-LAPD unit that had been set up to target L.A. gangs for a Racketeer Influenced and Corrupt Organizations (RICO) Act prosecution. Frankly, the gang task force was kind of a sore point with those of us on the bank squad, one of those intramural beefs that occur in every large organization. At the time, the Bureau brass was in love with the idea of RICO prosecutions against gangs, having had some success along those lines with street gangs in Washington, D.C. Consequently, the Bureau's gang task forces were getting the lion's share of the resources, in money and personnel, while the bank squad was being bled dry. And the gang task force was concentrating its efforts on crack-dealing operations and pretty much ignoring what we knew to be the bigger problem—that is, gang-related bank robberies.

Still, after a lot of bitching and moaning on our parts, Special Agent Hanlon and a few other gang task force agents had been assigned to concentrate their attention on armed robberies by gang members, bank robberies included. And as they got into it, the name that kept coming up was Casper, Casper, Casper.

By this time, we'd caught many of Casper's young bank robbers, mostly through their own ineptitude; we'd already locked up dozens of them, the juveniles through the state system, the eighteen-and-overs through the federal courts. And when we interviewed them, when we gave them the pitch about the benefits of cooperation, some of them agreed to help us out—up to a point.

It was Casper's idea to do that lick, they'd say. Cas made me do it. He said if I didn't rob that bank he'd tell everybody I was a buster and a pussyboy. He said I had to do my work for the Sixties or he'd whup my ass. I did the work and I took the risk, but Cas and C-Dog took most of the money, and now I'm in jail and they're sittin' fat and happy and bitched-up back in the 'hood. It ain't fair, man.

But when it came down to making that cooperation official, they wanted no part of it.

What? You want me to me to testify? You want me to go into court and say he did it? Shit, you must be fuckin' crazy, man. I'm scared of those big motherfuckers. I do that, they'll get their homies to fuck me up, fuck my mama up, fuck my little brother up. If I gotta do my time, I'll do my time. It's better than being dead.

Fear was what Casper had been counting on, and he had called it right. If the guy wouldn't testify, his cooperation in telling us about Casper was pretty much worthless; you can't build a criminal case solely on accusations by an anonymous informant. One informant told us that Casper had boasted that the FBI couldn't lay a hand on him, because he never went into a bank, never personally jacked a car, never left his prints on a gun. So Casper figured that even if one of his guys did roll over on him and agree to testify, it would just be his word against Casper's.

He was right on that one, too. A few times we actually had a Casper bandit who was reluctantly willing to testify in return for a reduced sentence. But when we'd put together an investigative report and take it to the Complaint Unit of the U.S. Attorney's office and ask them to file bank robbery conspiracy charges against Casper, the Assistant U.S.

Attorney on duty would look at us as if we'd dropped a load of cow flop on his desk.

Let me see if I've got this straight, he or she would say. You've got no physical evidence connecting this Casper person with the bank robbery in question—no prints, no bait money in his possession, no independent witnesses that can put him within ten miles of the bank. You've got no surveillance photos of him peeping out the bank or jacking the getaway car or handing a gun to the bandit. You've got no witness statements from tellers or passersby or any other decent law-abiding citizen that connects Casper in any way to this bank robbery. All you do have is the uncorroborated statement of one co-conspirator named Baby Insane or Li'l Lunatic or Skull, a co-conspirator with a criminal sheet that stretches back to when he was nine years old and who's making these allegations to shave time off his own bank robbery beef. You want me to stick my neck out and file this pathetic loser of a case? You really think, after any moderately competent defense attorney is finished with Mr. Insane or Mr. Lunatic or Mr. Skull, that a jury is going to have the slightest faith in your witness's testimony? Gimme a break. You want me to file on Casper? Fine. Bring me a case that's winnable. Meanwhile, get out of my office.

It was frustrating. Casper's bank licks kept piling up, people kept on getting terrorized or hurt or killed, and yet we couldn't touch the bastard, legally; we didn't have enough even to arrest him, much less convict him in court. I could almost hear the sonofabitch laughing at us.

Of course, if it had been a movie, as opposed to real life, it would have been simple: Disregarding the express orders of my SAC, a paper-pushing, desk-bound bureaucrat with no understanding of the street, and contemptuous of a legal system that lacks the moral courage to see justice done, I set off on a relentless personal quest to bring Casper down. Alone or, better yet, with a young, blond, and buxom female Special Agent partner, I unleash my own reign of terror in the 'hood, kicking down doors and slapping around Casper's homeboys and jacking up his girlfriends to squeeze them for information, without even a nod to probable cause, much less that pesky business of a warrant. I spend days tracking my quarry through the mean streets, without sleeping or eating or even once going to the bathroom. There's a car chase, a screaming 100-mph pursuit that leaves a swath of wrecked cars and demolished fruit stands across South Central, at the end of which my beautiful young partner takes a bullet in a shoot-out and dies in my arms, breaking my heart but hardening my resolve. Eventually Casper and I meet face to face, mano a mano, each of us firing dozens and dozens of rounds from our 9-millimeter semiautomatics without reloading, and he misses me every time and I don't miss him even once. Finally he is dead, the bank robbery wave is halted, peace reigns in the city. And through it all I don't have to write up even one FD-302 field interview report or one FD-430 bank robbery case initiation report or one affidavit in support of an arrest warrant or one motor vehicle accident report to explain in exhaustive detail exactly how it was that I came to demolish that fruit stand, thereby exposing the FBI to God knows how much in liability claims. Heroes don't worry about paperwork.

It didn't much help matters that Casper knew we were onto him. He probably suspected it all along, but if he had any doubts at all they ended the day some plainclothes cops from the LAPD's CRASH (Community Resources Against Street Hoodlums) anti-gang unit pulled his car over and jacked him up, looking for drugs or weapons. This wasn't unusual: he was a well-known Rollin' Sixties OG, a familiar face to every gang detail cop, and the occasional shake was simply part of the routine. They didn't find anything to tag him with, but they couldn't resist taunting him a little.

"Hey, Casper," they said. "You're big time now, aren't you? The FBI's been asking a lot of questions about you."

I guess it wasn't too surprising that word of the FBI's interest would eventually get back to Casper; like everybody else, cops gossip. But we certainly would have preferred that the CRASH officer hadn't chosen to mention it.

The certain knowledge that we were on his case made Casper more careful, but it didn't make the cocky bastard stop setting up bank robberies. As long as he kept his distance from the actual robberies, as long as most of his henchmen were too scared to testify, he figured he was legally bullet proof. Given the reluctance of the Complaint Unit prosecutors to file charges on him, it seemed that he was right.

It all made for a lot of crying into our beers at the end of the day, and savage barroom denunciations of candy-assed young prosecutors who were too chickenshit and too worried about their careers and conviction rates to file charges against Casper and take a chance that they'd lose.

That may not have been completely fair, but that was how we saw it. Somehow we had to find a prosecutor who'd be willing to wade into Casper's criminal organization like Samson wading into Philistines, someone tough, relentless, even ruthless. We needed a prosecutor with some serious stones.

This is hard to imagine. But as it turned out, the stones we needed belonged to a mild-mannered UCLA law professor named John Shepard Wiley, Jr.

And although Casper didn't realize it, pretty soon his young bank bandits were going to be a lot more afraid of the professor than they ever were of him.

◆ ◆ ◆

Professor John Wiley was restless.

It wasn't that he didn't love teaching; he did. He loved standing in front of a classroom of bright young faces and guiding them through the mysteries and intricacies of patent and intellectual property law. Infringement analysis, the doctrine of equivalents, enablement requirements—Wiley loved teaching that stuff, loved the calm intellectual atmosphere of the classroom. A top honors law school graduate from Boalt Hall at Berkeley, he had clerked for U.S. Supreme Court Justice Lewis Powell before joining the faculty at UCLA, and now after seven years in academia he was nationally known as one of the top experts in his field. He had a nice home in an upscale neighborhood of L.A. that he shared with his wife, Anne, and their two young children; Anne, also a lawyer, was the West Coast general counsel for NBC. He had an excellent salary, and tenure; at age thirty-seven, his life was solidly on track.

And yet, he couldn't shake the feeling that, as satisfying as teaching was, he was missing something, something real and fundamental about the law. He was an expert in the law of books and briefs, but he hadn't really seen the law in action, hadn't seen how it played out down in the trenches and on the streets. The same compulsion that drove him to skiing and rock climbing was pushing him to do something else in the world of law, something interesting, maybe even thrilling.

Like, for example, being a prosecutor, and sending criminals to jail.

Almost as a lark, Wiley wrote a letter to the U.S. Attorney's office for the Central District of California, headquartered in downtown L.A., and asked if maybe they could use someone with his qualifications. Naturally they leaped at the chance. An honors grad from Boalt? A former Supreme Court law clerk? A tenured UCLA professor and a nationally recognized legal expert?

Hey, Professor, come on down.

So Wiley took what he expected to be a two-year leave of absence from UCLA (it turned out to be four) and started off as a green Special Assistant U.S. Attorney in the white-collar crime division. He'd never handled a criminal case before, never argued a case in front of a jury, but the man was a certifiable legal genius; it didn't take him long to pick it up. He started off working some small-time fraud cases, bank embezzlements, guys keeping double books, that sort of stuff, and then quickly moved up to the Major Crimes Unit. He found himself fascinated with people, often very ordinary people, who turned to crime; it was a part of the human parade he'd never encountered before.

He also discovered that he liked working with cops and federal agents. It was a strange development for a guy who'd hardly ever even spoken to a lawman before, a liberal Democrat who had spent most of his life in the cop-unfriendly atmosphere of the ivory tower and we-are-the-world campus activists. He found that he liked the way cops and federal agents talked, and what they laughed at, and the cynical way they looked at the world. And what was perhaps even stranger was that cops and agents liked him back.

You have to understand that, in the cop/agent universe, lawyers in general rank even lower in esteem than journalists. Defense attorneys, of course, are beyond the pale; they're the assholes who put even bigger assholes back on the street, and to do it they'll cheerfully flay alive any cop or agent who takes the witness stand. But prosecutors, although ostensibly on the same side as cops and federal agents, are also considered suspect.

After all, it's the prosecutor who refuses to file a case on some dirtbag you've been chasing for months because he says you don't have enough evidence, the prosecutor who tells you your witnesses stink and your physical evidence is all fucked up and the case is an unwinnable piece of shit. He may be right, legally speaking, but in the cop/agent point of view he's just trying to protect his conviction stats, taking the easy cases, the slam dunkers, and letting the harder ones go.

Even if he files a case, it's the prosecutor who's probably going to plead it out and let the dirtbag get off with half the time he deserves, just to get the case file off his desk and avoid the hassles and risks of a trial. If it does go to trial, it's the prosecutor who's going to fuck it up in front of the jury and waste all the effort you've put into the thing. Or, if he wins, it's the prosecutor who's going to be high-fivin' with his lawyer buddies and acting like he was the Lone Ranger who took the unwinnable clusterfuck of a case that you had put together and, through an unprecedented display of courtroom genius, managed to turn certain defeat into victory.

That's a gross generalization, of course; there are a lot of good, dedicated, hard-charging prosecutors out there, guys that we are happy to work with. But in the cop/agent worldview, a prosecutor is basically just another lawyer until he proves otherwise.

John Wiley did just that.

Unlike a lot of prosecutors, Wiley never looked at a case from the perspective of a courtroom or a case file. He looked at it from the perspective of the victims eating carpet facedown and trembling on the floor, or being jerked out of their cars and pistol-whipped, or being shot down like a dog for no reason except that they were in the wrong place at the wrong time. Being new to the world of crime, Wiley still had the capacity to be outraged, and a finely tuned sense not only of the law but of right and wrong. Sure, he could feel compassion—and act on it—for some basically honest but perhaps not too bright person who in a moment of weakness had embezzled the company petty cash fund. Somebody like that could catch a break from Wiley.

But if you hurt somebody, if you preyed upon the innocent, the man was a total ball-buster. And unlike some prosecutors, keeping his personal conviction stats high wasn't his motivating factor; in a couple years he was going to be back at UCLA anyway. So if he thought a guy was guilty, and that he had a halfway decent chance of proving it in court, he'd come down like a shithammer.

Special Agent George Schroder—a veteran agent who is not easily impressed—and I had first worked with Wiley on what was known as the "Nasty Boys" case. And when we saw the way this mild-mannered professor knocked the Nasty Boys' dicks in the dirt, we fell in love with him.

The Nasty Boys—Clarence Sanders and Harold Walden—were a little like Casper, except without his brains. Both were members of the Rollin' Sixties, both were ex-cons in their early twenties, but unlike Casper they didn't have the cunning to get somebody else to rob banks for them. They did it themselves, starting out with a string of note jobs and then, following Casper's example, moving into takeovers. As thugs go, they were even worse than Casper's crews, raising the superfluous violence to new levels—hence the nickname I gave them. They'd burst into a bank, firing off rounds, terrorizing bank employees and customers, herding them into the vault and threatening to kill them, making females beg for their lives, sometimes ripping open their blouses and groping them. They seemed to get a kick out of scaring the hell out of people. They made some good scores, $20,000 here, as much as $150,000 there, and then blew it on nice cars, a fancy apartment, women, trips to Jamaica.

Their last hit, before their own basic stupidity caught up with them, was at a Great Western Bank in Mission Hills, in the San Fernando Valley, where they made off with $180,000 from the vault. After they split the loot, Sanders takes half of it, the cash bundles still banded with the name "Great Western Bank" printed on the paper straps. He does a little blow, then climbs into a metallic silver Lexus and blasts off up Highway 101 at a hundred miles an hour—literally 100 mph—to party with some friends in Santa Barbara. Naturally he clips another car and winds up in the median strip, unhurt but with the California Highway Patrol (CHP) on the scene. There he is, an ex-con gang-banger with pupils like pinholes and thousands of dollars of banded cash in his car; you don't have to be a racial profiler to decide that this looks hinky. The CHP hooks him on a reckless driving charge, then notifies us that they've got this player with big bundles of money from Great Western Bank in Mission Hills, and is there anything we might know about that? Well, now that you mention it, yeah, we have an idea where that money came from. Sanders is immediately on ice; a few months later, we pick up Walden in Detroit.

And then the case lands on John Wiley's desk in the Major Crimes Unit.

There are some things you do not do in John Wiley's world. In Wiley's world, you do not terrorize innocent people. You do not sexually assault women and make them cry and beg for their lives. You do not shoot guns and rob banks. This is not appropriate behavior. So Wiley whacked the Nasty Boys with the shithammer.

Ordinarily, these guys would have been looking at maybe fifteen or twenty years in the joint, the customary clip for armed bank robbery. It was enough time to satisfy society—or at least to satisfy most prosecutors—but usually not enough for the defendant to back up and say, Fuck it, I'm not gonna plead out, I want a trial. The dirty little secret of the criminal justice system is that everybody—prosecutors, defense attorneys, judges—wants to avoid the expense and risk and hassle of a trial. The prison time offered to a bank bandit in a plea deal is specifically designed to help avoid that.

But giving thugs like the Nasty Boys a dime and a half in the joint wasn't good enough for Wiley; that punishment wouldn't fit the crimes. So he started browsing around Title 18 of the U.S. Code—the basic federal criminal statutes—and came upon part of the sentencing code called Section 924(c).

Section 924(c) specifically addressed the use of a fully operable firearm in commission of any violent or dangerous federal felony. Under that section, the use of a gun in one violent or dangerous felony would add a mandatory five years, to run consecutively with the underlying sentence. (Consecutively means the sentences run back-to-back, not concurrently; if you get ten years on the basic charge and five for the gun, your total sentence is fifteen years.) For a second violent felony involving the use of a firearm, the mandatory extra time shoots up to twenty years—again, that's in addition to the time served for the underlying crime. A third gun count would get you another mandatory twenty years, and so on. In other words, if you were indicted and convicted for three violent felonies committed with a gun, you were looking at forty-five years just for using the guns, plus whatever time you drew on the basic crimes themselves. And federal judges didn't have a lot of wiggle room on the mandatory "gun enhancements." If the gun counts were charged in the indictment and the defendant was convicted, a judge generally had to dole out the time whether he or she wanted to or not.

The system placed enormous power in the hands of federal prosecutors, who decide how many counts to indict on. With a defendant who'd been involved in multiple gun-related violent felonies, a determined prosecutor could stack up enough mandatory sentences to keep that defendant in prison from now to the twenty-second century if he or she wanted to.

With the Nasty Boys, Wiley wanted to. Section 924(c) had only rarely been used in bank robbery cases before, but Wiley decided that it should be dusted off and applied with gusto; after all, if armed bank robbery wasn't a "violent or dangerous" federal crime, what was? So he started filing 924(c)'s on Walden and Sanders like a man possessed. When the filing was done, the Nasty Boys were looking at five counts of bank robbery and five 924(c) gun enhancements, for a total prison time of 185 years each.

The Nasty Boys could hardly believe it. Who is this hardass motherfucker? Fuck you, they told Wiley through their lawyers. If that's the way you're gonna be, we want a trial. Okay, fuck you, Wiley told them, albeit in the polite way lawyers talk to each other. I'll see you in court.

Which he did. The case went to trial, and Wiley put on a brilliant, almost airtight case; the jury came back with guilty verdicts on four of the five counts, and hung on the fifth. Nasty to the end, before his sentencing Walden told the judge the whole thing was "scandalous," and blamed the "white supremacist majority" for his problems—conveniently forgetting that a number of his terrorized victims were African Americans.

Wiley, meanwhile, called Walden and Sanders "violent nightmares come to life," and asked the judge to give both defendants every year they were eligible for. The judge wouldn't go for that, and found some wiggle room on the mandatory sentences. Still, he slapped Sanders and Walden with the longest sentences ever imposed for bank robbery: seventy-six and seventy-one years in prison, respectively, of which they'd have to do 85 percent before they were eligible for parole. You can do the math: If these guys ever do another bank lick, they'll be doing it in wheelchairs or walkers.

Based on what he'd done in the Nasty Boys case, George Schroder and I finally decided that if anyone could get Casper, it'd be John Wiley. So we went around channels in the U.S. Attorney's office, bypassing the more timid souls in the Complaint Unit and going straight to Wiley with an investigation report on Casper.

Wiley was astonished. This guy's using kids to rob banks for him? And he's done this dozens and dozens of time? You bet I'll take this case.

From that moment, Casper was doomed.

By this time Wiley had enough juice in the U.S. Attorney's office to command some resources. He brought in another young Assistant U.S. Attorney named Michael Reese Davis, an experienced prosecutor and grand jury expert with a soft Louisiana drawl and a country-boy habit of drinking water from a jam jar while he sat at his desk. Earlier, Davis had prosecuted a tax evasion case against Marvin Mitchelson, the famous divorce lawyer to the stars, putting him away for two years. It was quite a switch, going from white-collar crimes of the rich and famous to shoot-'em-up bank bandits on the streets of L.A., but Davis, too, was eager for a crack at Casper.

Wiley and Davis helped us come up with a game plan that would hold up in court. Instead of spreading ourselves too thin, and trying to attach Casper to a bunch of bank robberies, we'd concentrate on building strong cases in three to five robberies in which guns were used. With the mandatory gun enhancements, even a few counts could build up the potential prison time into a virtual life sentence. Some of our gang task force agents hoped that, faced with spending his life in prison, Casper might roll over and agree to work an undercover RICO prosecution against his fellow gang members in the Rollin' Sixties, and bring down the entire gang.

Given what I knew of Casper, I didn't think that was likely; Casper was a solid OG, and I doubted that he'd ever turn buster and rat out his homeboys. But I didn't say as much. RICO was the magic word in those days; it could open doors.

With a couple of respected prosecutors behind us—and by waving in front of the Bureau brass the tantalizing prospect of a RICO prosecution against the Rollin' Sixties—we were finally able to get the resources we needed to get Casper. Eventually, more than fifty FBI agents from the bank squad, the gang task force, the special operations group for surveillance, and field agents like George Schroder, as well as detectives from the LAPD Robbery-Homicide Division (RHD) bank team, would work the Casper case. It was a massive—and in my opinion, long-overdue—effort.

Part of it involved setting up a surveillance on Casper. Although we knew we'd never catch him actually going into a bank, if possible we wanted to get videotape of him peeping out a bank, meeting with the robbers, handing out guns and leading them to the job. Then we'd bag the robbers on their way out, explain the harsh facts of life to them, turn them and use them as witnesses, with their statements backed up by surveillance tapes and photographs. It would make for a strong case.

Unfortunately, it wasn't easy to surveil a guy like Casper—especially since, after his earlier little chat with the CRASH guys, he knew we were watching him. One problem, frankly, was racial. Although we'd come a long way since the J. Edgar Hoover days in terms of hiring black agents, we didn't have enough of them available to staff a full-press surveillance in South Central. As you might expect, putting white agents on surveillances in an entirely black neighborhood was problematic. A white guy stood out in Hyde Park like—well, like a white guy in Hyde Park.

And Casper was smart; he acted as if we were always watching, even when we weren't. Whenever he or his driver—he often had other guys drive him around—would venture out, they would make jackrabbit starts, sudden U-turns, take meandering routes through low-traffic residential areas, their eyes on the rearview mirrors all the while. We were pretty sure Casper made us on several tails, at which point we had to call it a day on the surveillance. Tailing a guy while he knows he's being tailed would just be a waste of government gas. We had aircraft surveillance on him at times, but he was savvy enough to drive through the approach zones to LAX airport, where air traffic was restricted and our aircraft couldn't follow. Although we managed to tail Casper on what we figured were some bank peep-outs, we were never able to tape him in an overt act of conspiracy. Driving by a bank that happened to later get robbed isn't evidence of a conspiracy.

But as clever as he was, Casper had two serious problems. One was that even though he knew that we were after him, the man still couldn't cure his addiction: despite the heat, he just couldn't stop setting up bank jobs. His other problem was that he couldn't stop his henchmen from getting caught.

And when we caught them, Wiley laid down the law: No more Mr. Nice Guy. From then on, when a Casper bandit got caught robbing banks, just copping to the robbery wasn't going to earn him any consideration at charging and sentencing times. The price of mercy had gone up.

Wiley and the FBI agents on the Casper task force would lay it out for them, and watch their eyes get big as they started to grasp the implications. You see, Mr. Bank Robber, Wiley would say, there's this thing called Section 924(c), and what it means is that you have two options. Option one is that you give us names, dates, and testimony in court against Casper, in which case we will treat you as if you're a basically decent but naive young man who made the mistake of falling in with some bad company. Option two is that you don't give us what we want, in which case we will treat you like the thug we actually know you to be, and we'll pile up enough bank robbery charges and 924(c) gun enhancements to keep you locked up for every single day of the rest of your miserable life. If you don't believe it, ask the Nasty Boys.

It was hard, maybe even brutal; but remember, these young guys had committed hard and brutal crimes. And it worked. Faced with a lifetime in prison, they started rolling over and giving us names of other Casper bandits. Agents from the Casper task force would roll out and pick those guys up on federal arrest warrants, and then they'd get the same eye-opening speech about the new high cost of doing bank licks. They'd think it over and, in most cases, give us some more names. They were more afraid of Professor John Wiley and his ball-busting 924(c)'s than they were of Casper and their other homeboys.

Eventually, we had dozens of guys lined up to testify, however reluctantly, against Casper and C-Dog. Even today I can't reveal their individual names or specific case histories. Casper knows who some of them are; the ones we eventually selected to testify are on the witness list we submitted to the court, and to Casper's lawyer. But I still can't put their names in this book. Let's face it, given their backgrounds, and criminal tendencies, many, probably most, are either back in prison on new charges or back in the street life; being publicly identified as snitches could ruin their day.

But I can say they ran from the high end to the low end of the criminal world, and everything in between: hard-core, violent gang-bangers with long arrest sheets who were trying to save their own skins; scared eighteen-year-olds, ordinary young men from decent, hardworking South Central families who had fallen under Casper's charismatic spell, and now were looking at spending the rest of their lives in prison; working guys who'd supplemented their incomes by peeping out banks or driving getaway cars for a few hundred bucks; broken-down crackheads, gun-waving sociopaths, mental defectives.

John Wiley interviewed all of them, trying to winnow out the bad witnesses, the ones that wouldn't play well with jurors.

The juveniles among them posed special problems. Although they weren't looking at life sentences under stacked-up gun counts—the federal system rarely prosecutes juveniles, primarily because there isn't a federal juvenile facility to put them in—they were still looking at being sent to the California Youth Authority for a long stretch. Most of them weren't hard core enough to take it, and decided to testify instead.

Some of them could break your heart. Wiley talked to one kid who'd done a couple of takeovers for Casper, a thirteen-year-old who'd been raised in a dirty, roach-infested South Central crackhouse with a half dozen half brothers and sisters. The kid had been shuffled in and out of county child protective services, but always wound up back in the neighborhood, sleeping on a couch in a house full of crackheads and hanging out on street corners. The kid's lawyer wanted him to cooperate, but Wiley knew that he'd be an ineffective witness. The kid couldn't remember where the robberies had happened, or what day of the week they were, and so on; a defense attorney would chew him up. But as he talked to him, Wiley realized that the kid wasn't being intentionally evasive. Instead, his development had been so stunted that he didn't even know the days of the week. He'd been passed through the school system until he was now in the seventh grade, and yet he didn't know that Thursday followed Wednesday, or that Monday was the day before Tuesday.

Another young kid Wiley interviewed brought home just how insulated these Baby Bandits were from the world most of us know. The kid described a bank robbing foray led by Casper to a place "where all the white people lived," a place where "the signs were written in Jewish." It turns out he was describing the Fairfax District of L.A., situated just across the I-10 freeway from the kid's South Central neighborhood, and yet he acted as though it was a million miles away. He admitted that he'd been frightened—not about robbing the bank but simply venturing into a place that was, for him, like another planet. The kid had grown up on some of the most violent, dangerous streets in America, and yet the largely middle-class—and yes, largely white and largely Jewish—Fairfax District had scared the hell out of him.

For Wiley, it was light-years removed from the bright, intelligent young faces that stared back at him in law school classes. It pissed him off that Casper would use such kids to do bank licks. It wasn't fair.

So the potential witnesses against Casper kept piling up, until finally we realized we had enough. True, for all our surveillance work, we still didn't have any physical evidence against Casper—no fingerprints, no bait money in his possession, no videotapes of him peeping out a bank. But with the cooperating witnesses stacking up, we decided we'd be able to assemble a pretty strong court case for conspiracy to commit bank robbery with the use of a firearm—not a perfect case, but probably good enough. And once we had sufficient evidence to arrest him, we couldn't in good conscience let Casper and C-Dog stay out there setting up bank robberies in the hope we could further bolster our case. Somebody could get hurt.

It was time for this to stop.

The end of the greatest bank robbery spree in American history came with a whimper, not a bang. In May 1993, we swore out a federal complaint, based on our cooperating witnesses' grand jury testimony, against Robert Sheldon Brown and Donzell Lamar Thompson for two counts of bank robbery and use of a gun; more counts would be added later. The word went out to our surveillance teams to pick them up. Thompson was picked up at his grandmother's house in Carson. Meanwhile, one of our surveillance teams was sitting on a house Casper sometimes lived in when they saw Casper roll up in a cab. The agents swarmed over him, guns drawn. Casper didn't resist, or even look all that surprised. He was a player, and getting arrested was just another day at the office. It wasn't until later that he learned just how deep in the shit he really was.

With Casper and C-Dog safely locked away in the federal Metropolitan Detention Center, tipsters and informants against them started coming out of the woodwork, further beefing up our case. Eventually Wiley and co-prosecutor Michael Davis got a federal grand jury indictment for six armed takeover robberies committed by Casper and C-Dog and their crews, all of them occurring between January and April 1993, plus related carjacking and assaults charges, plus the dreaded 924(c)'s. The charges didn't even begin to cover Casper and C-Dog's bank robbery careers, but in practical terms it wasn't necessary to file charges on any of the other eighty-five note jobs and ninety takeovers that they had organized. Altogether, the fifteen-count indictments were enough to send them to federal prison for 285 years each.

Wiley was looking forward to the trial, but in the end Casper disappointed him; he was smarter than the Nasty Boys had been. Faced with spending his life in prison if convicted by a jury, Casper, the Bank Lick King of the World, finally decided to do what so many of his henchmen had done before him—that is, cut a deal.

No, Casper told us through his lawyer, he wouldn't roll over on his fellow Rollin' Sixties gang members to help make a RICO case against the gang; he wouldn't give up anybody else. But he would plead guilty to the charged bank robberies in return for a reduced sentence: thirty years in prison. C-Dog decided to do the same thing, for a recommended sentence of twenty-five years.

There were bitter arguments on our side about whether or not to accept the deal. Some of our guys thought it was too easy on them, given their records. But you never know what can happen in a jury trial. Witnesses can back up or get caught in lies, the judge can throw out crucial evidence, the jury can fall in love with the defendant. Remember the O.J. case.

Finally Wiley decided, and I agreed, that it was a deal worth taking. Casper, then age twenty-three, would have to serve just over twenty-five years before he'd be eligible for parole; he'd be almost fifty years old before he got out. C-Dog would do twenty-two years, minimum.

The deal was done. In November 1993, Casper and C-Dog, wearing blue jail jumpsuits, stood before a federal judge for sentencing. Although they'd agreed to the plea bargain, they still bitched about it to the judge.

"I feel this proceeding, my incarceration, has been unjust," Casper said. "I just feel it ain't right. It's a low blow if I ever heard of one."

C-Dog, meanwhile, told the judge the case was "the beginning of modern slavery," and complained about our use of co-conspirators to make the case against them. "An individual would sell his mama if he was facing 125 years."

Maybe so. But Judge Stephen Wilson seemed more persuaded by the declarations that Wiley and I had filed with the court. My twenty-seven-page declaration traced Casper's three-year bank robbery career: The note jobs with crackheads, the gangs of gun-wielding young boys bursting into banks, the carjackings, the getaway school buses, the pistol-whippings and violence, the high-speed pursuits and deaths and woundings of his young henchmen, Casper's overall role as "the premier bank robber in the history of the United States."

Wiley, meanwhile, wrote about Casper and C-Dog as corruptors of youth and agents of urban terrorism.

> [Charles] Dickens invented Fagin as the exploiter and debaucher of youth to inspire horror and revulsion in his Victorian audience. Brown and Thompson inspire the same revulsion today. The difference is that Fagin was only fiction. . . . Brown and Thompson systematically caused unusual levels of violence.
>
> Every robbery savaged someone. Takeover robberies terrorize victims by the dozen. They shattered people's sense of security and well-being at work and in their cars and neighborhoods, where they live and drive and shop. Brown and Thompson worked relentlessly to make Southern California more violent, more traumatizing, more forbidding, more deadly, more laden with fear and loss and pain and grief. It lasted for years.

The recommended sentences stood.

The press played up Wiley's *Oliver Twist* angle. The story was reported in the *Los Angeles Times*, *The New York Times*, and others, with headlines like "Modern-Day 'Fagins' Admit to Series of Bank Robberies." But it was a one-day story, quickly forgotten. Most of the public remained unaware of the impact that a young gang member named Casper had on so many people's lives—and would continue to have. Because even though Casper was on ice, the epidemic of street gang bank robberies wasn't over.

Casper had let the evil genie out of the bottle. And to this day the genie is still doing bank licks.

✦   ✦   ✦

It had begun even before Casper's arrest. After seeing Casper's success, other members of the Rollin' Sixties started getting into bank licks—the Nasty Boys were just one example—and then it spread to other gang sets. The Rollin' 40s Crips, the Playboy Gangster Crips, the Eight Treys, the Harvard Brim Gangster Bloods, the P-Stone Bloods—the list of South Central gangs whose members were doing bank licks was almost endless.

And it wasn't just in L.A. Before long I started getting calls from FBI field offices from all over—in San Francisco, Denver, Phoenix, Las Vegas, Dallas, New Orleans, Atlanta. All of a sudden, out of the blue, they were getting these takeover bank robberies committed by members of L.A. street gangs, guys who had muled out some dope and then stuck around to do some bank licks, or had moved out of L.A. to escape a warrant and had set up branch sets of the Crips or Bloods and started doing bank robberies. What had been an L.A. phenomenon had quickly gone national, and FBI agents from Atlanta or Dallas were calling me to try to find out what in unholy hell was going on.

The explanation was simple. Thanks in large part to Casper, street gangs had discovered that bank robberies were more profitable than dope—although the risks were considerably greater, since eventually they almost always get caught. And they were acting on that discovery in record numbers. In the early 1990s, bank robberies nationally were pushing ten thousand a year, a new record, and a large percentage of them were street gang takeovers; the Casper phenomenon was metastasizing like a cancer.

It wasn't just in the big cities, either. By the late nineties, Casper-style bank robbers were hitting the heartland. In Winston-Salem, North Carolina, three members of the L.A. East Coast Crips—"East Coast" meant their turf was east of the Harbor Freeway in L.A.—pulled off a series of bank licks. In Des Moines, Iowa, some other East Coast Crips did the same. In Indianapolis, guys from the Rollin' Sixties and the Underground Westside Crips did a string of credit union jobs that ended in an L.A.–style shoot-'em-up freeway chase captured on live TV. In Mentor, Ohio, some P-Stone Bloods from L.A. pistol-whipped an elderly couple in a bank lick just for the fun of it.

And remember the aforementioned Li'l Scoobie, the fifteen-year-old bumbling Baby Bandit who caught a bullet from a security guard's gun in a Casper-organized bank robbery in Downey in 1992? Li'l Scoobie did some time in the California Youth Authority for that robbery, but the time obviously didn't teach him much, either about life or about how to pull off a successful bank lick. In 1998, having graduated to

Rollin' Sixties OG status, Scoobie was identified doing a bank robbery in scenic Spokane, Washington.

In L.A. the street gang bank robbery phenomenon continues apace. Although the numbers have never hit the same highs as when Casper was a player, takeover bank robberies still plague the city—more than two hundred of them in 2001 alone. Hardly a day goes by that armed young street gangsters don't burst into a bank in Orange County or Simi Valley or West L.A. or somewhere else and reenact the wild old days of Casper and crew. We routinely catch them and throw them in prison, and they're just as routinely replaced. The new generation of street gangsters seems to have limitless manpower reserves to draw on.

Because as long as all those lost boys are still standing on the corner, on streets that are long on despair but short on hope, the gangsters will never run out of boys who think they can easily become men.

Just by robbing a bank.

4

THE HOLE
IN THE GROUND GANG

The tunnel under the streets of Hollywood was a claustrophobe's nightmare, a descent into the dark dread of being buried alive.

It was just 3 feet high and 3 feet wide in some places, a little higher in others, but nowhere along the tunnel's 100-foot length could I stand up any taller than a miner's crouch. In parts of the passageway I had to crawl along the dirt floor on my hands and knees, like a rat in a drainpipe. The air inside was cool and dank, heavy with the loamy smell of fresh dug earth; there was no sound, no sense that 20 feet above my head the city was going on about its noisy business. When I briefly switched off the flashlight, just to see what it was like, that tunnel was as black and silent as a crypt.

I was an FBI agent, not a miner or a spelunker. Creeping through homemade subterranean passageways wasn't part of my job description—at least not until today. So it was hard to fight off the first flutters of panic.

It wasn't exactly a rational fear; after all, men had been crawling through this tunnel for weeks, and had gotten out alive, their arms full of loot. But it wasn't exactly an irrational fear, either. The tunnelers had been interested in speed, not safety, and had invested no time in shoring up the dirt ceiling with timbers or other supports. One small earthquake, even a tremor, and tons of dirt and rock and concrete would entomb me under the streets of Hollywood.

Still, even in those brief moments of rapid heartbeat and elevated blood pressure, I knew I had it relatively easy.

I was just a temporary tourist here. All I had to do was crawl through the tunnel, trying to get a feel for the thing—how they'd done it, who they might be. The bad guys, on the other hand, had had to dig the damn thing, by hand, with picks and shovels, sweating and burrowing like human moles, for weeks on end, until they finally made it to the point under the floor of the vault.

Being in that tunnel, seeing firsthand the conditions they'd had to work under, breathing the same stale air they'd breathed, I had to respect their balls and determination.

✦ ✦ ✦

And once again I was amazed at the efforts men will go to, the risks they'll take, to bust into a bank.

It was June 1986, and for weeks employees at the First Interstate Bank in Hollywood had thought something vaguely strange was going on. They kept hearing these noises . . .

It had started one evening the month before, when the branch manager was working late, trying to catch up on some paperwork after closing time, and she heard a kind of low, grinding sound, like somebody drilling something. She walked around inside the bank, trying to figure out where it was coming from, but then the noise stopped, and she decided it was probably just something going on outside. The bank was a two-story brick structure on the corner of Spaulding Street and busy Sunset Boulevard, at the foot of the Hollywood Hills just east of the Sunset Strip. There was always a lot of street work and heavy traffic rumbling along Sunset, and construction crews were putting up a new building directly across the street. The sound probably had something to do with that.

But then a week later the branch manager was working late in the bank, after closing, and damn it, there it was again, that whirring or grinding sound. This time it seemed to be coming from somewhere near the vault.

The vault was a concrete and steel box, 10 feet by 20 and 10 feet high, situated behind the teller counters at the southwest corner of the bank. It was what's known in the business as a Class I commercial vault, the typical style of vault for a branch bank like the First Interstate on Sunset. Constructed out of poured concrete and 5/8-inch steel rebar and steel mesh, its walls and ceiling were 12 inches thick, the floor 18 inches thick. The vault door was made out of 3 1/2-inch thick steel, with a thin layer of copper sandwiched inside to diffuse the heat if anyone tried to burn through it.

In short, it was a pretty sturdy box, although by no means impregnable. Anything built by humans can be breached by humans, including every bank vault ever made in the history of the world. In fact, the standard of security for any commercial vault is measured not so much by the thickness of its walls or the strength of its steel as by how long it takes to break into it—the so-called minimum time of attack. Under federal bank regulations, class I vaults have to be able to withstand one hour of attack by a knowledgeable person working under optimum conditions with state-of-the-art tools: industrial drills, high-temperature burn bars, and so on. Just one hour.

That may not sound like much time for a vault to hold off an attack. And it wouldn't be if a guy could simply sashay into a bank, set up his equipment, and start drilling away without worrying about anybody noticing. But he can't, because the vault has a second line of defense. In addition to the concrete and steel, bank vaults have alarm systems that, ideally, will notify security personnel long before the would-be vault buster has time to break through.

The vault at the First Interstate on Sunset was no exception. Inside there was a sound sensor that would set off a silent alarm at bank security headquarters if it picked up any noise; there were also heat sensors that would detect the rising temperature if anyone tried to cut through the doors or walls with a burning bar. The gearbox that controlled the locking bolts inside the door also had an alarm that would trip if anybody tried to drill through it.

As for a safecracker being able to turn the dials and hear or feel the tumblers moving inside, well, that's fiction—literally fiction. That popular image dates back to the early 1900s, when a play called *Alias Jimmy Valentine*, based on an O. Henry short story, featured a safecracker who sandpapered his fingertips to heighten their sensitivity and then managed to feel his way through a safe's combination lock. The only problem is that that was ridiculous even then, and even more ridiculous with modern vaults. I'll spare you the arcane technical details of tumblers and dogs and slots and other features of combination locks, but trust me: You could put your fingertips on a grinding wheel and they'd still never be sensitive enough to pull a Jimmy Valentine on a modern vault.

And as if all those security features weren't enough, there was also—and this was critical—a time lock on the vault door. At the end of each business day the bank manager would set the time lock—located on the inside of the vault door and therefore inaccessible from the outside after the door was shut—to determine when the vault door could be opened again. For example, if it was Monday evening, the manager would set the time lock to allow the vault to be opened the next morning at, say, 8:00 A.M.; if it was a Friday, and the bank was closed over the weekend, the time lock would be set to allow the vault to be opened Monday morning. And so on. Once the time lock was set and the door locked shut, even in the most dire of emergencies there was no way to open the vault door before the specified time except by drilling out the vault door—which wasn't something a bank did lightly. Those vault doors cost $10,000.

Altogether, then, the physical structure of the vault and the accompanying alarm systems made the vault at the First Interstate Bank seem like a pretty tough nut. Sure, during business hours, when the vault was open, gunmen might be able to force their way into the bank and take the loose cash out of the vault. But after hours, with the vault securely shut and the time lock set, there really was nothing to worry about. Nobody could possibly get into the vault.

Still, on that warm May evening in 1986, the sounds the First Interstate bank manager was hearing coming from the vault were too strange to be ignored. She had to tell somebody. And that's when the weakest link in the elaborate vault protection system—the human link—came into play.

The bank manager calls the First Interstate central security office downtown and tells the guy on duty about this noise she's hearing. He checks his console monitors and tells her, Nope, I got nothing here; the sound sensor alarm inside the vault hasn't activated. What you're hearing, he tells her, is probably just a rat running around inside the walls or something.

A rat? *A rat?* The bank manager can hardly believe it. If what's making that sound is a rat, it must be some kind of giant mutant rat out of a horror movie. The manager even holds the phone up against the vault door, so the guy downtown can hear the sound, but he checks his monitors again and, same as before, there's no alarm. Nothing to worry about, he says. Maybe it's just some construction in the neighborhood.

Okay, the bank manager figures. He's the expert. And now the sound has stopped anyway.

But a few days later, on a Saturday, the vault's sound sensor alarm does go off, and the alarm signal shows up on the central security office monitors. Not that this sends the security guys catapulting out of their chairs or anything. Ninety-nine times out of 100—no, make that 999 times out of 1,000—a vault alarm does not, repeat, does not indicate that somebody has actually breached the vault, or even tried to. Vault alarms go off all the time, usually because of electrical problems. Most vault alarms use ordinary phone lines to send an alarm signal to the bank security or alarm company headquarters, and whenever the boys at Ma Bell start working on the line, even miles away from the vault, it can break the circuit and trip the alarm signal. Sometimes dust or moisture accumulates on the electrical contacts and shorts the circuit, or maybe a bank employee forgets to set the time lock at closing time and sets off the alarm when he opens the vault door the next morning. Motion detector alarms, which are set to detect movement all the way across a large room, have been known to go off when a spider crawls across the sensor.

The point is, an alarm can mean anything—and almost always it means nothing. After 1,000 false alarms, the very human response is to assume that the 1,001 alarm is—ho hum—just another false alarm. No need to get excited. And on that Saturday afternoon in Hollywood, nobody did.

Nevertheless, when a vault alarm goes off, there are procedures to be followed. So the bank security office notifies the cops and then calls the branch manager at home and tells her about the alarm, and she comes in and meets the cops and a security guy at the bank. Together they look around, but they can't see anything, or hear anything. Probably just another short in the system somewhere, the security guy decides. Happens all the time.

But weird things continue to happen. Later that week, the bank's power fails and the phones go out; an electrician comes in and gets everything up again by flipping the breaker switch, but he can't figure out what shorted the electrical system in the first place. Bank employees start joking about the "poltergeist" that has taken up residence at the First Interstate.

Then, on Saturday, June 7, while the bank is closed, an assistant manager comes in to catch up on some work. She's sitting at her desk, shuffling some papers in total silence, when all of a sudden the bank is alive with the sound of music. For no reason, the Muzak system has come on—and while in the course of an ordinary business day the music system is sort of a low background noise, in the confines of an empty bank the sudden, unexpected instrumental strains of "Yesterday" or "Would You Like to Ride in My Beautiful Balloon?" can be pretty startling.

In fact, the assistant manager is freaked out. And it's not just the music. When she goes over to check the Muzak controls, which are situated near the vault door, she hears this hissing and popping noise, like an electrical short. So she calls bank security, and yeah, they're getting a vault alarm. So again they come out and check out the bank, and again they can't find anything. Of course, because of the time lock on the vault door they can't open the vault and check inside—but really, why would they bother? Obviously, no one is drilling out the door, or attacking the vault walls with a jackhammer.

And they don't even think about checking *under* the vault, because, well, why would they? The floor of that vault is 18 inches of solid concrete and steel, sitting on the ground, with no crawl space under it. They couldn't check under the vault if they wanted to. So they get the Muzak turned off and then leave; so does the assistant manager.

Then on Saturday evening the central alarm lights up again, and the local alarm, the outside alarm bell that was a feature on older banks, starts clanging away, too. The security guys once again alert the branch manager, who tells them, in essence, screw it, she's not going down to the bank again for another false alarm. So the security shift manager tells his guys to, quote, "shine it on" and wait for the maintenance guys to come in on Monday and fix the goddam thing. Meanwhile, the outside alarm bell on the bank exterior wall keeps ringing and ringing and ringing, calling for help that is not on the way. After a few hours the alarm bell literally beats itself to death and falls silent.

At that point, the bank vault's 12-inch thick walls became as effective as plywood, its elaborate electronic security system nothing but a worthless tangle of wire and dimestore lights. All the security systems couldn't overcome a bad short in the human element.

Monday morning, 8:05. The branch manager and assistant manager come in, getting ready for a normal business day. The vault time lock automatically disengages, the manager dials in the combination, swings the steel vault door open and—

Oh my God!

We got the call at the bank squad a few minutes later. Burglary at the First Interstate, 7700 Sunset. Yeah, they got into the vault. Probably been in there all weekend. Took the cash and hit the safe deposit boxes. A bunch of 'em.

Uh-oh. See, it's one thing when somebody steals cash from a large bank chain. Although the money isn't insured by the FDIC—most large banks are self-insured against theft, and therefore have to eat the loss themselves—a stolen few thousand, even a stolen few hundred thousand, isn't going to send a major financial institution spiraling into bankruptcy. Hell, one commercial loan gone bad can easily cost them ten times that much, and the shareholders still manage to sleep at night. It's all part of the cost of doing business.

But private safe deposit boxes are another matter entirely. An average bank vault will contain hundreds of them, of varying sizes, some as big as airport baggage lockers, others just 3 inches by 6 inches by 18 inches deep, each equipped with two locks—one that the customer has a key to, one that the bank has the key to. Banks don't make a lot of money renting the boxes; they're mostly just a service for their customers, to give them a place to store, presumably safely, anything they think is important: wills, insurance policies, photos of the honeymoon trip to Mazatlán, original artworks, licit cash, illicit cash, marriage licenses, gold, birth certificates, diamonds, zirconium, bronzed baby booties, real estate deeds, love letters, negotiable bonds, silverware— you name it. Anything and everything that anyone wants to protect from theft or fire can be found locked away in the boxes.

The thing is, there's no FDIC insurance for the contents of safe deposit boxes, either; no one except the boxholder even knows what's in them. And when a vault gets hit, the losses to the boxholders—or at least, as we'll see, the claims of the boxholders—can easily run into the millions of dollars. When their supposedly impregnable safe deposit boxes turn out to be all too pregnable, the boxholders start to howl and the lawsuits start to fly: against the bank, against the alarm company, against anybody with pockets deep enough to tickle a lawyer's money bone. Which means that the pressure on the FBI to crack the case and retrieve the stolen property increases exponentially.

So, when I heard that the burglars had hit the boxes, I knew this was going to be a major shitstorm. We mobilized almost the entire bank squad, a dozen guys or so, and headed up to Hollywood.

The bank was closed, with a sign on the door directing customers to another FIB branch—without, of course, specifying why. The last thing a bank is going to tell its customers is, "We apologize for the inconvenience, but while we were sleeping, a person or persons unknown snuck into our supposedly secure vault and stole your money and negotiable bonds and your great-grandmother's diamond brooch." But the bank manager and assistant manager were there, standing outside the open vault door wearing "I can't believe this is happening" faces. A couple of LAPD uniformed officers were there; they'd been the first to respond to the call, and were securing the scene.

And some of the BAD guys were there, too.

BAD was the LAPD's Burglary-Auto Theft Division; the detectives at the bank were members of BAD–Burglary Special, an elite unit of fifteen or so detectives who specialized in high-end break-ins and property theft: purloined payrolls, jewelry store burglaries, commercial safe-crackings, fine art thefts, high-profile heists of every description. The Burglary Special guys operated with citywide jurisdiction, and only took the big cases, the sort of cases that might end up in the newspapers, or involve somebody important enough or powerful enough to personally get the chief on the phone. If somebody broke into your house in L.A. and stole your 18-inch color TV set, detectives from one of the LAPD's eighteen divisions would handle the case, when and if they got around to it. But when thieves broke into Cher's house, or ripped off Don Johnson and Melanie Griffith's jewelry, or stole some original European masters from a filthy-rich Saudi sheik in Holmby Hills, BAD-Burglary

Special caught the case. Detectives Dennis Pagenkopp, Tom Donnelly, Doug Sims, Troy Galloway—a lot of those BAD boys were department legends; they had forgotten more about working high-end burglaries than most cops would ever know.

And despite all those jurisdictional turf battles that preoccupy the top brass of every law enforcement agency, we were happy to see them there, and to have them on this case. The FBI's expertise was in bank robbery—that is, the use of force or fear of force to steal money from a person. Burglary, which is the surreptitious theft of money or valuables when nobody's looking—which is what we were dealing with here—is an entirely different criminal investigatory discipline. As we'll see, given the difficulty of breaking into modern bank vaults, it had been more than a decade since we'd had to handle a vault burglary in L.A. For the BAD-Burglary Special guys, on the other hand, burglaries were their bread and butter.

But even the BAD guys had never seen anything like this.

More than a hundred safe deposit boxes inside the vault had been pried open with crowbars or popped open with hammer drills and lay scattered all over the floor. The wheeled money carts that held the cash from the tellers' drawers were empty, as were the safe boxes where the vault teller kept her reserves of cash; eventually the bank determined that $172,000 of the bank's cash was missing.

And there, in the middle of the vault floor, was a hole—a trapezoid-shaped, 20- by 25-inch hole just big enough for a man to squeeze through. Below the hole there was only blackness.

It didn't take a genius to figure this one out: tunnel job. Somebody had dug a tunnel under the vault and busted up through the floor. The question was, from where?

Well, somebody had to do it. Somebody had to play Alice and go exploring down the rabbit hole. After some discussion—"You wanna go first?" "Uh, I dunno, do you want to go first?"—Alice turned out to be Burglary Special Detective Dennis Pagenkopp, a slim, athletic veteran.

So Pagenkopp borrows a flashlight from one of the uniforms and lowers himself through the hole in the vault floor. He drops down into a hollowed-out chamber about 4 feet across and about 5 1/2 feet deep—just big enough and deep enough for a man to stand almost upright and drill and chip away at the concrete floor of the vault. On one side of that chamber there was a narrow passageway, just 3 feet high and wide, that led to yet another chamber, slightly larger than the first. And on the side of that chamber there was another hole, also 3 feet high, slanted sharply downward under the foundation of the building and headed toward—hell, it could have gone all the way to China for all Dennis knew.

But Dennis wasn't Burglary Special for nothing; crawling into strange places was part of the job. Holding the flashlight in front of him, he creeps into the passageway, like a Vietnam tunnel rat crawling under Cu Chi, and starts downward. But the incline is steeper than he'd thought, and suddenly he's sliding down the passageway, headfirst, like someone barreling over the Banzai Falls at Soak City USA. Yeah, it's a short slide, just 7 or 8 feet, but Dennis has no idea what he's sliding into, which significantly increases the pucker factor.

But finally—*thump!*—he lands at the bottom of the chute. He starts shining the flashlight around and sees that he's in another large, excavated chamber, a huge one, the ceiling 12 feet high; it's like a goddam cathedral in there. At the top of the chamber he can see some of the building foundation, and a broken electrical conduit that has some wires hanging out and exposed; Dennis figures the tunnelers tapped into the underground power line to run their drilling tools—which would explain why the bank had been having so many electrical problems.

On one side of the large chamber there's another passageway that runs in a straight line due east: it slopes gently downhill and it's a tight fit; Dennis has to duckwalk to get through it. But then it levels out and he can almost stand up. The guys who dug this thing knew what they were doing; it's been dug by hand with shovels—Dennis can see the spademarks on the walls—with a rounded ceiling that would offer more resistance to cave-ins than a flat ceiling. Which is a good thing, because there's no shoring anywhere along the route. Every 20 feet or so, shelved niches have been cut into the walls, presumably to serve as resting places for lanterns until the tunnelers could tap into a power source and string up some lights. The tunnel stretches off into the darkness toward who the hell knows what.

This is the part of the horror movie where the audience starts yelling, "Go back, you idiot! Go back!" Dennis is certain—pretty certain—that there's nobody down here, that the burglars are long gone. But still. Slowly, carefully, he shuffles along the passage.

And finally the tunnel ends. It ends at a hole that's been cut into the side of a concrete pipe 4 1/2 feet in diameter, a pipe that's part of the city's vast underground network of storm sewers.

The tunnelers had come in through the storm sewer system, cut through the side of the sewer pipe, excavated the tunnel, cut their way into the vault, taken the loot, and then escaped back into the storm sewer system.

And from there the trail could lead almost anywhere in the city.

Eventually, we all took the tunnel tour, some of us to take measurements and look for evidence, some, like me, just to get an appreciation for the thing. In a way, it was awe-inspiring. Christ, it must have taken these guys weeks, maybe even months, to dig this goddam thing. It showed a lot of planning, determination, discipline, and yes, balls.

No doubt about it: We had a bona fide caper on our hands.

Capers are, by definition, crimes in which cunning and intelligence and careful planning trump weapons and violence, crimes where the payoff is big, the methods stealthy, and nobody gets hurt. When a jewel thief in a tuxedo slips out of the masked ball and steals the duchess's diamond tiara from the safe hidden behind the cognac in the liquor cabinet, that's a caper; when an ex-con gang-banger puts a cap into a Beverly Hills jewelry store owner and does a smash-and-grab on the Rolexes under the glass counter, that's not a caper. Since the overwhelming majority of criminals tend toward the gang-banger model—that is, they're lazy, potentially violent, firmly entrenched on the low left side of the IQ bell curve, and seldom own tuxedos—it figures that true capers are extremely rare.

That's especially true in the world of L.A. bank vault heists, which is ironic given the fact that Hollywood has been the source of an endless stream of movies featuring clever crooks who manage to defeat state-of-the-art security devices and make off with the swag from a bank vault. The truth is, there've been far more movies made about bank capers in L.A. than there've been actual bank capers in L.A. or even on the entire West Coast. When you hear about a caper crew hitting a bank vault, it's almost always on the East Coast and in the Midwest.

There are various reasons for that. Eastern cities are older, for one thing, and so are their banks and bank vaults. In L.A. a fifty-year-old hamburger stand is a contender for historic building status, but in Boston or New York or Chicago, century-plus buildings are common-place—and they're a lot easier to bust into. Same with the vaults and alarm systems; generally, the older they are, the less effective they are. There's also the organized crime (OC) factor. Most bank vault jobs have some OC connection: connected guys have the skills, the access to sophisticated burglary tools and, most important, the stolen goods fenc-ing network needed for a successful vault job. But traditional organized crime in L.A. has always been pretty much a shirttail cousin to the mob families back East; it's never amounted to much.

And then there's the whole Left Coast, laid-back attitude thing. Pulling a vault caper takes a lot of time, a lot of planning, and a lot of hard physical work; it's a hundred times quicker and easier to storm into a bank, stick a gun in somebody's face, and take the money. Maybe it's something in the palm trees and the sunshine, but L.A. bank bandits never seemed to develop the kind of discipline and work ethic that a caper requires.

And it was a good thing for us, too. True, a Special Agent or a cop may be able to work up some professional admiration for a crime that is bold, brilliant, and audacious. The problem is that crimes that are bold, brilliant, and audacious are inevitably the work of criminals who are intelligent, disciplined, and professional, guys you can count on not to leave much if anything behind in the way of clues. Therefore, from a professional law enforcement perspective, capers are the absolute worst kind of cases. They promise nothing but long hours, mountainous paperwork, fretting bosses, and aggravated ulcers, plus a slim chance of ever putting anybody in jail.

Sure, if you manage to solve a caper, you are in retrospect a hero, an investigative genius; you'll walk into the bull pen the next day and your buddies will call out: "Hey, everybody! It's Sherlock fucking Holmes!" But given a choice between working an inept crime committed by some moron or working a caper, your wise lawman will choose the moron every time. It's a lot easier on the stats—and on the blood pressure.

Over the years, we've had a few bank robbery crews that showed a little caperlike flair. For example, there was a Canadian bank crew that pretended to be building an addition to a bank in Hollywood over a weekend—they had phony work orders, construction company trucks, hard hats, the whole shot—and used it as a cover to knock down the bank's wall and bust into the vault. It was a bold move and a good score, and they might have gotten away with it, except that when they got back to their safehouse with the loot, they tried using gasoline to wipe the place clean of fingerprints. The fumes hit a pilot light on the stove and the Canadians got cooked so bad they wound up in the hospital, and ultimately in prison.

We also had a two-man crew of YACS—members of an East Coast organized crime group composed of immigrants from Yugoslavia, Albania, Croatia, and Serbia—who would cut holes in a bank's roof, rappel down to the bank floor on ropes like Batman and Robin dropping into the Bat Cave, and then force the startled bank employees to open the vault. The Batman & Robin Bandits, as I naturally called them, came to grief when they left behind some ski masks that had saliva on them. Some cops from the Anaheim Police Department tailed one of them to a McDonald's, then fished his Coke cup and straw out of the garbage when he left. Saliva on the straw matched the DNA on the ski masks, and Batman & Robin were on ice.

And in the sixties and early seventies we'd even had a couple of half-baked tunnel jobs. In one, some guys tried to tunnel from a rented house in South Central L.A. to a Bank of America next door, but their timing was seriously flawed. When they were halfway to the vault, the bank permanently closed for business, because—and this is the good part—Bank of America officials had decided that the bank was already being robbed too frequently by ordinary, run-of-the-mill holdup guys. In another tunnel case, this one in Southgate, south of L.A., some guys tried to tunnel from an empty furniture store to a bank across the street. These guys actually managed to make it under the vault and start cutting a hole in the floor; the problem was that the hole they were cutting was directly underneath a change safe, a wheeled cart that banks use to store nickels, quarters, and dimes. Those carts can easily weigh 1,000 pounds, and when the burglars busted up through the vault floor, the change safe fell into the hole like a cork in a bottle. That was the end of that caper.

But those were the exceptions—and all of them ended in failure. The fact is that in at least two decades before the 1986 Hollywood tunnel job, there'd been only one more or less successful bank vault heist in the L.A. area that truly rose to the level of a bona fide caper.

True to tradition, it involved a crew from back East—a family of professional bank burglars from Ohio known as the Dinsios. And it was a classic example of how the FBI can break a professional caper.

Amil Dinsio, thirty-six, was the leader of the crew, which also included his elder brother James; Amil and James had learned the fine points of burglary from their dad, Amelio Dinsio, a master burglar in the Youngstown area with connections to the Youngstown-Erie Mafia. During the 1960s and early 1970s, the Dinsio crew had pulled off half a dozen successful vault jobs in Ohio and the East Coast, and while they were well known to law enforcement, no one was ever able to make a case on them—and because of their mob connections, the local cops never seemed to try very hard.

The Dinsios might have continued to thrive if they'd stayed in their own neighborhood. But in early 1972 Amil and his wife took a trip to Southern California to visit some relatives, and Amil turned it into a busman's holiday, looking around for likely fat scores. He finally settled on the United California Bank in the Monarch Bay section of Laguna Niguel, in Orange County south of L.A., a seaside neighborhood of wealthy retirees and highly paid professionals—the sort of people who keep treasure locked up in bank safe deposit boxes. After peeping out the bank for a few days, Amil went back to Cleveland and put the crew together: his brother James, a brother-in-law, a couple of cousins, six guys in all. In February 1972, they flew out from Cleveland to L.A. together, first checking into a motel in Lynwood and then renting a pricey condominium in an exclusive Laguna Niguel neighborhood about a mile away from the bank.

The bank was a one-story structure with a false mansard-style flat roof, situated in a shopping center and set back from the street. The vault was a standard class I, constructed in 1965, with 12-inch concrete and steel walls and ceiling; it was equipped with inside sound detectors connected to a central alarm center and an outside "local" alarm—basically just a big bell—mounted on an exterior wall of the bank.

Late on a Friday night in March, after all the stores in the shopping center had closed and the place was deserted, the Dinsio crew climbed up to the roof on ladders, pausing to spray expanding insulating foam in the housing of the exterior alarm to immobilize the striking arm. Once on the roof, they tapped into the electric line of the air-conditioning unit, plugged in a saw, and easily cut a hole through the 3/4-inch plywood-and-roofing-tar roof, then dropped down into the crawl space between the roof and the vault ceiling.

After neutralizing the internal alarms—Amil was an expert at rewiring and bypassing alarm systems—the crew drilled sixteen 1-inch-diameter holes into the vault ceiling in a circle and then stuffed the holes with dynamite. They piled up sandbags on top of the charges to muffle the sound and direct the explosive force downward, then unreeled detonator wire out of the roof and over the side, and—*kaboom!*—they detonated the dynamite.

It was a lot louder than they had thought it would be, but nobody noticed; or if they did, nobody called the cops. After a couple of hours of watching for any cop activity, the crew climbed back into the bank and found a neat, almost perfectly circular 2-foot hole in the vault ceiling. All that was left was the web of steel rebar across the hole, but that was easily cut with an acetylene torch.

It was getting late, and they couldn't take the chance that in daylight somebody might spot the hole in the roof, so the crew resealed the roof hole and went back to the condo for some sleep. Saturday night they came back, climbed onto the roof, reopened the hole, dropped down into the vault, and set to work.

There wasn't much bank cash in the vault, just $50,000 or so, which probably was to be expected. The richer the neighborhood, the less likely a bank is to have a lot of cash on hand; poor and working-class people get cash for their paychecks, while wealthier people deal in checks and credit cards. But it wasn't cash that the Dinsios were interested in. It was the five hundred safe deposit boxes that lined the interior walls of the vault. For a bank burglar, safe deposit boxes are like gift boxes under a Christmas tree; you never know what you're going to get, but you're hoping Santa's going to be nice to you.

And Santa was very nice to the Dinsio crew.

When bank employees arrived Monday morning, they found 458 safe deposit boxes drilled out and opened. Total loss estimates would range from $2 million to $8 million in cash, negotiable bonds, gold, and jewelry, making it one of the biggest—maybe the biggest—bank heists in U.S. history up to that time.

Well, put the word "biggest" together with "bank heist" and you're going to get the FBI's undivided attention, especially since J. Edgar Hoover was still the FBI director. (Hoover died suddenly about a month later.) For the Los Angeles division of the FBI, the Laguna Niguel caper was a division special, meaning just about everybody dropped what they were doing and pitched in. The press was all over it, too, pumping up the cleverness of the burglars and dubbing it the *"Mission: Impossible"* heist.

The problem was, given the professionalism of the crooks, there wasn't much to go on at first. We interviewed bank employees and boxholders, checked names against records of known safecrackers and felons, knocked on doors looking for witnesses, anybody who might have seen or heard anything. We also ran down the tips that poured in, most of which were some variation on the theme of "My ex-husband just bought a new car for that slut he left me for, and my friend whose husband's cousin is a salesman at the dealership told me he paid cash. I think he stole it from that bank!" But none of it amounted to anything. Weeks went by without a break.

Ironically, the break finally came from another bank burglary far away, in a place where things like this were expected to happen. In May, six weeks after the Laguna Niguel job, a bank in Lordstown, Ohio, got hit by vault burglars for $500,000 in cash that the bank had on hand in preparation for payday at a nearby General Motors plant. What made the Ohio job particularly interesting was that the burglars had foamed the outside alarm bell, cut a hole in the roof, and then bypassed the alarm system before attacking the vault. From the M.O. it certainly looked like the same guys. And FBI agents in Cleveland wondered if maybe the famous Dinsio crew might be involved.

(If it seems strange that the same crew would pull another job just six weeks after the multimillion-dollar heist in Laguna Niguel, consider the economics of the thing: cash is worth face value, sure, but when you lay off stolen goods through a fence—diamonds, rare coins, even negotiable bonds, which are numbered and can be traced—you're usually only going to get maybe 15 or 20 percent of the value, tops. Divide that by half a dozen guys on the job and, yeah, they're making a living, but they can't take a year off to lie on a beach in the Bahamas.)

So FBI agents started checking the names of known members and associates of the Dinsio Youngstown crew against travel records and—

bingo!—we found that five members of the crew, Amil included, had booked a flight together to L.A. in February, a month before the Laguna Niguel heist, traveling under their own names. Agents from the FBI L.A. office started interviewing every cab driver who worked the airport, and finally Special Agent Paul Chamberlain, the lead agent on the case, found an immigrant from Ghana who remembered picking them up. He described them as being five of the toughest guys he'd ever seen, out-of-town types who talked with funny accents; even a guy from Ghana could tell that these boys hadn't grown up in Malibu. The cabbie's memory of them was particularly vivid because after he'd dropped them off on a street corner in Lynwood, a working-class suburb just south of L.A., they'd tipped him $100, which in 1972 was a week's pay.

We canvassed the area motels, flashing the Dinsio gang's mug shots, and finally found a motel clerk who remembered renting them a room. A check of the motel phone records showed calls from their motel room to a residence in Tustin, an Orange County town, and to a real estate agent who handled rental properties in an upscale neighborhood near the bank.

And from there the Dinsio gang's caper started to unravel.

The Tustin house belonged to a boyhood friend of one of the Dinsio gang members, Amil's thirty-eight-year-old brother-in-law, Christopher Mulligan; the friend had gone to school with Mulligan back in Ohio. After the bank job Mulligan had stashed one of the cars the crew had used, a gold 1964 Oldsmobile, in the unsuspecting friend's garage and then left for Ohio. When agents searched the car, they found drills and other burglary tools hidden in the empty spare tire compartment, but while the Dinsio crew had carefully rubbed down the tools to remove any fingerprints, they weren't quite careful enough. A flashlight found in the trunk was clean, but one of the batteries *inside* the flashlight yielded up Amil Dinsio's well-documented prints. An even bigger mistake was that the burglars had also left three gold coins in the car, coins that matched the description of some of the loot taken from the bank. With the friend's cooperation, Mulligan was lured back to Orange County and arrested.

Meanwhile, the call from the Dinsios' motel to the real estate agent led us to an exclusive condo complex next to the Laguna Niguel golf course. (Newspaper accounts at the time generally referred to the $500-

a-month rented condo as "posh"—which indicates how much real estate you could rent for $500 back then, and also just how big a score a $5 million bank heist was at the time.) Like the Oldsmobile, the condo had been thoroughly rubbed down with alcohol to remove any prints—but again the Dinsios made one little mistake. Special Agent Roger Goldsberry, a former cop and the L.A. bank squad's forensic specialist (he later became the Bureau's leading expert on firearms forensics), opened the dishwasher and—Hey, what's this? They'd forgotten to turn on the machine! Roger gathered up the dirty dishes, glasses, and flatware and personally processed them for latent prints. The gang's prints were all over them.

One set of those prints belonged to a Dinsio cousin named Phillip Christopher, who was on federal parole back in Ohio for a truck hijacking. Christopher's problem was that he had forgotten to mention to his parole officer that he was leaving Ohio to pull off a bank heist in sunny Southern California—and leaving the state without permission and plastering your prints all over a highball glass in a California condo used by a bank burglary crew was a pretty clearcut violation of the terms and conditions of his parole. Incident to Christopher's subsequent arrest for violating parole, FBI agents from the Cleveland office found $30,000 in cash in a garment bag in Christopher's closet, including two damningly special five-dollar bills. The bills were mementos of a trip that an Orange County woman had taken to Dallas in 1969, and before she tucked them away in her safe deposit box at the United California Bank in Laguna Niguel she had thoughtfully written down the serial numbers, which she provided to us after the heist. Christopher had a lot of explaining to do.

A few days later, Amil Dinsio, who'd been under surveillance, was arrested outside his home in Boardman, a suburb of Youngstown. A grand jury later indicted Amil's brother James and two of Amil's nephews, Harry and Ronald Barber. Ronald Barber was arrested in January 1973 in Rochester, New York, and James Dinsio was nabbed a couple months later in Ohio; but Harry Barber was in the wind and wouldn't be caught until later.

Meanwhile, some of the loot from the Laguna Niguel job started turning up. A kid playing in a vacant lot near Amil's home in Boardman got the surprise of his young life—and a reward—when he happened to dig up a jug containing $98,000 in cash, some of it from the Laguna Niguel job, some from the Lordstown burglary. In July, four months after the burglary, a survey crew working on a steep brush-covered hillside just off Sea Island Drive in Laguna Niguel found a gunny sack stuffed with a million bucks' worth of non-negotiable securities, stock certificates, and other stuff the burglars wouldn't have been able to fence; after the burglary they'd separated it out from the good stuff and tossed it down the hill.

There was more. After tailing Amil's brother James, agents spent a week digging up a field outside of Youngstown with picks, shovels, and a bulldozer, and finally found a buried stash of $1.4 million in negotiable securities taken in the Laguna Niguel job. A few months later, another $175,000 in negotiable securities turned up when a Beverly Hills public relations man with low-level organized crime connections— in Beverly Hills, every guy with no real job is either an actor or a public relations man—tried to use them as collateral for a $100,000 loan from a bank in Chicago.

(That's a standard organized crime method of laundering stolen bonds: You buy them from the thieves at 15 or 20 percent of face value, but you don't cash them in; the bonds are numbered, and the numbers might be checked against a stolen list before the money is paid out. Instead, you pose as a legitimate businessman and use them as collateral on a bank loan for, say, half the face value; bankers are much less likely to check out the bonds if they're simply holding them as collateral—and in some cases the loan officer may even be in on the deal. Once you get the loan cash you simply disappear, and when the bank tries to cash the bonds to cover the default, hey, sorry you guys, those bonds were stolen last year out of a vault in Laguna Niguel. Unfortunately for the Beverly Hills P.R. man, the bankers in Chicago were a little more conscientious than most. He was arrested and charged with interstate transportation of stolen securities.)

All told, then, about $2.7 million of the swag was recovered. But that left a couple million or so unaccounted for—and the Dinsio crew wasn't about to tell us where it was. Their response to our proffered deals in return for cooperation was a uniform "Fuck you."

So they all went to trial—Amil, Mulligan, and Christopher first. The trial itself was a slam dunk, but there were several sideshows. A jailhouse snitch reported an attempt by Amil to buy an alibi for $30,000, and there was another alleged plot to bribe or murder a witness. There were even some fears that the Dinsios were targeting FBI agents or their family members to disrupt the case. When a member of Special Agent Chamberlain's family started getting some telephone threats, suspicion naturally fell on Amil, who'd made no secret of how much he hated the FBI in general and Chamberlain in particular. Special Agent Jim McCauley and I were detailed to go down to county jail and give Amil an official talking-to about the high risk of fucking with the FBI, or with anybody the FBI cared about—and in those constitutionally less restrictive times, a talking-to always had the potential to expand beyond just talk.

But Amil, a dark, curly-headed guy with deepset eyes and a hard face, made a pretty convincing case: Yeah, he told us, I hate the FBI and I hate that fucking Chamberlain, but hey, we don't fuck with families— ever. We tended to believe him, and it later turned out that the threats to Paul's family member were unrelated to the Dinsio case.

But again, those were sideshows. In court, where it counted, the trial lasted five weeks and the jury took just two days to convict Amil, Mulligan, and Christopher of conspiracy, bank burglary, and larceny. They all got twenty-year sentences. Amil was unrepentant, giving a lengthy speech about the unfairness of the judicial system and calling the FBI "the biggest frame artists in the world." James Dinsio and Ronald Barber went down for fifteen years each. Harry Barber stayed in the wind until 1980, when he was found living in a small Pennsylvania town under the protection of the local sheriff; he got twelve years, and the sheriff was indicted.

None of them actually did more than twelve years in the jug. This was before mandatory minimum sentences, and the federal parole boards back then were considerably more lenient than today, especially with non-violent crimes like the Dinsio caper. In fact, Phillip Christopher was paroled after just three years and got a job in Cleveland repairing voting machines for the Cuyahoga County Board of Elections— which may tell you something about the sanctity of the electoral process in Cuyahoga County.

Amil, meanwhile, went back to his old ways after being paroled in 1984. In 1992, he was convicted of burglarizing a bank in North Carolina, and later earned himself a spot in the Prison Inmate Bogus Lawsuit Hall of Fame when he filed a $15 million lawsuit against the bank he had burglarized. Amil claimed that the bank had inflated the amount of the loss, which earned him a longer prison sentence. The lawsuit was thrown out.

There was one other coda to the Laguna Niguel caper. As it turned out, the Dinsios hadn't been the only people who were interested in ripping off the United California Bank. Shortly after the burglary, the bank sent out notices to the boxholders asking for a list of their lost valuables. When the missing property reports started coming back in, the bank's lawyers noticed that an alarming percentage of the claims seemed to be—how shall we put it?—somewhat excessive.

In fact, some of the boxholders, knowing that they were the only ones who knew what was—or wasn't—in their boxes, let their greed out for a romp, claiming that they'd lost a quarter million in cash, jewels the size of the Hope Diamond, gold ingots by the score, and so on. The bank lawyers weeded out most of the clearly fraudulent claims by inviting the claimants in for a chat and then introducing them to a local IRS agent who'd been invited by the bank to sit in on the discussion. Under those circumstances, a number of boxholders suddenly decided that, gosh, now that I think about it, I guess I didn't have a quarter mil in unaccounted-for cash in that safe deposit box after all. Eventually, however, after a lengthy lawsuit, the bank paid forty-seven boxholders $1.3 million in damages for unrecovered losses, ranging from gold and jewelry to $40,000 in negotiable bonds issued by the Kentucky Turnpike Authority.

All in all, then, the Laguna Niguel caper was a mixed bag: the burglars all went to prison, but not for nearly as long as they should have, and some of the losses were recovered, while millions weren't. The heist was a good example of how a professional burglary crew operated—and how they could screw up on the small details. We'd caught some breaks, and the massive cross-country investigation had been brilliantly handled by Paul Chamberlain, Roger Goldsberry, and scores of other FBI agents. For the FBI, the Laguna Niguel caper was a "win" on the scoreboard.

And that score stood for fourteen years. In all that time, while thousands of L.A. banks were robbed at gunpoint, no one ever hacked their way into a Southern California bank vault and made off with the swag.

But then someone decided to dig a tunnel under the streets of Hollywood. And unlike the Dinsios, these guys weren't making any mistakes.

✦ ✦ ✦

Alligators. He knew it was silly, but LAPD Detective Doug Sims couldn't stop thinking about alligators—giant, sewer-ranging, man-eating urban alligators.

It was a few hours after the tunnel at the First Interstate in Hollywood was discovered, and Doug and a dozen other detectives and FBI agents were fanned out into the L.A. storm sewer system. They didn't really expect to find the crooks, of course; those boys were long gone. But maybe they had left some evidence behind.

There are some 2,600 miles of storm sewer pipes under the city of Los Angeles, ranging in size from 12-inch street gutter drainpipes to huge underground culverts big enough to drive a bus through. The pipes are arranged like veins in a huge leaf, the smaller pipes emptying into larger pipes and the larger pipes emptying into still larger ones, until finally the main arteries empty into the Los Angeles River or Ballona Creek, and the water flows out to the ocean. In a heavy rainstorm the storm sewer pipes, even the largest of them, will be filled to bursting as they struggle to carry off billions of gallons of rainwater that run off hillsides and down street gutters. But even in the dry season—say, from April to November—the pipes will always have a trickle of water running through them, an inch or two deep. People by the millions are watering lawns, washing cars, hosing off sidewalks—and that water runs down the gutters and into the storm sewer system.

True, you don't have to deal with raw sewage in the storm sewers; nobody's toilets empty into them, or at least they aren't supposed to. Sanitation sewers for toilets and sinks and showers are a completely different and separate underground pipe system. Still, think of every kind of noxious, disgusting substance that you've ever seen on a lawn or a sidewalk or a street gutter, and that's what you'll find washed into the storm sewers: dog crap, grass clippings, cigarette butts, weedkiller, candy wrappers, beer cans, illegally dumped industrial solvents, motor oil, condoms, rotting leaves—every imaginable form of urban detritus is in there, creating a potentially dangerous environment. The biologicals can build up and decompose, creating deadly pockets of methane gas, and the water trickling through those pipes is so full of toxics it can peel your skin.

It's pretty disgusting, all right. Throw in the utter darkness inside the sewers, add a pinch of claustrophobia as you're duckwalking through a 4-foot-diameter pipe, then start thinking about all those urban myths you've heard—about people buying little baby alligators as pets and later dumping them into the sewers, where they grow huge and fat on a diet of rats and winos and the occasional passing Burglary Special detective—and you've got a recipe for a bad case of the heebie-jeebies.

Doug Sims was a big, burly, barrel-chested guy, a hard-core cop, and in his head he knew damn well there were no goddam alligators down there, or any other man-eating fauna; hell, even the rats got washed out in every big rainstorm. Still, even without the alligators, it was spooky. Doug couldn't help but notice that the Department of Public Works guys who were guiding them through the sewers were equipped with methane detectors and oxygen bottles, while he was protected by nothing more substantial than a pair of rubber boots and an LAPD T-shirt. Slogging through the muck in those sewers was enough to make him briefly wish he'd gone into some other line of work.

And there wasn't much payoff for it, either. The tunnelers hadn't left much behind, just a few abandoned hand tools, some sandbags, some tire tracks. It was enough to figure out the how of the thing—but the who of it was going to be a little tougher.

We decided there'd been at least three, maybe four of them working underground, plus a lookout up top. They had accessed the storm sewer system about a half mile north of the bank, near the intersection of Hollywood Boulevard and Nichols Canyon Drive, a narrow street that wound its way up into the Hollywood Hills. Next to the road was an open concrete storm channel that carried water runoff downhill until it got to Hollywood Boulevard, at which point it went into a 54-inch-diameter underground concrete pipe.

Sometime in the night, several weeks before the burglary, the burglary crew had lowered some four-wheel all-terrain vehicles (ATVs) into the open channel—from the tire tracks we found in one of the sewer pipes, they appeared to be Suzuki Quads—then broken the lock on the grate that covered the mouth of the storm sewer pipe. They loaded their heavy tools onto the ATVs and drove into the sewer pipe. Hunched over on their ATVs—remember, the pipes they were riding through were only 4 1/2 feet in diameter—they drove south, then east, then south again through the sewer pipe that ran under the middle of Spaulding Street, until they got to the point due east of the bank; that would have been easy to determine by measuring the distance from a manhole cover further north on Spaulding.

They set up a gas-powered generator to provide electric power, and then used an industrial concrete saw to cut a 2 1/2- by 3-foot rectangular hole through the side of the 4-inch-thick concrete sewer pipe. It would have been noisy, but so what? At night, no Department of Public Works employees would have been down there, and even in the daytime their maintenance guys don't venture into the smaller pipes unless there's evidence of a blockage or some other problem. The crew knew that the chances of someone stumbling onto the hole in the side of the pipe were pretty small.

Once they removed the section of the sewer pipe, they started digging with picks and hand shovels, using a surveyor's transit and a compass to keep the tunnel shaft properly aligned. The soil was relatively easy to work. Los Angeles is built on an alluvial fan, the buildup of eons worth of silt and small gravel washing down from the mountains, so the earth was soft and relatively free of large rocks and heavy clay. As they got deeper into the tunnel, they used wheelbarrows to haul the dirt out to the sewer pipe.

It was backbreaking labor. There was a huge amount of earth, more than 3,000 cubic feet, that had to be dug out, loaded into a wheelbarrow, and then humped back to the tunnel entrance; we figured they would have had to make something like fifteen hundred wheelbarrow trips, of steadily increasing length, bent over a wheelbarrow in a dark, narrow, poorly ventilated tunnel. They would empty the dirt into the sewer pipe and then go back for more—again and again and again, seemingly endlessly.

As anyone who's seen *The Great Escape* knows, the secret tunneler's biggest problem is how to dispose of the excavated dirt without anyone noticing it. The British POWs in the movie hid it in their pants and dropped it around the exercise yard, but our guys had an easier solution. Using sandbags, they built a temporary dam just upstream from the tunnel entrance, backing up the trickle of water in the sewer pipe, and forming a reservoir about 2 feet deep. At the end of each working day—or rather, night—they'd knock down the temporary sandbag dam and the rushing water would carry the dirt downstream; later, when we searched the sewer system, we found a mud flow 2 feet deep downstream from the tunnel.

We figured it took them a month of hard labor to get under the vault, working at night and then climbing back up to the surface before daybreak to eat and sleep at some rented safehouse. Instead of traveling all the way back to the entrance to the storm drain to climb out, they'd parked a truck painted to look like a city public works truck by a manhole a half block from the bank, and used that for ingress and egress; neighbors later reported seeing the truck there at odd hours, and the manhole surrounded by orange warning cones. The topside man with the truck would be able to keep an eye out for any unusual activity at the bank—cops, bank employees looking around, whatever—and also keep the diggers fueled with hot coffee. Afterward we found an enormous number of Styrofoam fast-food coffee cups that had collected downstream from the tunnel.

They had almost certainly timed the vault entry to take place early on in the Memorial Day three-day weekend, which would have given them an extra day to bust into the safe deposit boxes. But once they got under the vault, they had run into problems cutting their way through the 18-inch vault floor.

They had set up a large industrial boring drum pointed up toward the bottom of the vault, tapping into the bank's electrical system for power—and in the process, causing the electrical problems that had so mystified the employees in the bank. On the boring drum they mounted a water-cooled core bit 18 inches in diameter, a heavy-duty metal cylinder with a cutting edge of industrial diamonds; water for cooling the machine was pumped in through a hose leading back out to the sewer pipe. The diamond-studded bit—which costs about $2,000—will cut through concrete and steel like an apple corer through a Golden Delicious, but it's hard to work with. The base of the boring drum that turns the bit has to be firmly mounted or the bit will travel.

Which is what happened to our guys. When they started drilling, the core bit started to shimmy, and they couldn't steady it. We could see from the marks on the bottom of the vault floor that the bit had been creeping all over the concrete. (That initial drilling attempt, incidentally, most likely was the "rats or something" that the security guy had told the branch manager she was hearing on the Friday evening at the end of May.)

Finally, the crew said the hell with the core bit and started chipping away at the vault floor with concrete saws and hand-held drills; that took them an extra week. Once they were almost through the floor, they set up hydraulic jacks on timbers and broke through the remaining few inches of concrete, then climbed up into the vault and set to work drilling and prying open the safe deposit boxes. The topside man would have alerted them by two-way radio if cops or the security guys showed up to check on the alarms, at which point they'd sit tight until the security guys decided it was a false alarm. Then back to work.

By late Sunday night or early Monday morning, it was time to knock off. They gathered up the loot and their tools and loaded them onto the ATVs in the sewer pipe. They went back into the tunnel and swept it clean—we didn't even find any footprints in there—then drove back to the above-ground culvert north of Hollywood Boulevard and loaded all their stuff onto a truck.

And then they vanished.

Oh, it was a hell of a caper, all right. They'd gotten $172,000 of the bank's cash, and had hit 114 safe deposit boxes. Seventy-four of those boxes were unrented, and thus a waste of time, and of the remaining boxholders, only thirty-six reported losses; the others either didn't have anything in their boxes, or else they didn't have anything in the boxes that they wanted to tell the FBI about. This was, after all, Hollywood, and if you were keeping drugs or drug money or stolen merchandize in your safe deposit box, well, you weren't going to blab about it; you took your hit and kept your mouth shut.

Still, the contents of the thirty-six boxes for which losses were reported amounted to a treasure trove: jewelry, gold, silver flatware, some ancient Persian artifacts, an 1855 first edition of Walt Whitman's *Leaves of Grass*, an untitled sketch of a young girl by Henri Matisse, two works by Raoul Dufy; Michael "The King of Pop" Jackson's dad put in a claim for some gold coins and cash he had in one of the boxes.

Eventually, the bank paid out $2.5 million to the boxholders for their losses—and even that was considered a low-end figure on the total loss.

So it was a pretty good score. But there was something strange about this heist, something that didn't fit. The truth was that, despite their success, these guys hadn't seemed to know very much about burglarizing a bank.

Yes, their tunneling had been professional and expert, and they had seemed to know that the alarms they had set off wouldn't lead to anyone opening the vault to check it out. But the way they had attacked the safe deposit boxes inside the vault seemed amateurish, almost desultory. Although the locks on the larger boxes had been carefully drilled out with impact drills, most of the smaller boxes had been pried open with crowbars, which left flanges of jagged metal that prevented opening the boxes around them; consequently, for every box they pried open, they had closed off access to the ones on the top, bottom, and sides of the opened one. They could have gotten into a lot more boxes if they'd used a sledgehammer and a two-headed punch to pop out the double locks on the boxes—which is exactly what a professional crew like the Dinsios had done down in Laguna Niguel.

So, one working theory was that these guys were professional tunnel types but only amateur crooks. We wondered if these were miners or construction workers or storm sewer maintenance crews, guys who had seen one caper movie too many and decided to try a bank heist—and had miraculously succeeded.

It was a solid theory. Certainly there was nothing in this job that matched the M.O. of any known professional burglary crew, not in L.A. and not anywhere else in the United States that we could determine. So BAD detectives and FBI agents spent weeks checking out construction and mining companies and specialized tools outlets, looking for leads. They also checked out anyone who had access to the Flood Control District's sewer maps, or guys who'd worked on sewer projects for the city.

But there was another possibility, too: What if the tunnel crew's target had been one particular safe deposit box, something so big, so valuable, that it alone would have justified all the work and risk that had gone into the tunnel?

We had some basis for that theory, as well. After the tunnel story hit the news, we started getting a lot of helpful phone-in advice from the citizenry: it was a gang of Vietnam veterans, former tunnel rats, callers suggested—forgetting that the while the U.S. military's tunnel rats explored Viet Cong tunnels, they didn't dig them. No, others suggested, it was the VC themselves who'd dug the tunnel, sneaking in among the flood of Vietnamese boat people in the early eighties and turning to crime to bankroll the commie government back home. No, wait, it was a gang of urban troglodytes, derelicts, and winos who inhabited the sewers and somehow got it together to rob a bank. As usual, the callers were long on theories and short on specifics.

But there was one call that seemed promising. Two days after the burglary, the lead agent, Special Agent Tom O'Quinn, got an anonymous call from a guy who said he knew exactly who had pulled off that vault job. The caller sounded rational, well spoken, obviously intelligent. He told Tom that a guy with organized crime and drug connections —let's call him Johnny Glick—had set up the job with a professional crew from back East. Their target was a specific safe deposit box that contained $3 million in laundered drug cash. Glick and his girlfriend, whom the caller named, had rented a safe deposit box under the girlfriend's name so they could peep out the vault and get the layout, then brought in the crew to dig the tunnel and hit the vault and grab the drug dealers' cash. No, the caller didn't want to say any more, not yet, he was in some danger here; but he said he'd call Tom O'Quinn back in a day or two with more information on the tunnelers—oh, and don't try to trace the call or you'll never hear from me again.

Well, it could have been the same sort of bullshit tip that follows every high-profile crime—except that an FBI criminal records check did indeed turn up a guy named Johnny Glick, formerly of Los Angeles, current address unknown, an aging, low-level organized crime guy with a forty-year-long record for theft, assault, pandering, and drug dealing. And yes, one of the bank boxes had been rented to someone with the same name as Glick's alleged girlfriend.

It was pretty intriguing. It could explain why the crew had worked so hard, for so long, to hit that particular bank: A $3 million cash score, as opposed to ripping off coins and jewelry and artwork that you'd have to fence at bargain basement prices, would have been well worth the effort. Of course, if that was the plan, they wouldn't have just hit the one targeted box and left the rest alone; that would have drawn an arrow to the boxholder, and maybe given the FBI a place to start working back from. Besides, once you're in the vault, why not pop a few other boxes see if you can stumble onto some gold or diamonds? So, the theory went, they hit the target box first and then started popping other boxes as camouflage, and for the extra gravy. As for the sloppy prywork on some of the boxes, what difference did it make? They weren't really interested in those boxes anyway.

It was either a solid lead or one hell of a coincidence. Besides, we didn't have much else. And Tom O'Quinn, a veteran agent with a quiet, easy-to-trust demeanor, was an expert at working sources; he was confident that the guy would call back and he could squeeze more specific information out of him.

Unfortunately, we had an Assistant Special Agent in Charge at the time—let's call him ASAC Huha, short for "ASAC Head Up His Ass"— who like too many upper-level management types thought he knew more about investigating a case than street agents did. ASAC Huha insisted that we put a trap and trace on O'Quinn's line to find out who the caller was when he called back—this on the lame assumption that the guy would be calling from the phone in his own den or something. Tom bitterly resisted, words were exchanged, but ASACs must have their way. The trap and trace was set up through the main switchboard at the FBI field office, and sure enough, when the guy called back two days later he heard some distinctive clicks on the line. He hung up and never called back. Tom was furious; ASAC Huha continued his relentless upward climb through the bureaucracy.

In the end, though, maybe it didn't matter. Months later, we finally located Glick living in a cheap apartment house in Las Vegas. He was put under surveillance for a while, but nothing hinky developed. At last Special Agent Jerry Hines, a former Army helicopter pilot who'd taken over the case, decided, What the hell, let's jack him up and ask him about it. Sweat him a little about this mysterious box with millions in dope money inside it.

So agents from the Las Vegas field office knock on Glick's door and tell him about the phone call and suggest that perhaps an explanation is in order. But Glick, who is pushing sixty and down on his luck, offers up a pretty convincing "What the fuck are you talking about?"

You say somebody dropped a dime on me? Hey, I got a lot of enemies; somebody's just trying to screw me. And yeah, maybe my girl-friend—*ex*-girlfriend now—rented a box at that bank, but so what? She wanted a place to keep all that fancy jewelry I said I'd buy her and never did. Besides, you guys really think I'm gonna rip off some major drug dealers for millions of dollars and then sit out here in this desert dump with my name on the mailbox, waiting for them to come and find me? You found me, so could they—probably quicker than you guys did. Shit, if I had that kind of money, I'd be long gone. Look somewhere else, guys; I didn't have nothing to do with it.

And the truth was, no, Glick didn't look good for this one; he didn't seem to have enough brains, or style, for a caper like this. And his ex-girlfriend backed him up, sort of. That broken-down old pimp pulling off a million-dollar bank caper? Don't make me laugh.

The problem was, nobody else was looking good for this caper, either. Canvassing construction and mining companies hadn't produced any leads. We hadn't even seen any of the loot turn up. The BAD detectives' extensive network of informants hadn't reported anybody trying to fence any of the distinctive items stolen from the bank boxes, and legitimate dealers hadn't seen any of the stuff, either. After the burglary, we sent circulars to art dealers and rare book stores and jewelers associations across the country, asking them to let us know if anybody was offering up a certain Matisse or a first edition of *Leaves of Grass*. Nothing.

A criminal investigation is like a living thing; you have to feed it to keep it alive. As the weeks and months went by, with no life-sustaining clues or leads to chew on, the investigation started to waste away. First Interstate had put up a $20,000 reward for information on the bur-glars—a lousy $20,000 on a multimillion-dollar bank heist; Jesus, those bankers were cheap—but that certainly hadn't turned any heads. Eventually the extra agents and detectives who'd been assigned at the start were peeled off to work on newer, fresher, more promising crimes. After all the evidence, such as it was, was collected, the tunnel was pumped full of popcorn concrete and sealed. Finally only the lead special agent and the lead BAD detective were left on the case, to pursue new theories or check out old leads—when they had the time from their other cases. Mostly they waited for a break, a break that just wouldn't come.

It was frustrating. Once again we were forced into the Lawman's Paradox: while we certainly couldn't encourage or condone violation of Title 18, U.S. Code, Section 2113(b)—that is, burglary of a federally insured financial institution—we needed these guys to pull off another bank job. We needed them to hit another bank, somewhere, with the same M.O., just as the Dinsio crew had done after the Laguna Niguel job—and maybe this time they would leave behind some more clues, something we could work with.

You know the old saying: Be careful what you wish for.

✦ ✦ ✦

Saturday morning, 3:00 A.M., August 22, 1987, a little more than a year after the Hollywood tunnel job. The branch manager of the Bank of America at the corner of Pico and La Cienega is sound asleep, as you'd expect any decent banker to be at that hour, and the phone next to the bed starts ringing.

This is bank security, sir. Sorry to disturb you, but we've got a vault alarm down at the bank.

Huh? What? What time is it?

Three A.M., sir. We had an alarm at 11:30 P.M., but it reset itself, so we figured it was a false alarm. Then we had another at 1:30 A.M., it reset again, and now we've got another one. We thought we should notify you.

Uh, yeah, right. Christ, three o'clock in the morning. Well, look, there's a construction project right across the street. They probably got a wire crossed or something. Can you call the cops and ask them to swing by and take a look?

Already done, sir.

Okay, great. It's probably nothing. I'll go down in the morning—later in the morning—and take a look.

Yes, sir.

Well, okay, who wants to crawl out of bed at three o'clock in the morning on a weekend and drive in to work because there's some hobgoblin in the wiring? And even if the bank manager retained some dim, sleepy-eyed memory of the Hollywood tunnel job from a year earlier, which was doubtful, what were the chances that this was a repeat? Hell, there were 3,500 banks in L.A. Why think yours was the target of a once-in-a-lifetime—or even twice-in-a-lifetime—caper?

So the manager goes back to cutting Zs, and an LAPD black-and-white cruises by the bank, a one-story brick building surrounded by nail salons and auto repair shops and Middle Eastern mom-and-pop markets. Nothing out of the ordinary; all quiet at the corner of Pico and La Cienega. Then at 6:00 A.M. the vault alarm activated and didn't reset itself; at the Bank of America security center the alarm light kept blinking and blinking. Something was going on here.

This time the bank manager heads down to the bank and meets the cops. They check out the lobby—all okay—and the bank roof and exterior walls—all okay. But the bank manager isn't satisfied. He decides to open up the vault and take a look inside.

But wait a minute. I said earlier that FDIC vault specifications require class I vaults to be equipped with time locks that, once set, make it impossible to open the vault door before the specified time. And true enough, the vault at the Bank of America was equipped with a time lock—which in the ordinary course of events would have kept the vault locked until Monday morning.

But Bank of America brass had never liked the time lock system. Yeah, they had the time locks, but they didn't set them. Instead, they used a double combination system on the vault, meaning that it took two employees, with separate combinations, to open the vault door. The Bank of America guys figured that was sufficient security—and the advantage of not employing the time lock, obviously, was that it allowed after-hours access to the vault in an emergency, or if something seemed hinky.

And something seemed hinky here. So the manager calls in the assistant manager, who has the second set of vault numbers, and with the cops standing by they dial in their respective combinations and swing open the vault door and—

It was holy shit time all over again.

It was the same guys, no question. They'd refined some of their tunneling skills and upgraded some of their equipment; as far as the tunneling went, it was an even more sophisticated operation than the Hollywood job. Still, it was them; the Hole in the Ground Gang was back.

But this time they'd screwed up.

They had come in from one of the larger storm sewers, a 10-feet-tall by 15-feet-wide main line that ran under La Cienega Boulevard, a major West L.A. thoroughfare. Using the same kind of 18-inch core bit that they'd tried on the First Interstate vault—but more solidly anchored this time—they cut a perfectly round, 18-inch-diameter hole through the 10-inch-thick reinforced concrete wall of the storm sewer. Since the main lines of the storm sewer system are often traveled by city maintenance workers, who surely would notice a fresh hole in the wall, they had covered up the hole with a circle of plywood when they knocked off for the night, mortaring it over to make it blend in with the concrete.

Eighteen inches isn't much of a hole, barely wide enough for a slim man to squeeze through (a standard sewer manhole is 24 inches in diameter). You could pass shovels through it, and the concrete boring machine and core bit would just make it through. But this time they had to cut their wheelbarrows in sections, pass them through the hole, and then bolt them back together with metal straps. It worked just fine. As they dug the tunnel, they shoveled the dirt back out through the hole and into a trailer attached to an ATV, and then they hauled it downstream to dump it and let the water flowing through the sewer carry it away undetected. During the day they'd stash the ATVs in a smaller side sewer pipe.

The tunnel itself was a little shorter than the Hollywood tunnel, about 70 feet long, and somewhat more luxurious. It was about 4 feet wide in most spots, and at least 5 1/2 feet tall throughout. Two-by-fours were used for shoring in some portions, and electric lights were strung along the ceiling, powered by a gas generator. When they got under the vault, they made sure they could keep their boring machine and core bit steady; they drilled up into the bottom of the vault floor and sunk lag bolts to attach the inverted frame of the electric boring machine. Once that was done, the rest was easy. They cranked up the machine and cut another perfectly round, 18-inch-diameter hole through 18 inches of concrete and steel rebar that made up the vault floor.

Once again, the tunneling work was brilliant, the concrete-cutting work even better. Even under optimum conditions it's not easy to run a boring machine and get such smooth, round cuts—and standing in a storm sewer or hunched over in a hand-dug chamber under a bank vault are hardly optimum conditions. In fact, later, when BAD Detective Dennis Pagenkopp showed crime scene photos of the core bit holes to guys who were in the concrete-coring business, they whistled with professional admiration. Hell, they said, if you catch these guys, have 'em call us when they get out of prison.

But if the Hole in the Ground Gang had honed their construction skills since the Hollywood job, they hadn't improved their basic knowledge of vaults and vault alarm systems and bank security procedures. Professional bank burglars like the Dinsio crew would have known that Bank of America didn't use the time lock system, that someone could open the vault at any time—and if they didn't know it they would have found out. Bank of America was the biggest bank chain in California, with tens of thousands of current and former employees who could have been tapped for inside tips on the bank's operations. At the very least, if our tunnel boys had been smarter about the security system, they would have intentionally set off the alarms for a week or two before the vault entry—as they'd unintentionally done on the Hollywood job—to make the security guys think there was a glitch in the alarm system, and thus ignore the inevitable alarms on vault-busting day.

But they didn't. We figured they were actually in the vault for less than an hour before their outside man radioed that the cops and the bank manager were coming into the bank. They'd had time to bust open the wheeled cash cart where the bank tellers stored their working currency, but not one of the safe deposit boxes had been opened before they heard the tumblers on the vault door clicking open and had to scramble back down the hole in the vault floor and run like hell.

They took $98,000 in bank cash with them, but they left stacks of bundled cash sitting on a counter in the vault; that's how fast they scooted out of there. Ninety-eight grand, divided four or five ways, for a job that had taken weeks to pull off. By bank caper standards, it was nothing. They also left behind some coveralls and a Harley-Davidson T-shirt in the vault, along with their safe box breaking tools; in the tunnel they left behind the boring machine and the core bit, some shovels and a wheelbarrow, the Honda generator, their electric lighting system. And in a small side sewer line near the storm sewer outlet at Ballona Creek they left behind a Suzuki Quad ATV with the serial numbers filed down.

We found all that stuff. And then we found something we could hardly believe.

A couple days after the Bank of America job, LAPD Burglary Special Detective Doug Sims was back in the sewers again, sloshing through 2 inches of water and still trying not to think about giant sewer 'gators. With a city public works guy acting as a guide, they were walking through the large storm sewer that runs under La Cienega, looking for any evidence that the initial searches might have missed. About a mile north of the entrance for the Bank of America tunnel, as they're passing under Wilshire Boulevard in Beverly Hills, Doug notices some fresh concrete patchwork on the side of the storm sewer.

What's that? Doug asks the public works guy.

The guy looks at it, shrugs. Patch, he says. The walls crack, we patch 'em. Happens all the time.

Wait a second, Doug says. He takes the butt of his flashlight and starts tapping along the storm sewer wall. *Thud, thud, thud, thud—thonk! Thonk thonk thonk thonk thonk!* Doug looks at the public works guy: That sound hollow to you? It sure as hell does. So they scrape away the mortar and, sure enough, there's a piece of plywood fitted into a perfectly round 18-inch core bit hole cut through the sewer wall. And behind that hole there's open space that leads off into blackness.

It's another goddam tunnel! And it turns out that this one leads to an excavated chamber directly underneath the vault at the Union Federal Savings and Loan in the 8400 block of Wilshire Boulevard, in the splendor of Beverly Hills. The Hole in the Ground Gang had already sunk lag bolts into the floor of the vault, just waiting to attach the boring machine and the core bit and start drilling up through the floor of the vault.

At this point all of us—FBI agents, Burglary Special detectives, the public works guys—are in absolute awe.

Two tunnels! *Two banks!* At the same time—unbelievable.

The Bank of America was closed on Saturdays and Sundays, but the savings and loan was open Saturdays, closed Sundays. So we figured they had planned to hit the Bank of America vault on Friday night, clean it out on Saturday, and then bust into the Beverly Hills savings and loan on Saturday night and clean it out on Sunday. We estimated that if they'd been able to pull off both jobs, taking the bank cash and hitting all the safe deposit boxes—and this time they'd had much more professional box-busting tools with them—they could have gotten away with a face-value take of anywhere from $10 to $25 million. It could have been the biggest bank burglary in the history of the world.

The audaciousness of the thing was stunning—but it was also more than a little weird. The question was, why? Why double your work, and your chances of being detected, by digging two tunnels simultaneously? Why try such a complicated caper? Yes, it was dazzling, and bold, but somehow it wasn't—well, professional. It was almost as if there was a thrill angle to it, a desire to do something that had never been done before, just to show you could. Weird.

And who knew if they had stopped there? We started getting these nagging mental images of a network of tunnels under every bank in West L.A., of the ground beneath us laced like a prairie dog village with holes and chambers and secret passages, of waking up one morning and finding five or ten or a hundred bank vaults simultaneously breached and stripped, and legions of bankers and boxholders screaming for vengeance and immediate compensation. Every sewer line in West L.A. would have to be searched, every patch job inspected; it took weeks.

We also wondered if, after being screwed on the Bank of America job, they might try to come back and make good on the Beverly Hills tunnel. After all, they wouldn't necessarily know we had found it. Maybe they had balls enough to come back for a second try; given the balls they'd shown already, that didn't seem out of the question. So there was some discussion about keeping the discovery of the second tunnel a secret, then staking out the storm sewers, or even sealing an FBI agent or an LAPD detective inside the Beverly Hills tunnel with some food and water to wait for the tunnel boys to come back.

But finally we decided it wouldn't work. For one thing, after we found the second tunnel, traffic on busy La Cienega Boulevard had to be stopped completely for a few hours, until engineers could take a look and see if there was any chance of a Mercedes with somebody important in it crashing through the asphalt and into the tunnel. Catching bank bandits is one thing, but it'll take a backseat to warding off civil liability every time. The street closure caused a hellish traffic jam, and news reporters saw cops popping in and out of manholes like a giant game of Whack-a-Mole; there was no way we could keep the second tunnel out of the news. Besides, there was no place to hide a stakeout team in the sewers—and frankly, there weren't a lot of volunteers.

So finally, after all the evidence was gathered, the two tunnels were pumped full of popcorn cement and the entry holes sealed. Meanwhile, FBI agents and the Burglary Special detectives started looking at the evidence the tunnel boys had left behind.

The vehicle identification number on the Suzuki Quad had been filed down, but the crime lab guys were able to raise the letters with acid. Detectives traced it to a dealer in Hollywood, whose records showed that it had been purchased more than a year earlier by a "Robert Spaulding"—Spaulding of course being the name of the street in Hollywood where the Hole in the Ground Gang had dug their way into the First Interstate Bank the year before. That was a cute touch, and it removed any doubt that we were dealing with the same crew as last time.

A check of area dealers showed that three other ATVs had been purchased under the name "Spaulding" or "Spalding" in Hollywood and El Monte, a suburb of L.A. "Spaulding" had also purchased some of the recovered tools from a Hollywood supplier. The buyers, who always paid cash, were described as white males, early thirties, slim and muscular, dressed in construction-style clothes, speaking accentless American English, and short-haired in a long-haired era. One dealer thought they looked military, like *Top Gun* types.

The 18-inch core bit also had a serial number on it. It turned out it had been purchased in the San Francisco Bay Area by a guy who arrived at the construction supply store in a taxi—same physical description—and said he needed it for a rush job in San Diego. He paid cash.

There was one other significant piece of evidence. The crime lab guys found one partial fingerprint on the Suzuki Quad, and that print was fed into the computerized print data banks in the United States, Canada, South America, and Europe. At the time, computerized print records were still in their infancy, and contained print records on only about 2 percent of all suspects who'd been arrested. So it was a long shot, and the fact that it was only a partial made it even longer. It was too long; there was no hit.

So it was the same story as the first time. Dozens of agents and detectives worked the case at first, searching the sewers, questioning construction and mining company workers, tracking down the tools, examining records, checking out tips—and nothing panned out. Every agent and detective wanted to crack the case—if for no other reason than to know who these unbelievable sons of bitches really were—but eventually, as the months went by, frustration set in, other cases came up, the ardor cooled. Even the so-called victim couldn't muster up much interest in the thing; as annoying as it was to have to fix that hole in the floor, no boxholders had to be compensated, and the $98,000 the burglars took was, for a bank chain the size of Bank of America, basically chump change.

Sure, whenever they had time, the lead agent or detective would pick up the case file and give it a shake, checking out a new angle or an old theory. In 1989, eighteen months after the second set of tunnels, Dennis Pagenkopp and the Burglary Special guys got the NBC reality crime show *Unsolved Mysteries* to do a segment on the three tunnel jobs. The show generated a couple hundred telephone tips, but it was the usual tipster circus: tunnel rats, troglodytes, Chinese commies burrowing through the earth. One caller insisted, for reasons that were unclear, that it was Hopi Indians. Absolutely nothing solid to work with.

And it still goes on. Every time that *Unsolved Mysteries* episode is repeated in syndication—the last time was in 1998—more hopeless tips trickle in.

But it's too late. After five years, in 1992, the statute of limitations on the crimes had run out. Even if we found them, even if the Hole in the Ground Gang took out a signed, full-page ad in the *Los Angeles Times* that said: "We did it!", all we could do is take them down to the Scotch & Sirloin and buy them a no-hard-feelings beer. No criminal charges could be filed.

Once again, and for all eternity, the Hole in the Ground Gang had gotten away clean. And never again, to this day, anywhere in America, has anybody ever tunneled their way into a bank vault.

Still, even after all these years, I wish I could buy them that no-hard-feelings beer. I wish I could find out how they did it, and why. I wish I could answer the question that every agent and detective who worked on the case still wonders about: Who were these guys?

✦ ✦ ✦

Everybody has their own theory, each probably as good as the next. The one thing that everybody seems to agree on is that they weren't a professional burglary crew; they appeared too suddenly, made too many technical mistakes on the burglary side, and then disappeared too completely for the professional criminal scenario to fit. In the criminal world, talk about a score like that inevitably gets around. Somebody brags, guys make deals to lighten up their own troubles with the law, somebody drops a dime, the stolen swag starts to surface, the burglary crew pulls another, similar job somewhere else.

That was what had happened to the Dinsio crew years before. In fact, it was largely because the Dinsios were professionals that we'd been able to catch them. Their M.O. was familiar, they had criminal records and prints on file, they had the fencing contacts to try to move the stolen goods, which tracked back to them. All of that had worked against them, and allowed us to put the case down.

But none of that happened with the Hole in the Ground Gang. No brags, no deals, no dimes, so swag, no matchable prints. The irony is that if only they'd been professional criminals, with all the baggage that entails, we might have been able to match them with the evidence we had.

So, the working theory on the Hole in the Ground Gang is that they were regular guys who simply got a wild hair up to do a bank heist—or three bank heists—and then melted back into the straight world, never to be heard from again. From there you can weave your own story line. This one is mine:

I see two, maybe three men, sitting around after work one day in a bar in some windblown desert town, with dust in their hair and hard-hat tan lines on their faces and cold beers in their hands. They're brothers, or cousins, or at least the tightest of friends, guys who went to a small-town high school together, the sort of wild but not mean blue-collar kids who liked cars and dirt bikes. They did some half-assed teenaged crimes, joyriding, maybe a burglary that they never got caught for, but they don't really have criminal hearts; it was the thrill, not the gain, that motivated them.

They're not well educated in the formal sense, they never gave a rat's ass about school; they're not college boys. But they're smart, resourceful, and they aren't afraid of big machines and hard work. They spent high school summers on the road crew, or doing pissant labor for their uncle's construction company, and after graduation some recruiter got to them, and they all signed up together for some high-adrenaline military specialty—Army airborne, Marines, something with a little are-you-man-enough juice to it. But Vietnam was over, no wars loomed, and to their disappointment they never got into the shit. Yet the military bearing and discipline stuck, even after they got out.

They're still young, late twenties, early thirties, still single, no wives, no kids, no mortgages. For years now they've been following heavy construction projects all over California and the West—bridges, dams, subway tunnels, storm sewer projects—as journeymen steelworkers or machinists or carpenters or heavy equipment operators. The money's good when they're working—in fact, it's almost more than they can spend—but the money isn't enough. They may not even realize it, but they need excitement, action, something different.

On this day, in this bar, in this godforsaken town, they're bullshitting as usual. Maybe one of them has seen a caper movie the night before, he's talking about it, how these movie bad guys pulled off this really cool score. And suddenly one of them tosses this off: Shit, we could do something like that. We could rob a bank.

And that's how simple it is. That's how regular guys get into crime—with a half-assed idea that lands on a barroom table amid a field of half-empty Marlboro packs and dead-soldier beer bottles.

Everybody laughs. Yeah, right. Rob a fucking bank.

No, I'm serious. We could do it.

Yeah? How?

He thinks a minute. Well, if it was me, I'd dig a tunnel . . .

Dig a tunnel—Jesus! But it's a fun game, the sort of beery bullshit that has bounced around a million barrooms. Nobody even dreams that any of it is serious. They keep talking about it, throwing out ideas, and the other guys say, No, that's not the way, we should do it this way—just talking, of course. Pretty soon the ideas dry up, and they move onto other things—sports, the barmaid's ass, that asshole foreman on the pipeline job.

But for one of them, the leader, the catalyst of the group, the idea won't go away. The next day he's still thinking about it, and the next, and the next. He's a brooder, a thinker, the kind of guy who's able to look into the future and see his own face on the bodies of the broken-down older guys he works with every day—and he doesn't enjoy the vision. Maybe he wishes the idea wasn't there in his head, but there it is, and it has to be dealt with; the only alternative is more life as he now knows it, forever—and fuck that. Just fuck that.

He would never use the word, of course, probably wouldn't even understand it in the context. But he's a romantic. And finally, after weeks or even months, he passes through the door.

I'm gonna do this. I'm gonna do this bank robbery thing.

Yeah, sure. But they see his face. You're serious?

You fuckin' A I'm serious. I'm not gonna bust my hump for the rest of my life just so I can get old and die in a goddam trailer park. Are you in or are you out? If you're out, say so, I'll find somebody else.

It's a challenge, a question of balls. These guys aren't criminals, but none of them wants to be left behind. And it's not like they're going to stick guns in some old lady's face; nobody's gonna get hurt. Slowly, over days or weeks, they each do a personal life assessment and decide: Okay, what the fuck, I'm in. How much you think we'll get?

I dunno, a million, two million—whatever.

Holy shit.

But for the leader, at least, the money is almost secondary. Somehow it's the doing of the thing that matters most.

So they start to plan, seriously now; they're meticulous, or at least the leader is, going over every possible angle. They realize they need more hands, so they bring in one or two other guys, cousins maybe, or lifelong friends, guys they can count on to be cool and never talk, for love or fear or money. Maybe they check out a library book on vaults, to figure out the specs, how much concrete and steel they'll have to cut through, what tools they'll need. They think that digging the tunnel and cracking the concrete is going to be the hard part, not paying much attention to bank security procedures or alarm systems. Maybe one of them dated a teller once, somebody who mentioned time locks, and the frequent false alarms, and they figure they'll be long gone before anybody can check the vault. They're not worried about that part of it.

They pick Los Angeles because one or all of them had worked on a sewer project there; they know the sewer system layout, and how the public works guys who maintain the sewers operate. They pick the First Interstate Bank on Sunset for no other reason than that after scoping out the ground, it's the closest bank to the open flood channel in Nichols Canyon where they can access the storm sewers with ATVs and equipment. They rent a couple of cheap crackerbox apartments in Hollywood or in the Palms neighborhood, someplace where nobody will pay any attention. One of them rents a safe deposit box under a phony name, so he can pace off the vault dimensions and location inside the bank. Pooling their money, they buy some ATVs and an old DPW truck, some two-way radios. They steal a boring machine off a construction site—hey, in for a dollar, in for a dime; those goddam things are expensive—and buy a new core bit, and some shovels and wheelbarrows.

D-Day. Gut-check time. They get their courage up—Fuck it, let's go—and pretty soon they're hunched over on their ATVs, rolling through the storm drains. They set up at the entry point, electric generator roaring, sparks flying, the scream of a saw blade on concrete reverberating through the pipe. It takes them a full night to cut through the pipe, and the next night they start digging. They spend weeks at it, night after night, digging dirt and hauling dirt, digging and hauling, the hardest sort of mind-numbing, backbreaking physical labor. And they're doing it all by lantern light, in a close, cramped little hole under Hollywood.

Finally, they get under the vault, just in time for the long Memorial Day weekend, but the goddam core bit won't work, it won't cut through the bottom of the vault; it keeps traveling on them, they can't steady it. So they start cutting away with a hand-held power saw. It's slow, miserable work, standing bent-kneed in a small earthen chamber, holding a 12-pound saw over your head in a choking cloud of concrete dust. It takes them a week to get close enough to drill a triangle of connector holes up through the last few inches of the vault floor. Then they set up a hydraulic jack and bust through the last couple inches of concrete.

Damn it! The topside man radios down to the tunnel man: There's an alarm bell clanging away on the outside of the bank. Tell 'em to sit tight. So they squat there, in the hole, for an hour, two hours, three hours, wondering if somehow, after all that goddam work, they're gonna get screwed out of the payoff. But no, nobody shows up at the bank, and finally the alarm bell just stops. What the hell? Let's go.

So they squeeze up through the hole, and they're in the vault. They can hardly believe it, but they're in the fucking vault! There are two of them inside, covered in a thick coating of white concrete dust; in the lantern light, they look like ghosts in overalls. They hit the bank cash carts first, prying them open with crowbars, scooping the cash into empty sandbags and dropping them down the hole. They don't bother counting it, but it feels like a lot. Then they start on the safe deposit boxes, the big ones first, on the theory that the bigger box the more valuable the stuff that's in it. One of them takes a hammer drill to the box locks.

But it's slow work, slower than they'd thought, ten minutes of drilling per lock, two locks to each box. At this rate, they're never gonna get all the boxes open. So now it's Amazing Kreskin time: Which boxes *feel* rich? That one, then that one, then that one—but the psychic vibes aren't working, and half the time, more than half the time, the goddam box they work so hard to open is empty. With the other ones, all the stuff in them goes straight into the bags and down the hole, where the tunnel man drags it out to the mouth of the tunnel. They don't even bother to look at it. Hey, if it's in a box it must be worth something; we'll sort it all out later.

Time, time, time. After weeks of work, it comes down to a few short hours before the bank's going to open up again. One of them starts prying open some of the smaller boxes, at random—eenie, meenie, minie, moe—but they're constructed with relatively small tolerances, and the crowbar work is flanging the metal, shutting off access to the adjacent boxes. Doesn't really matter; they're out of time anyway. They still have to pack up their equipment, load it and the loot bags on the ATVs, sweep the tunnel free of tracks, drive through the sewer pipes to the open storm channel, haul the stuff out, and load it onto the truck. Gotta go. Gotta go, now!

Back at the apartment, they're bouncing around, too wired on adrenaline and relief to feel as exhausted as they actually are. I can't believe we fucking did it, man. I can't believe we pulled this off! Hours later they're still toasting each other over beers and watching the news reports, and they laugh when some cop flack calls it a "daring" heist by a "highly professional" team of criminals. They feel like something out of the movies.

And they're rich, or at least it seems that way at first. It's only later, when they start to do the arithmetic, that the hard economics of bank burglary start coming into grim focus.

Yes, they got $172,000 of the bank's cash, which is, lump sum, a lot of dough. But subtract $20,000 or so for equipment and incidentals and living expenses, then divide what's left five ways, and it only works out to—what—about thirty grand apiece? For two months of dangerous, backbreaking work? It's not exactly a ticket to retirement.

Sure, there's a few clumps of cash from the boxes, a few hundred here, a few thousand there, but if they dreamed of stumbling onto suitcasefuls of millions of dollars in drug cash, well, it's time to wake up. Your high-roller criminals, your major drug dealers, don't march into a bank with millions of dollars in suitcases and put it in a box that any FBI or DEA agent with an active imagination and a talent for writing affidavits might get a search warrant on. That kind of money, you put it someplace safe.

Maybe there's some gold coins and gold bars, stuff ordinary people put in a safe box; that can be passed off at weight value. But the rest, the negotiable bonds, the loose diamonds, the jewelry, they really don't know what to do with it. Some of it, like the ancient Iranian artifacts, that old poetry book, that old French drawing of the young girl, hell, they aren't even exactly sure what it is or if it's worth anything. They aren't professional criminals, they don't have a fencing network to fall back on, nobody they can trust to move negotiable bonds or diamonds, even at 10 or 15 percent. Maybe they can unload some of the stuff for pennies on the dollar at a pawnshop, but they can't sell it to any reputable dealer who knows what it's worth. They just have to hang on to it for a while.

So the months go by, and there's no heat; it's pretty clear that the FBI isn't going to figure out who they are. Nobody's even come close. But the money runs out quicker than any of them could have imagined. They're spending it like sailors on shore leave, a new Harley here, a trip to Hawaii there; the money burns right through their pockets.

And finally, after a year, it's another what-the-hell moment: Let's try another one. We did it once, we can do it again. Except this time we'll really blow their freakin' minds. We'll do *two* vaults, on the same weekend, and this time we know what we're doing, we'll have the right tools to get into all the boxes. This time we'll strike it rich.

But they don't. Again they think that it's the tunneling and getting into the vaults that's the problem, not the alarms. They don't know that Bank of America doesn't use the time lock system, that the bankers and the cops can get into the vault any time they want. After weeks of breaking their backs and eating dirt, they haven't been in that Bank of America vault for thirty minutes when the topside guy radios them: Shit, man, there's cops all over the place, they're going into the bank!

So they stand there in the vault, silent, listening, thinking that whoever's out there will go away. But suddenly they hear the combination lock on the vault door clicking, clicking. Holy shit, they're coming in! They grab what cash they've already got bagged up and drop down the hole, leaving tens of thousands of dollars just sitting there in the vault, and all the safe deposit boxes safe and secure. They abandon everything, bolting out of that tunnel and through the hole, scared shitless, then roaring through the sewers on their ATVs, fishtailing and kicking up water like a Suzuki TV commercial, running for their freedom, their lives. And when they get away, when they're safe, and they count what they've got, it's a lousy $98,000—minus expenses, split four or five ways.

For all the work they did, all the risks they took, it's nothing. Nothing.

Inevitably there are bitches, arguments, recriminations: "Big fucking score," you said. "We'll be rich," you said. Shit. Of course, nobody's going to rat anybody out, they're all too close for that, and besides, why would they? For that lousy $20,000 reward First Interstate offered after the Hollywood job? And since they aren't professional criminals, they aren't going to get picked up on another charge they'll want to deal their way out of. So they'll tell no one—not a wife, not a girlfriend, no one. It's a secret, forever.

But it's also the end. No more. Never again. We did it, and yeah, it was cool, exciting, but it wasn't worth it. For them, crime, even brilliant crime, just didn't pay.

So they go back to their lives, following the construction work around, here six months, there a year, living in temporary apartments in cheap neighborhoods in the cities, or baking in trailer parks in high summer in the middle of nowhere. The years go by, they're getting older now, in their mid- to late forties, they're thinner of hair and thicker of waist; it's doubtful they could squeeze through an 18-inch-diameter hole in the floor of a bank vault, even if they wanted to. Although their lives have finally gone in separate directions, they still get together every now and then, to crack some beers and talk in guarded, coded phrases about that long-ago "special job" they did when they were young; the wives most of them finally settled down with have no idea what the boys are talking about, and they've long learned not to ask.

All the money they took is long gone, of course, and the stuff they stole out of the bank boxes on the first job—almost all the stuff—is gone too, pawned for pennies or burned or buried or put in a plastic bag and tossed in a Dumpster. They never did figure out what to with it, and keeping it was dangerous. But one of them, the leader, the planner, couldn't stand to part with every reminder of what they'd done. He held onto some of the junk, a couple of items that none of the other guys cared about.

He's holding on to them still.

And so, in my imagination, I see a trailer sitting in a mobile home park in Pahrump, Nevada, or outside Bakersfield, cooking in the sun. Inside, it's clean and orderly, the home of a guy who is disciplined, meticulous, a man who lives by himself and likes things just so. There's a small TV, a mustard-colored couch, a fridge well stocked with beer, a battered hard hat sitting on a Formica table, and a pair of dusty work boots resting on a dull green linoleum floor. It's a totally unremarkable place, with almost nothing at all to indicate that its occupant once did something amazing.

But in the bedroom, on top of a particle-board chest of drawers full of tightly rolled socks and neatly folded underwear, there's an old book of poetry that someday the man who lives here might just read. And over the bed, encased in a Wal-Mart frame and hanging from a nail driven into the wood veneer paneling, there's an untitled sketch of a young woman, a kind of free-flowing line drawing, a series of loops and swirls that show the idea of the woman more than the details of her. He's been dragging it around with him for years now, and while he doesn't know much about the drawing, he likes it. It's important to him.

It's by some guy named Matisse.

5

INSIDERS

She was young and beautiful, an intelligent but naive and overly romantic woman who dreamed foolishly of living happily ever after. He was older, worldly, handsome, a man with soft eyes and a malignant heart—and a wife and two children at home. She wanted him desperately, and would do anything for him; he used her shamelessly, without remorse, and never really loved her.

It's the script of a thousand soap operas, the grim blueprint for a million tragedies, a million broken hearts. But what sets this particular tragedy apart is that it involves more than just tears and a heartache.

This tragedy also involves a bank robbery.

It started at ten minutes after nine on a Thursday morning in November 1997, in the University Village district near the University of Southern California, a green island of ivory towers and rich white kids and three-bucks-a-cup gourmet coffee joints surrounded by the sea of gritty ghetto that is South Central L.A. An Armored Transport Services truck rolled up to a Bank of America on West Jefferson Boulevard, just across the street from the university campus, and stopped by the front entrance of the bank, its engine running, the armed driver locked inside behind bullet-resistant glass. In the back, two armed uniformed guards unlocked the truck's back door from the inside and stepped out. While one held his drawn pistol loosely at his side—then standard operating procedure—the other guard loaded three large plastic bags onto a small cart, which he pushed into the bank.

Within the plastic bags was money, cash money, a lot of it, $722,000 to be exact, all of it crisp and clean and neatly compressed into bricks, then shrink-wrapped in plastic. It was interesting money, for a couple of reasons.

The first was that the block of cash was unusually heavy on the higher denominations of bills. About half a million dollars of it was in fifties and hundreds, twice the usual amount of large bills the bank would get in a routine cash shipment. The high percentage of large bills was a critical factor in what was about to happen. As it was, that three quarters of a million in cash weighed only about 40 pounds. But if most of the bills had been twenties, the stack would have weighed twice that, some 80 pounds, a heavy, bulky load for one man to carry—and you can't easily steal what you can't easily carry.

The second reason the money was interesting was because there was absolutely no reason for it to be there. The bank already had in excess of $2 million in cash locked away in steel boxes inside the vault, more than enough to service the USC kids' ATM withdrawals through the coming Veterans Day weekend, to cash the payroll checks and public assistance vouchers of local residents, and to handle the commercial cash needs of area businesses. The bank simply didn't need another three quarters of a million dollars in cash.

Nevertheless, a few days earlier, someone at the bank had ordered the cash brought in, and the Armored Transport Services guys had delivered it from the Bank of America's main cash depository. After the hoppers took it inside and into the vault, the assistant manager and the customer services manager did a quick count of the cash bricks—a more complete count would be done later—and signed for it. Ordinarily, the cash would then have been quickly unwrapped, with the stacks of smaller bills—fives, tens, twenties—placed in double-locked metal boxes inside the vault, while the half million in fifties and hundreds would have been locked away in even more secure safe deposit boxes in the vault. That was a standard bank security measure; the more you spread the money around, the harder it is to steal.

But today, for some reason, the cash shipment wasn't broken down and locked away. The plastic bags full of cash were placed on a wheeled metal cart in the counting room, a small adjunct to the vault. And there the money sat, a fortune in cash, compact and lightweight, nicely bundled together, almost as if it were asking for somebody to come in and take it.

Five minutes later, somebody did.

He was a tall, well-built, good-looking African-American man with a wide, well-trimmed black mustache and a gold stud earring, wearing an expensive gray suit, a white shirt with a floral print tie, a black beret, and sunglasses. Hanging from a shoulder strap under his suit, hidden from view, was an M-11 semiautomatic assault pistol.

At 9:15 A.M. the man in the suit walks in the front door and takes his place at the end of a line of a dozen or so customers who are waiting their turns for one of the tellers. He stands there for a moment, shifting his weight from side to side, seemingly impatient—which isn't all that unusual among bank customers stuck at the end of what always seems like an interminably slow line.

As he looks around, the man in the suit sees another man enter the bank, walk up to a freestanding counter in the lobby, and start filling out a deposit slip. The man is younger, also African-American, wearing a white running suit and tennis shoes and a baseball hat. They don't acknowledge each other, but the man in the suit knows that the man in white is carrying a small handgun concealed in his pocket; he's the backup or "layoff" man, the guy who's going to keep an eye on things while the man in the suit does his business.

Everything is ready. The only thing standing between the man in the suit and a fortune in fresh cash is the bandit barrier.

The bandit barrier is a 1 1/2-inch thick wall of clear, bullet-resistant Plexiglas that stretches from the top of the long teller counter to the ceiling of the bank, separating the tellers and the vault area from the customers in the lobby. Business is conducted through windows and drop slots at each teller station, and access through the bandit barrier from the lobby is only possible through locked doors at each end of the counter.

The presence of the bandit barrier in this bank, or in any bank in L.A., is actually somewhat unusual. Although similar but smaller bullet-resistant barriers are a common fixture at self-serve gas stations and rough-neighborhood liquor stores throughout Southern California, banks have traditionally resisted using them. That's partly because they're expensive to install, upward of $40,000, depending on the size of the bank. But mostly it's because, in bankers' minds, bandit barriers conflict with the warm, customer-friendly image that banking corporations spend millions of advertising dollars trying to cultivate: Welcome to our happy banking family . . . We're here to serve you. But if you don't mind, we're going to keep our money and your suspicious-looking, potentially bank-robbing hide on opposite sides of a bullet-resistant wall.

During the explosion of takeover robberies in the early 1990s, when armed bandits were hopping over L.A. bank counters and cleaning out the teller drawers four or five times every single day, some hard-hit banks—Bank of America in particular—finally decided the hell with customer-friendly, we gotta do something about all these goddam robberies. So they put in bandit barriers, and at those banks the numbers of robberies, particularly takeover-style robberies, plummeted. After all, if you're a bank robber with an IQ anywhere above room temperature, why hit a hard target when there were so many other softer, unbarriered ones?

But on this day, the good-looking man in the nice suit with the M-11 assault weapon accessory isn't worried about the bandit barrier. He has a plan.

As the man in the suit is fidgeting in line, he sees a young woman named Errolyn Ramirez, the bank's customer service manager, walk across the lobby and use a key to unlock the door to the bandit barrier at the south end of the bank. The man in the suit suddenly breaks out of the customer line and starts walking toward her, and the now-unlocked door. He's almost up behind her when an unarmed uniformed bank security guard named Bernard Mordi sees him coming and intervenes. The security guard isn't worried by the man's actions; he can't see the gun under the guy's suit. Still, he's a conscientious sort, and customers aren't supposed to approach bank staff as they're opening the barrier door.

Can I help you, sir? the security guy says.

I have to get to my safe deposit box, the man in the suit says.

That's fine, sir, but you'll have to go to the safe deposit teller window and fill out the access form.

The man seems a little disconcerted, agitated, as if he's been thrown off stride, but he doesn't argue. He says okay and walks over to the safe deposit box window just a few feet away. Ramirez, the customer service manager, closes the barrier door behind her—it locks automatically—and walks to the safe deposit teller window where the man is waiting. She passes the safe deposit access form through the teller tray, and the guy starts to fill it out. At that point, Ramirez will later tell us, he suddenly opens his jacket to show her the assault weapon and says, in a low voice that only she can hear, "Open the fucking door or you'll be the first to die!"

Now, Ramirez is separated from this guy and his gun by 1 1/2 inches of Plexiglas—but remember, it's bullet-*resistant* Plexiglas, not bullet-*proof* Plexiglas. She is in fear for her life. So she hits the door access button and buzzes the guy through the barrier door, just as if she were admitting a bona fide customer to the safe deposit box area. Nobody else in the bank—the unarmed security guard included—notices anything unusual.

The thick steel door to the vault is open, as it always is during business hours, but there's a locked Plexiglas "day gate" at the vault entrance. Ramirez opens it with her key. With the bandit behind her, she walks into the vault, past the safe deposit boxes, to another locked, stainless-steel door; behind that door is the counting room, a drab 15-by 15-foot room stacked with bank records in cardboard boxes and metal lockers containing the bank's operating cash. Ramirez opens the door with her key.

Two other bank employees, assistant manager LaPortia Davis and teller Rhea Edwards, are inside the counting room, getting ready to inventory and lock away the $722,000 Brinks cash shipment. Davis is annoyed, because the money should already have been broken down and locked away by now. As the door opens, they see the guy in the suit standing behind Ramirez—and that black, mean-looking gun he's holding.

What the . . . ?

"Get down!" the man with the gun shouts, pushing Ramirez forward and to the floor. "Don't look at me! I want the money that Armored just delivered. Don't touch those fucking pagers or I'll blow your fucking heads off!"

This guy obviously knows the drill. The "pagers" are actually remote silent alarm activators that Bank of America had started issuing to its employees, a higher-tech version of the alarm buttons under the teller counters. Clipped to belts or clothing, they allow employees to send out a silent alarm from anywhere in the bank.

"I want the money"—the guy says again—"It's not worth dying for!"—and Davis, the assistant manager, has to agree with him there.

"It's right there!" she says, pointing at the metal cash cart; the $722,000 is sitting there, still inside the three clear plastic bags. The guy walks over and grabs the bags with both hands; the M-11 is hanging from the strap, leaving his hands free. He walks toward the door, then turns and says, "Stay there and don't touch those fucking pagers!"

Then he's out the door of the counting room and heading back toward the lobby. Davis waits about half a second and then starts hitting her remote alarm button like she's playing a GameBoy. The electronic signal immediately activates the bank's two-eleven silent alarm system and starts the 35-mm surveillance cameras in the lobby clicking away at two frames per second. Ramirez seems to be reaching for her remote alarm, too.

The cameras in the lobby pick up nice, clear shots of the man in the suit walking out of the bandit barrier door and through the bank lobby. The eyes of Bernard Mordi, the security guard who had spoken with him earlier, also pick him up—and those eyes don't like what they see. Here's a guy coming back through the door of the bandit barrier with three clear plastic bags chockful of cash in his hands—which means he either just retrieved a suspiciously large amount of dough from his safe deposit box or else he's just pulled off a robbery. The guy in the suit clears up any confusion on that score when he looks at Mordi and shouts: "Close your eyes! Don't look at me!" The guy keeps walking, shouting at bank customers who are staring wide-eyed at the commotion: "Move! Get out of the way! Don't look at me—I have a gun, I'll blow you up. *Don't look at me!*" Then he's out the door.

Bernard Mordi doesn't chase him or anything; nobody would expect him to. He's unarmed, and bank standard operating procedure calls for bank employees to cooperate with armed bandits.

Mordi's job right now is to observe and then summon help. As the guy with the money is walking out the exit door, Mordi runs over to the customer service desk in the lobby and picks up a phone—and suddenly he notices there's a guy standing right next to him, a guy in a white running suit and a baseball cap, with a gun in his hand. The man presses the gun into the Mordi's side and says, "Put the phone down, fool, or I'll shoot!"

Mordi drops the phone receiver likes it's on fire. "Step back," the guy with the gun tells him, and he instantly does. The man in the running suit stands there for a moment, then he turns and sprints out of the bank. Mordi runs to the door and sees the man in the suit and the guy in white getting into a white Ford Windstar van in the parking lot, with a getaway driver behind the wheel. The van—which will turn out to be stolen, and will later be found abandoned a few blocks away—screeches out of the parking lot and disappears.

And that was that. Only ninety seconds had passed since the man in the suit had first approached the customer service manager as she was opening the bandit barrier door. The robbers had been fast, efficient, professional—and given the size of the take, incredibly lucky.

In fact, too lucky.

The call from the Bank of America alarm center came in to the bank squad just a minute or two after the robbers got away. As usual, Linda Webster, the veteran bank squad civilian radio dispatcher, took the call and confirmed that the two-eleven alarm was a "good" one—meaning that it was a bad one, that it wasn't a false alarm, that a robbery had in fact gone down. As she had done on thousands of previous bank robberies, Linda then called the bank and talked to the manager to quickly get some basic information on the bandits: physical description, getaway vehicle, and so on. She immediately broadcast that information over the FBI and LAPD radio frequencies, the hope being that an LAPD black-and-white or a passing Bureau car might be able to tag these guys before they dumped the getaway car.

That done, Linda started asking the bank manager a series of more detailed questions about the robbery. And pretty soon a certain distinctive odor started rising up from this bank robbery.

Wait a minute. The bandits got three quarters of a million dollars? That had just been delivered five minutes before, still neatly shrink-wrapped? In a bank that I knew from past experience was equipped with bandit barriers? And they made it through those barriers and into the vault and out again in ninety seconds? Without anyone else in the bank even realizing at first that a robbery was going down?

I'd been working bank robberies for thirty years and I knew this was too slick, too easy, too perfect to be an ordinary bank lick.

Given the size of the loss, and my suspicions, three agents went to the bank—Andy Chambers, John McEachern, and Brenda Cotton, the lead case agent—along with LAPD Robbery-Homicide Division (RHD) Detectives Brian Tyndall, Greg Grant, and Steve Laird, who shared joint jurisdiction with the FBI. They were all experienced bank robbery investigators, and within minutes of getting the basic details on the robbery they were all thinking the same thing I was.

Special Agent Brenda Cotton had picked up on another anomaly: the robber had come in without a bag: No briefcase, no satchel, no pillowcase, nothing. Even the lamest takeover bank bandit knows that if you're going to hit the vault, those bundles of cash aren't going to fit in your pants or in your pockets, so you better bring something to stuff the money in—unless of course you already know that the money's going to be neatly laid out for you, encased in plastic bags.

Shortly thereafter I talked it over with Brenda and the others. And after looking at all the factors, reviewing all the angles, every one of us came to the same conclusion:

Inside job.

✦ ✦ ✦

It happens all the time. A bank employee starts looking at all the cash that passes through his or her hands every day and thinking how nice it would be if some of that money just happened to come home with her at closing time.

It's understandable. There she is, standing behind a counter all day, her back aching, her arches falling; customers are sullen after waiting in line, and maybe her supervisor is on her case for this or that—and for all the hard work and aggravation she's pulling down a grand total of what, twenty or twenty-five grand a year? Meanwhile, she's handling millions of dollars in cash over the course of a year, for a financial corporation that has billions—and really, when you look at the thing in a certain way, who would be hurt if a tiny piece of those millions and billions wound up in her purse?

Of course, the vast majority of bank employees are honest, hard-working folks who are trying to support their families and would never even consider stealing from their employers. Even among the few who are seriously tempted, it's usually just a passing thought, a daydream of minor riches; they'd be too afraid of getting caught. Given the tens of thousands of people who work in banks, the amount of cash they handle, and the number of seeming opportunities to steal some of it, the amazing thing isn't how common bank employee thefts are, but how rare.

Still, maybe half a dozen times a year in L.A., the forbidden daydream becomes an actual felony. Out of greed, desperation, or love— yes, love—a teller or other bank employee figuratively crosses to the other side of the teller counter and becomes a bank bandit.

And the sad part is just how easy it is to catch them when they do it.

The bank employee thefts take one of three basic forms: giveaways, "phantom bandits" (those are the two most common types), and inside jobs. (Embezzlements, cooking the books to illegally transfer money from one account to another, are a separate crime, and are handled by the FBI white-collar crime unit.)

Giveaways involve tellers who are "robbed" by someone they know—usually a husband or boyfriend, almost invariably some lowlife who's been in trouble with the law before. The boyfriend walks up to her window posing as a customer, the teller hands over the money, the boyfriend leaves, and then, when he's well away from the bank and the surveillance cameras, the teller hits the alarm buttons and reports that she's been robbed by an unknown bandit.

Nine times out of ten in giveaway robberies, the whole thing was the boyfriend's idea. The teller only went along with it because he talked her into it. He kept saying, Aw, c'mon, baby, do it for me, show me you love me, nobody'll ever know, that's my girl—and finally she'd break down and say okay, just to keep this worthless bastard in her life.

And more often than you'd think, even after she's caught, when she's crying and sobbing and saying she's sorry, she still won't give the worthless bastard up. She won't tell us his name, or testify against him; she loves him, don't you understand? Even if we know who the robber is, without her testimony we can't make a case on him. He'll talk to her over a jailhouse phone, or visit her in the lockup and breathe sweet nothings through the glass: I'm sorry, baby, I'll get you out of this, I'll wait for you, I swear, don't say nothing to anybody. And she'll take the fall. She'll spend a year or two in Dublin Federal Correctional Institution, her life ruined, while he's running free.

The "phantom bandit" jobs are more individual. A teller simply scoops the money out of his or her cash drawer when nobody's looking, stuffs it into a purse or a backpack, and then reports that he's been robbed by someone posing as a customer, a robber who is conveniently long gone. As I've said, in most one-on-one robberies the other people in the bank aren't even aware that a robbery's been committed until the teller reports it, so the story has some initial plausibility.

The problem is that even though the tellers work in a bank, and may have secondhand or even firsthand experience with bank robberies, they simply don't know enough about the bank robbery business to make their stories fly. In both giveaways and phantom bandit jobs, they drop clues all over the place.

How much money was taken? Five thousand? Wait a minute, the "drawer limit" for tellers in this bank is only two thousand; kind of a coincidence that the "victim teller" checked out more money from the vault, in violation of bank cash control policies, just before she was robbed, isn't it? And how about that description of the bandit? A short white man with a hat—that's the best she can do? And as vague as that description is, how come nobody else in the bank remembers seeing anyone like that in the bank when the "robbery" occurred?

Another thing: How come we don't have a picture? How come the teller didn't hit the two-eleven alarm button and activate the surveillance cameras? Okay, maybe she couldn't do it during the robbery, but she could have done it when the robber was on his way out of the bank. She says she was scared? She says the bandit told her that he knew she lived on Elm Street and that he'd come to her house and kill her if she told anybody, and that's why she waited several minutes to tell anybody about the robbery? C'mon. It's not like one-on-one bandits do research; no real bandit is going to know she lives on Elm Street.

And there's something else. You say the victim teller is relatively new on the job, and is chronically late, and offers up lame excuses, and doesn't get along well with the other employees, and is overall the sort of employee who makes her supervisors wonder what the hell the guys in Human Resources were thinking when they hired her in the first place?

No, it's never all of those things, but it's always a couple of them. In all but a few cases, a victim teller is exactly that—a victim, someone who is understandably shaken by the experience, and you treat them with compassion and consideration. And you don't walk into every bank robbery investigation suspecting the victim teller. But when the flags start going up, when your bullshit antennae start to quiver, it's time to sit your victim teller down for a little chat. And nine times out of ten, he or she just doesn't have the heart to see it through.

I remember one guy, a teller at a Crocker Bank in the Mid-Wilshire District, who reported a one-on-one note job robbery. Jack Williams, a veteran RHD detective, and I responded to the two-eleven call and interviewed the victim teller in the employee lunchroom. He was a young white kid in his early twenties, a flaky-looking sort who kept nervously fingering his tie throughout the interview. And he had good reason to be nervous; he was waving red flags like it was a May Day parade.

His story was that a white male, early thirties, (vague description), had approached him at his teller window and robbed him of $4,500 (twice the cash drawer limit) and that he'd been too scared to push the two-eleven button because the guy had said he had an accomplice who was across the street behind a bus bench with a rifle pointed at the teller's head, and that he, the teller, had looked out the bank window at the bus bench and had actually seen the "sunlight glinting off the rifle barrel."

At this point, Jack and I are rolling our eyes. "Sunlight glinting off the rifle barrel"? Who is this guy, Louis L'Amour? Okay, sure, maybe a bank robber would *say* that he has an accomplice with a rifle across the street; bandits often make bogus threats to tellers. But the teller claims he actually *saw* a guy with a rifle? We're really supposed to believe that on busy Wilshire Boulevard, with motorists and pedestrians all over the place, in the bright light of day, there was a bona fide sniper crouched behind a bus bench that nobody else except the teller happened to notice?

C'mon, son, that's enough lying for one day. If there's something you want to get off your chest, now's the time to do it. And in the end the kid couldn't muster up the stones to stick by his story. He finally gave up the cash, which he had stuffed in his backpack when nobody was looking, and told us that he'd needed the money to buy a car and go to junior college. He knew that bank tellers in the area were robbed all the time, and who would suspect anything if he said he'd been robbed, too?

In a way it was sort of pathetic; most giveaways and phantom bandit cases are. You're dealing with low-level employees, working grunts, who in a moment of weakness trade their freedom for a lousy four or five thousand bucks. In practical terms, they would have been better off quitting their teller jobs and taking up the bank robbery business full time; they probably could have robbed six or a dozen or twenty banks and gotten a lot more money before they got caught, instead of being nailed their first time out of the box.

Most of the time, unless they have a prior record, and if they cooperate and confess, the justice system is relatively merciful on these guys. After all, the amount stolen was small, nobody was waving a gun around, nobody got hurt.

But there's another, far more insidious form of bank employee collusion in robberies. That's the inside job, in which an employee plays a key role in an armed takeover. That's when things start getting serious.

Sometimes it's just a matter of a bank employee telling an accomplice or group of accomplices about how the bank handles security procedures. Where are the two-eleven alarm buttons located? The surveillance cameras? Where do the tellers keep the bait money in their drawers? Do they have dye packs and tracking devices, and what kinds? Do tellers at this bank get a reward for slipping a dye pack into the stolen money? Is there a security guard, and what time does he usually break for lunch? What's the bank policy on robberies, total cooperation or subtle non-cooperation? Who has the key to the vault day gate? Having the answers to all of those questions can significantly increase the robbers' take, and reduce the chances of getting caught.

Sometimes the employee takes an even more active role. If there's a scheduled cash delivery from an armored car company, the employee may tell the robbers when it's coming, or have them wait nearby and then call or signal them to let them know when it has arrived and the armed guards have driven off. And in some cases the employee—usually a manager or an operations officer—will spike up the robbery take by ordering an unusually large delivery of cash from the armored car company.

That's a major red flag, because FBI agents and cops don't believe in coincidences. If you're a bank officer who usually orders, say, $250,000 or so on your once or twice-weekly cash deliveries, and then you suddenly order a delivery of three quarters of a million dollars, which just happens to get stolen two minutes after it's delivered, by robbers who seemed to know exactly where it was—well, you'd better have a damn good business reason for ordering that extra money. Because every arrow is pointing back at you.

Sometimes the insider will realize that, and try to come up with a seemingly valid explanation for the large shipment: The holidays were coming up and customers were going to need more cash, he'll say, or there was a rumor about an armored car guard strike and he wanted to stock up—whatever.

But again, in most cases the insiders have a hard time holding up under scrutiny. After all, they're not professional criminals; banks won't hire anybody with an adult felony record, and it takes at least several years of unblemished employment to rise to a bank officer position. And again, usually the bank robbery wasn't even their idea. They simply fell in love with the wrong man, or fell in with the wrong crowd, someone who used them, who talked them into it. Although they are vital to pulling off the bank robbery, they are also the weakest link in the chain.

An insider case from the 1980s illustrates the point. It started when four young black males hijacked a van in the wholesale produce section of downtown L.A. in the predawn hours, in the process viciously gunning down the owner of the van, a twenty-two-year-old Vietnamese immigrant named Tuong Truong.

After burying Truong's body in a garbage pile, they drove to the Family Savings & Loan on South Crenshaw, one of the most successful black-owned financial institutions in L.A., an institution that specialized in giving home loans to working-poor South Central families who couldn't get loans from the mainstream banks. Moments after an armored truck had delivered a cash shipment to the S&L, three of the bandits stormed in wearing Halloween masks and waving a shotgun, an M-16, and a 9-mm handgun, while the fourth bandit waited in the stolen getaway van. The bandits fired one shot in the air to show they were serious, then put everybody on the floor and went straight to the cash shipment sitting in the vault. They got away with a quarter of a million dollars—at the time the biggest bank robbery take ever in L.A.

Except for the senseless murder of young Truong, it was a pretty straightforward bank lick. But when I got there fifteen minutes later, I saw something strange. Some other FBI agents and LAPD cops were already there, as well as an L.A. Fire Department paramedic unit; the paramedics were clustered around a man in a suit who was lying on the floor. I knew there'd been a shot fired, and I thought at first that maybe the man had been hit. But no, he hadn't been shot. It turned out that the man was the S&L's assistant operations manager, a guy named Norman Bond, and he was apparently having some sort of post-traumatic fit. He was rolling around and convulsing on the floor and shouting, "Oh, my babies, my babies!" (he was the father of twins) and, "Why me, Lord, why me?" Over and over and over.

Now, I've been to bank robbery scenes where the walls were riddled with dozens of bullet holes and bodies were lying on the floor in huge slicks of blood. And while some of the bank employees and witnesses at those scenes may have been screaming and crying, or even catatonic with shock, I'd never seen any of them go into convulsions and roll on the floor. But after one little round fired in the air, this guy was screaming and flopping around like Linda Blair in *The Exorcist*. He was acting a lot more traumatized by the robbery than he had any right to be.

So I waved one of the paramedics aside and said as much. The paramedic agreed. There's nothing wrong with him, the paramedic said; his vitals are all normal. We gotta transport him to the hospital, but if you ask me, it's bullshit. He's faking this.

From that moment on, the assistant operations manager was at the top of our list—and it certainly didn't help Norman's case when we learned that he was the one who had ordered the cash shipment that had been so conveniently stolen just minutes after it arrived, a cash shipment that also turned out to be about three times larger than normal. So, after he checked out of the hospital—the docs couldn't find anything wrong with him—we called him into the FBI office for a chat.

And as expected, Norman just couldn't stand up to the pressure. After the robbery he had heard about the murder of Tuong Truong, and it had shaken him badly. He was a family man, not a killer. He couldn't live with it. When he got to the FBI office, he told Special Agents Jim Keenan and Wayne Bourque that there was something he had to tell them.

Yeah, he said, he did it. He ordered the extra cash and told the bandits when it would arrive. No, it hadn't been his idea. He had met a couple of the robbers at a Nation of Islam storefront mosque in South Central, and they got friendly. They knew he worked in a savings and loan, and they came up with this idea to rob it, and he said no, but they kept working on him and working on him, telling him how easy it'd be, how no one would ever know, how no one would get hurt. He had the two babies at home, he needed money, and finally he gave in. He never dreamed they would kill somebody. His emotional collapse right after the robbery was supposed to divert suspicion away from himself, to make him look like a traumatized victim. But he guessed that maybe he'd overdone it, huh?

Yes, Norman, you sure as hell did.

(Norman Bond ID'd the bandits and agreed to testify against them in return for a reduced sentence. Two of the bandits were convicted for the bank robbery, although not for the murder, and took fifteen-year jolts. Another, Gregory Lewis, twenty-eight, the one who had actually shot Truong, was captured in Colorado and convicted of federal murder charges under a new law that made homicides in connection with a bank robbery a federal crime. The fourth bandit, Derrick Stevens, twenty-seven, the getaway driver in the robbery, fled the state and reinvented himself as Derrick Anderson, a food services executive who held top positions at three East Coast colleges. Sixteen years later, a Maryland college student spotted one of the hundreds of thousands of Wanted posters we'd put out on Stevens and thought it looked a lot like Mr. Anderson in the campus cafeteria; the student notified police, who questioned Stevens. Stevens fled before he could be arrested, but he later surrendered to the FBI.)

The robbery of the Family S&L had been easy to spot as an insider job—and it was the insider himself who proved to be the weakest link, the key to solving the crime.

That would also be true in the University Village Bank of America robbery. Within hours after the man in the suit and the man in white had fled, we had a pretty good suspicion as to who the bank insider had been. Based on past experience, I also suspected that when confronted, she would tell us what we needed to know.

And the guy who put her up to it should have known that, too.

Given his own experience, his position in life, the man in the suit with the floral tie and the assault weapon accessory should have known that the woman who loved him just didn't have the heart to be a bank robber.

✦ ✦ ✦

She was twenty-six years old, a striking young woman with long, raven-black hair, dark eyes, and a flashing white smile set off against cocoa-colored skin. Born in Belize, a small, sleepy Central American country where Latin American and African-Caribbean cultures had met and mixed, Errolyn Cheri Ramirez was raised by her grandparents after her mother moved to Los Angeles to look for work. At age fifteen, she would later testify, she was raped by a family acquaintance, an experience that left her emotionally scarred and vulnerable. The following year, hoping to change her life, she moved to South Central L.A. to join her mother and afterward became a naturalized American citizen.

Ramirez and her family were part of the South Central you usually don't hear enough about: the middle-class and aspiring middle-class folks who work hard, pay their taxes, and try to raise their children right amid gangs and drugs and poverty and crime. Errolyn was a smart girl, a good student at Dorsey High School, where she joined the LAPD Police Explorer Scout program, in which young people learn about police work and sometimes assist police in security and crowd control at public sites. She stayed with the program while attending Mount St. Mary's College, not far from USC, rising to the rank of sergeant. She also worked part time at the concession counter at the Baldwin Hills Theaters movie complex.

That's where she met him.

She was just nineteen at the time, and had never had a real boyfriend; he was thirty, and married with two kids, moonlighting as a security guard at the theater. He was handsome, the sort of man women went crazy over, with soft eyes and an athlete's body—in fact, he told her, he had been an athlete, a world-class track star. But it was his personality that attracted her more than his looks: he was someone she could talk to. During the lulls between show times, they would talk, and she found herself telling him things about herself, confiding her problems to him. Eventually she even told him what had happened to her in Belize, something she had never told anyone else about, ever. He was sympathetic and gentle, and despite all the reasons not to, she fell in love with him.

The affair would last seven years, seven long years of waiting for something that was never going to happen—that is, living happily ever after, the two of them, together. Later she would say that he became emotionally abusive and controlling, and dangerously possessive, following her to make sure she wasn't seeing anyone else, jealously berating her if she appeared to so much as look at another man. And maybe that was partly true. But it also seems likely that despite all the disappointments, she still loved him—and she believed, beneath it all, that he loved her, that someday he would make good on his many, many promises and marry her.

Her family eventually found out about it and tried to get her to break it off. He's not going to leave his wife, they told her, no matter what he tells you; guys like that never do, he's just using you. You're wasting the best years of your life. So she lied to her family, telling them that it was over, that she had broken up with him.

In the meantime, she went on with her daytime life. After graduating from St. Mary's, she'd gotten a job as a teller at the Bank of America at 29th and Crenshaw, in South Central L.A.; she was a good employee, conscientious and hardworking. In August 1997, after five years with Bank of America, Ramirez was transferred to the University Village branch and promoted to customer service manager, the third highest job in the branch. Part of her job was to keep track of the bank's cash reserves, and to order cash shipments.

It's unclear when the boyfriend first brought up the idea of robbing the bank—or at least it's not known by anybody but the two of them, and neither of them will say. But he knew that she ordered and determined the size of the cash shipments to the bank, and that she knew exactly when they would arrive. He was experienced enough in crime to know that she could give him access to the vault, and that if she didn't hit her alarm pager there would be no surveillance photographs of him. He'd go in, take the money, leave before anybody else in the bank even knew what was happening—and then she could report that she'd been robbed.

Given the kind of person she was, he probably joked about it at first, to test her reaction, plant the seed. Hey, you know what? We should rob your bank, ha-ha! If she sloughed it off, he kept bringing it up, again and again. The kicker was that it would be a way for her—for them—to finally realize her—their—dream of a life together. He was only earning $55,000 a year in his job, and like cheating married men since the dawn of time, he didn't have the money to support a wife and kids and a mortgage at the same time he was springing for romantic dinners and vacations with a girlfriend. He was already $17,000 deep in credit cards, and $20,000 in debt to the IRS, and he couldn't afford a divorce—unless of course he could get his hands on some big money. Then they'd be free, together, forever—and nobody would know.

Later it became clear that she was never interested in the money itself; in fact, she never wanted or received a dime of it. She wasn't in love with money; she was in love with the wrong man.

She must have thought that no one would figure it out, that no one would suspect her. Certainly he would have encouraged her to think that. And given his knowledge of criminal behavior, he should know, right?

But the truth is that from the first, everything pointed straight to her. After all, our investigation showed that it was Ramirez who had ordered the unusually large cash shipment, with the unusually high percentage of large-denomination bills. It was also her job to see that the cash was immediately broken down and locked away inside the vault, which it wasn't. Despite being separated from the bandit by the Plexiglas barrier and two locked doors, she had quickly acceded to the robber's demand to open the door to the bandit barrier—and had done so without hitting the two-eleven alarm button on her belt. She had quickly opened the day gate to the vault and the locked counting-room door. And in the opinion of one of the other bank employees inside the vault, Ramirez had only pretended to hit her remote alarm button after the armed bandit fled.

Individually, each of those circumstances could be explained away as simple sloppiness or incompetence or fear or coincidence. Yet, taken together, they drew an unmistakable picture. It wasn't nearly enough to make an arrest, much less put a court case together. But it was enough to take the next step.

It was time to put Errolyn Ramirez "on the box." Which is to say, it was time to give her a polygraph test.

✦ ✦ ✦

Polygraphing the bank employees is standard procedure whenever we suspect an inside job. True, under the Fifth Amendment of the U.S. Constitution, no one can be forced to take the polygraph test if he or she doesn't want to. And California state law says the bank can't require an employee to take a polygraph test as a condition of continued employment. I think we can all agree that those are admirable protections of sacred individual rights and liberties.

But with that said, let's come back down from Planet ACLU and talk about how it really works.

Okay, Mr. Bank Employee, we're with the FBI and we're investigating the armed robbery of your bank, and we'd like you to take a polygraph test—not that we think you did anything wrong, of course. We just want to eliminate you as a suspect and move on in our relentless search for the real criminal. We really appreciate your cooperation and assistance in this because . . .

What? You don't *want* to take a polygraph test? Well, Mr. Bank Employee, we're surprised and, frankly, a little disappointed. Everybody else at the bank is perfectly willing to take the test, but not you? Why not? There's nothing to worry about; if you didn't do anything wrong, the polygraph will prove it. You didn't do anything wrong, did you? No? Well, are you hiding something? No? Then why won't you take the polygraph?

To an FBI agent or a police detective, a potential suspect's refusal to take a polygraph is almost as good an indication of guilt as taking the test and blowing it. The refusal isn't admissible in court, of course; for that matter, neither are the results of the polygraph test, whichever way it goes. But if there are other indicators of guilt, it's a pretty good sign that you're on the right track.

And as far the bank is concerned, they can't fire you for refusing to take the polygraph test—but they can always find something else to fire you for. And you'll still be just as unemployed.

So almost always the bank insider will agree to take the test. She's looking at it the same way we are: If I don't take the test, they'll know I'm guilty. She takes it and hopes for the best—but seldom does it turn out that way.

A polygraph machine isn't a lie detector; it's just a stress detector. When you're hooked up, the machine measures three stress indicators: two metal finger-plates measure your galvanic skin response—that is, the electric conductivity of your skin, which increases when you sweat. A blood pressure cuff on your arm measures your blood pressure and pulse, which increase when you're under emotional stress; and two pneumographic tubes wrapped around your chest and abdomen measure your breathing rate. Throughout the test the readings from those devices feed into the machine, which uses four pens to display them as lines of peaks and valleys on a rolling chart. It's sort of like an earthquake seismograph, measuring the hidden rumblings and shakings going on inside the human body.

But the machine can't tell what those peaks and valleys mean. Does the graph show a higher-than-normal pulse rate, heavy sweating, rapid breathing—all indications of nervous stress? Of course it does. Of course you're experiencing nervous stress—you're taking a polygraph test. Determining the difference between that understandable nervousness and outright deception is an art, not a science—and that's where the polygraph examiner comes in.

It's not like what you see on TV. It's not just a question of strapping you into the machine and asking, "Is today Tuesday?" "Do you live on Elm Street?" and "Did you callously betray the trust and confidence of your Bank of America family by ordering too much money and having your gun-toting low-life boyfriend come in and steal it?" It's a lot more subtle. Examiners' techniques vary, but most polygraph examiners use some version of the "probable lie test"—that is, the examiner maneuvers you into lying about an irrelevant or "comparative" question so he can compare those responses to the responses on the relevant question.

For example, say you're a young applicant for the FBI who's going through the required pre-employment polygraph testing. The real purpose of the test is to determine whether you've ever been contacted by a foreign agent, whether you're a spy. But in the pre-interview, before you've even been hooked up to the machine, the examiner will chat for a while to establish rapport with you—and then, seemingly out of the blue, he'll start telling you how seriously the Bureau takes drinking and driving.

That's right, he'll say, the Bureau doesn't want anybody who's ever taken a drink before getting behind the wheel. In fact, he'll say, he's going to ask you about that on the test, right along with the questions about whether you're a foreign agent. But it's just a formality. You don't have to worry about the drinking question, the examiner will say, because he has studied your background and he knows you certainly aren't the sort of vile, irresponsible person who had ever mixed drinking and driving. Are you?

It's all bullshit on the examiner's part, a pure setup; you are being hustled. The truth is that as long as you didn't make a habit of it, the Bureau really isn't worried about whether you ever drank before driving. But you don't know that. You're sitting there remembering the time you got beered up at the college frat party and swerved your way home—but you're convinced that if you admit that little incident now, you'll blow your chances of getting into the Academy. So you take a gulp, shake your head and say, No, I never drank before driving. You know it's a lie, and more important, the examiner knows it's a lie, because just about everybody at some time in their life has had at least one drink before fishing out the car keys.

So when you, the hapless applicant, are finally hooked up to the machine, which question are you now most worried about? On which question is the machine going to show you're under the most stress? You're not worried about the "Are you a foreign agent?" question anymore; you know you're not a foreign agent, and when the examiner asks you that question your stress reactions will be base-line normal. But when the examiner asks you, "Have you ever had a drink before driving?" you show a huge reaction. You're lying, and you know you're lying, and the needles on the machine are whipping up and down so fast they're practically slinging ink on the walls. In short, if you show a bigger reaction on the irrelevant question (drinking) than on the relevant question (spying), you're telling the truth on the question that really matters: You're not a spy.

On the other hand, if you really are a foreign agent, are you going to show the most stress when asked about drinking and driving? Of course not. You're not worried about that; your responses on that question will be normal, or at least "small-lie" normal. Your high-stress question, the money ball, the point in the test when the machine will go wild, is on the foreign agent question—because that's a more important lie than the drinking question.

That's a simplified version, of course. In practice, a polygraph test is highly complicated and nuanced, a long (two hours minimum) mind-game between the examiner and the subject. And the results aren't always definitive. Some subjects are easier to test than others, and different polygraph examiners sometimes arrive at different conclusions from the same test results, which is why polygraph tests aren't admissible in court.

Still, when an experienced polygraph examiner tells me my suspect blew the box, ninety-nine times out of a hundred I know I've got my man—or woman.

And Errolyn Ramirez blew the box.

Shortly after the robbery, the bank's assistant manager had told Ramirez that the FBI and the cops wanted her to come in for a polygraph exam. It was no big deal, she said; she, the assistant manager, had already taken one herself and had done fine. (We had tested the assistant manager first to remove her as a suspect or accomplice and to narrow the focus on Ramirez.) If this news struck Ramirez like a dagger in the heart, which I suspect it did, she didn't show it. She said okay, and hoped for the best.

It was 8:30 A.M. on December 16 when Ramirez, dressed casually in jeans and a blouse and dark jacket, reported to the LAPD's Parker Center headquarters in downtown L.A. for her scheduled polygraph exam. (The FBI examiners were booked up, but the LAPD had a polygraph examiner available at the time. Since it was a joint jurisdiction investigation with Robbery-Homicide, either would do.) She waited for a while in the lobby, probably wondering what she had gotten herself into, but not knowing how to get out of it. Finally she was escorted to a small room on the fourth floor, where veteran LAPD polygraph examiner Ervin Youngblood was waiting.

A first-rate examiner, Youngblood went through the process described above, trying to put Ramirez at ease, speaking in a soft, non-accusatory voice, telling her that the main purpose here today was to clear her as a suspect. He went over the test procedure with her, subtly planting the comparative questions and explaining the relevant questions. He read her her *Miranda* rights, and explained that she was under no compunction to take the test, and she said she understood. Then he hooked her up to the machine, and slowly, carefully went through the questions, watching as the needles moved up and down on the rolling graph paper.

After it was over, Youngblood left the room, examined the results, and then came back with the bad news: In his opinion, he told her, when she answered "No" to the key questions—Did you have prior knowledge of the robbery? Did you assist in planning the robbery? Do you know the men who committed the robbery?—she was clearly being deceptive.

Ramirez didn't protest, didn't say there'd been a mistake, didn't insist that there must be something wrong with the machine. In other words, she didn't do any of the things that your normal, average, innocent person would do when a machine calls her a lying bank robber. She simply nodded and said, "Can I go now?"

Can she go now? Well, legally speaking, of course she can go now. This is America. She didn't have to come to Parker Center in the first place, she didn't have to submit to the polygraph—as the *Miranda* warning had informed her—and she wasn't under arrest. She could walk out of there any time she damn well wanted to.

But did we want her to leave? Were we finished with Errolyn Ramirez? Hardly.

So Youngblood, as he knew by training and experience to do, didn't directly answer the question. Well, he told her, there are some people who'd like to talk to you. Ramirez shrugged resignedly.

The people who wanted to talk to her were FBI Special Agent Brenda Cotton and LAPD RHD Detectives Brian Tyndall and Gregory Grant. Youngblood had already told them that Ramirez had failed the test. Now they ushered her into an interview room, a spare, windowless cubicle with a bare table and four metal chairs, and started trying to get past the lying and into the truth.

Although they hadn't planned it that way, the detectives and the FBI agent were basically another rendition of the venerable good cop–bad cop interrogation method you've seen a million times on TV: One cop is the nice guy, your friend who just wants to help you; the other is the mean bastard who wants to take your goddam head off.

In this case, Special Agent Cotton was the soft voice, the sympathetic ear. One of the Bureau's first African-American female agents, and a veteran bank squad member, she was a slim, strikingly attractive woman with an outwardly gentle demeanor wrapped around a tough inner core—tough enough to have earlier made her a standout on the Atlanta FBI field office's SWAT team.

Tyndall and Grant, meanwhile, were the outwardly hard cases—Tyndall a middle-aged white guy with close-cropped hair, not tall but beefy; Grant a black guy, big and imposing-looking, shaven-headed, built like a linebacker. Tyndall had twenty-six years on the department, seventeen of them as a detective; Grant about the same. They'd seen and heard it all. Cheerful, friendly guys in real life, if you were looking at them from across a table in an interview room it was hard not to feel intimidated—especially if you had something to hide.

So they all sit down in the interview room and it begins. It will go around and around, for a couple of hours, but essentially the interview of Errolyn Ramirez boils down to this:

Errolyn, Detective Grant says, if there's something you want to tell us, now's the time to do it.

Ramirez sits there, silent, not looking at them, not saying anything.

Look, we know you were involved. It's time to start being honest here.

Nothing. It's like she's a million miles away.

We're trying to help you, Brenda tells her.

Look, Errolyn, Tyndall says, you think it's just a coincidence that you're the only one at the bank we brought down here for a polygraph test today? No, it's not a coincidence. There were reasons for that, and you know what those reasons are. And you didn't do very well on the test, Errolyn. The examiner said you were deceptive, and believe me, that guy's the best, he knows his business. If he says you're lying, you're lying. Now, it's time to start getting in front of this thing.

Silence.

You ever think about prison? Ever think about what it's like in prison? Young girl like you, I don't think you could survive prison. You need to start thinking about yourself. This could be your last chance to do yourself some good.

Can I call my mother? Ramirez suddenly asks. I want to talk to my mother.

Brenda and the detectives look at each other. Well, why not? They aren't getting anywhere with her so far, and at least she didn't demand a lawyer, which would have shut the thing down right there. Might as well play along. Besides, sometimes it helps, sometimes Mom will come in and tell the suspect to do the right thing.

I'll call her for you, Tyndall says, what's the number? She gives it to him, he goes out to the squad room and makes the call, leaves a message that Errolyn is downtown and wants to talk to her mother. He comes back into the interview room.

Errolyn, I'm going to show you something, Grant says. He takes the bank robbery surveillance photos out of an envelope and lays them on the table in front of her. One of them is a nice, crisp, clean "8 by 10" glossy of the man in the suit walking through the bank lobby with the plastic bags of money in his hands.

Ramirez picks up the photo and stares at it, for ten seconds, twenty, thirty, in total silence, shaking her head slowly back and forth, as if she can hardly believe it. She doesn't say so, but this wasn't the way it was supposed to be. The plan, the way he had laid it out to her, was that no one except her was supposed to be in the vault when he came in and took the money, so no one would activate the alarms and start the cameras running. But LaPortia Davis and Rhea Edwards had been in there, unexpectedly, and LaPortia had hit her remote alarm. There weren't supposed to be any pictures of him.

Who is it? Who's the man in that picture? Tell us who it is, Errolyn.

How did I get myself into this? Ramirez says, aloud but mostly to herself. It is in itself an admission, a crack in the dam. The detectives and Special Agent Cotton feel it now; she's going to start talking, she's going to give him up. But not just yet.

Who is it, Errolyn?

You guys know who it is, she tells them.

No, we don't know who it is. That's why we're asking you.

Ramirez almost smiles then, as if she's onto the game.

You must know who it is. If you've been following me, you know who this is.

But no one's been following her; no one's been sitting on her apartment, or tailing her car; no one needed to. Ramirez really doesn't have a clue as to how a bank robbery investigation is conducted—or even much of a clue as to how the world works in general. She proves that a moment later when she grasps at what she hopes will be her ticket out.

What if I can convince him to give the money back?

What? Give the money back? Brenda and the detectives are trying not to roll their eyes. They're thinking, What planet is this gal from? Sure, lady, this guy—and you—stole three quarters of a million dollars at gunpoint, but if he'll just give the money back, we'll all let bygones be bygones and forget the whole unpleasant incident. So long. No hard feelings. Give us a break.

But what they say is, We'll talk about that later. Right now, tell us who the man in the photo is.

I was surprised when he did it, Ramirez says—another admission. I didn't think he would do it.

We understand. Who is it?

But Ramirez is still thinking that maybe there's wiggle room here.

Can the investigation be done discreetly, she asks, with no media, so no one gets embarrassed?

Embarrassed? She's looking at up to fifteen years in the joint and she's worried somebody will be embarrassed? That's not even worthy of comment.

Tell us who it is, Errolyn.

Brenda can see she's close, she wants this thing over with. But she just can't say the name.

I can see it's hard for you to say the name, Brenda says. But can you write it down for us? You don't have to say it. Just write it down.

Ramirez shakes her head.

Are you afraid of this person? Brenda asks, gently.

Ramirez thinks that one over. Yes and no, she finally says.

Brenda, looking at her, thinks, No, she's not afraid of him, not really; she's afraid for him. She's mad at him for getting her into this, she knows in her heart he's a bum, a bad guy, but she loves him. Despite everything, she still loves him; that's what makes it so hard.

Tyndall takes out a steno notebook and a pen and pushes it across the table. Write it down, Errolyn.

Ramirez picks up the pen and tries to write, but her hand is shaking. She starts to write, stops, starts, stops. She puts the pen down.

But finally she has to do it. She's an ordinary woman in an extraordinary situation, a basically law-abiding person who did a bad thing, something she knows was wrong, and she just can't hold up in a police interview room with two cops and an FBI agent who know she's guilty.

With a heavy sigh, she reaches into the purse she has clutched in her lap and pulls out a business card. She puts it faceup on the table. Without speaking, with a trembling finger, she points to the surveillance photo of the man in the suit, and then to the business card.

Everyone in the room can see the business card. Everyone can see the distinctive gold-embossed oval with the picture of L.A. City Hall on it. Tyndall sees it and goes deathly white, Grant sees it and goes ghostly gray. Brenda sees it and thinks, Uh-oh.

Tyndall picks up the business card.

This is the bank robber? Tyndall says, looking at the name. You're saying *this* is the man who robbed the bank?

Ramirez nods. He's my boyfriend. I told my family I wouldn't see him anymore, but. . . . Her voice trails off.

Tyndall and Grant give each other "Holy shit!" looks. They both know it's true: they can see the truth of it in the face of the young woman sitting across the table from them. Suddenly they're catapulting out of their chairs and bolting for the door, leaving Ramirez in the room with Brenda Cotton. Before, Brenda had almost felt sorry for Errolyn Ramirez; now she's feeling sorry for Tyndall and Grant.

But there's still work to be done. Ramirez is more than just a suspect in a bank robbery now; if she's willing to deal, if she wants to play Queen for a Day, she's also a potential star witness in what's bound to be a major investigation and a bona fide public relations shitstorm. She needs to be handled carefully.

Wow, says Brenda, I can understand why you were so reluctant to say who he was. I know it must have been hard for you. But you did the right thing.

But Ramirez is still distant, unresponsive. All she says is, Can I go to the bathroom?

Meanwhile, Tyndall and Grant are standing in the Robbery-Homicide Division captain's office, wearing the anxious faces of guys who have very big and very bad news for the boss.

Uh, Captain? Tyndall says. You aren't gonna believe this, but, that bank robber?

Yeah, what about him?

He's one of ours.

Ours? Whaddaya mean, one of ours?

Ours. We hate to tell you this, Captain, but his name is David Mack. And he's an LAPD cop.

✦ ✦ ✦

Officer David Anthony Lorenzo Mack. Age thirty-six, a onetime world-class track star, nine years with the LAPD, nominated for the Medal of Valor for saving his partner's life in a fatal shoot-out with a drug dealer, happily married to a woman with a good job with the Xerox Corporation, loving father to two children, block captain in the neighborhood association in the solidly middle-class, predominately black Leimert Park district, coach of his kid's soccer team, adviser and role model to youth. To most of those who knew him, or thought they did, the man was pretty damn close to being perfect.

"David Mack is a good person . . . [of] the highest moral character," Carl Lewis, the track and field star who won nine Olympic gold medals, would write of him. "During all the years I have known David, he has been a moral man who never broke the law," wrote the internationally renowned track coach Joe Douglas. "I love my dad and he loves us," wrote Mack's eleven-year-old son. And so on, from neighbors, teachers, fellow cops, community leaders: David Mack was "trustworthy," "loyal," "dedicated," "courageous," "devoted," "a man of honor." The very notion that David Mack was a bank robber was simply ridiculous.

Ironically, nobody would have been too surprised if he'd gone bad early in life, given the hard hand that had been dealt to him. Born in a whorehouse in Compton, Mack was the son of a prostitute and an unknown father, and as a boy he was passed around to a succession of informal foster families. Although he was bright, he didn't learn to read until he was thirteen, when a friend's mother took him under her wing. Raised on some of the toughest streets in America, with his background, the natural progression might have been for him to join a gang, do drugs, spend his teenaged years in and out of juvie, then graduate to the bigs when he turned eighteen and wind up in Folsom or Ironwood or Pelican Bay, totally screwed for life.

But David Mack had a gift that saved him from that: He could run.

He wasn't just a superior runner, he was a great runner, with the sort of talent that gets you noticed and opens doors. Finally taken in by a family that cared about him—although never officially adopted, Mack would always refer to the couple as his mother and father—he was able to escape the streets and put his energy into track. He was a star at Locke High School, dominating the conference in the mile and the 400 and 800 meters, and after graduation he landed a track scholarship at the University of Oregon. He majored in criminology—from a young age he had always talked about wanting to be a cop—and in 1982 he took first place in the 800 meters at the NCAA Men's Outdoor Track and Field Championships.

In his junior year, disenchanted with the Oregon athletic program—he complained of unfair treatment of black athletes in the department—Mack dropped out of college and joined the Santa Monica Track Club in L.A., founded by Joe Douglas and home to such track superstars as Carl Lewis. Under Douglas's coaching, Mack became one of the preeminent 800-meter runners in the world, winning meets throughout the United States, Europe, and Asia. Like his teammate Lewis, he was considered a top contender for the 1984 Olympics in L.A. But just before the Olympic qualifying trials he suffered a leg injury, similar to a stress fracture, that blew him out of competition that year. Although he continued with the Santa Monica Track Club for several years, and helped set an American record in the 4-X-800-meter relay in 1986, his dominance in the event was over. Married to his college sweetheart, with two young children at home, he needed a career outside athletics—and for that he turned to the LAPD.

Later there would be rumors and bitter speculation among some LAPD officers that Mack had been a "consent decree hire"—that is, a less than qualified candidate whose problems were ignored by the department in order to get more minority officers on the force and get the Justice Department civil rights lawyers off the department's back. But that wasn't so. At age twenty-six, Mack was a world-renowned athlete with two years of college, no serious juvenile record, a literate, articulate family man without any history of drug use—not even steroids. In short, he was an ideal hire on those factors alone; his race was just icing on the consent decree cake. The LAPD was happy to have him—and at his graduation from the Academy in 1988 his entire extended family turned out to smile and cheer him on.

Mack spent several years in uniformed patrol in the LAPD's Southeast and Rampart divisions, two impoverished, high-crime sectors of the city. Like a lot of cops, to help make ends meet he also worked part time, in uniform, as a security guard—including at the Baldwin Hills Theaters, where one of the concession clerks was a nineteen-year-old girl named Errolyn Ramirez.

By all accounts he was a good young cop, self-confident, a little jock-cocky perhaps, maybe even a little arrogant, but an aggressive officer in a department that valued "pro-active" policing. Years later, Mack would describe his policing style this way: "I never wavered from day one on what type of officer I would be," he wrote. "I have walked through many doors alone, believing I would never come out alive. I've responded to many crimes in progress with partners who wanted to wait for backup, but I went in alone. Some of my peers labeled me 'fearless,' some 'crazy,' others 'a hard charger.' I know fear, and I live with it. But I won't follow it."

That was exactly the kind of aggressive young cop they were looking for in the field enforcement section of the LAPD Narcotics Division.

Field enforcement was the absolute front lines, the muddy trenches of the war on drugs. It wasn't *The French Connection*, where detectives pursue sophisticated European heroin rings, and it wasn't the DEA chasing South American drug lords through the Colombian mountains. Instead, LAPD field enforcement involved going undercover to catch the bottom feeders, the lowlifes standing on a street corner peddling ten-dollar rocks, the gang-bangers running a crackhouse in some hopeless ghetto battle zone, the bikers cooking up a batch of meth in the trailer park. Depending on their basic appearance and the nature of the target, young officers like Mack would pose as gang-bangers or pony-tailed white bikers or tattooed ex-cons, negotiating drug buys or sales on street corners or in crackhouses and then having a backup team swoop in and make the arrests. Known in the business as "buy-busts," it was dirty, gritty, dangerous, and often violent work that required young cops like Mack to assume the walk and talk and bad-ass style of the people they were arresting. As a member of the West Bureau Narcotics field enforcement team, Mack spent years playing the role of the swaggering, pimp-rolling, motherfucker-this-and-motherfucker-that violent street gangster. He was utterly convincing in the role. He had to be. His life could depend on it.

Of course, the undercover cops were supposed to be able to turn it off and on at will, to go from their street persona back to their cop persona without any grinding of the emotional gears—and most of them could. But almost any cop who's worked undercover narcotics will tell you: If you do it long enough, you're never going to be quite the same.

Just how violent the job could be was illustrated on the night of October 26, 1993. Mack and another young undercover officer, a Puerto Rican–born ex-Marine named Rafael Perez, were looking to do a buy-bust on Cambridge Street, a grim little strip of urban blight in the Wilshire Division just west of downtown L.A.; their backup team, connected to them by hidden microphones in the car, was waiting around a corner.

When a twenty-nine-year-old crack dealer named Jesse Vicencio approached Mack's car, Mack told him they wanted to buy some rock, and handed him twenty bucks through the open car window. According to the official report, Vicencio threw the money down and then pointed a chrome-plated handgun at the undercover cops, demanding to know if they were Bloods or Crips. While the gun was pointed at Perez, Mack drew his weapon from under his shirt and fired four times, then five more times, then four more times, emptying his weapon. Vicencio fell dead without ever firing a shot.

At the time, Vicencio's body hitting the pavement didn't register as even a tremor on the social Richter scale of L.A.; the *Los Angeles Times* didn't print so much as a line in the paper about it. It was just another brief instant of violence on a forgotten street in a losing war, easily ignored. But years later Mack's partner, Perez, would tell the newspaper: "David Mack was a hero that night. David Mack saved my life." From that moment on, Perez idolized Mack, and became one of his closest friends.

Maybe the shooting happened exactly that way. The LAPD's Officer-Involved Shooting Unit investigated and found the shooting to be "in policy," meaning it was justified. Mack was even nominated for the department's highest award for courage, the Medal of Valor, although it was later knocked down to a Police Medal. But given what happened after, to both Mack and Perez, eventually there was speculation that maybe Vicencio hadn't really been armed, that the gun found next to his cold dead body was a "throw-down," a cheap, disposable, untraceable weapon that cops plant on a suspect to justify a shooting that might otherwise be questionable. If so, it meant that Mack had already crossed the line from good cop to rogue cop.

But no one thought so at the time. Mack's supervisors always gave him high marks, and his reputation among his fellow officers was of a tough, cool-under-fire cop, the sort of guy you could depend on.

Nevertheless, in 1994, Mack requested transfer out of Narcotics Division and back to uniformed patrol. He was assigned to the West L.A. Division, a quiet, upscale, low-crime, low-stress division where domestic arguments and noise complaints, not shoot-outs with drug dealers, constituted the bulk of an officer's workload. Because of his experience and leadership abilities, he was made a training officer, someone who would teach young rookies fresh from the Police Academy how to handle themselves on the streets.

Mack later said he requested the transfer back to patrol because he wanted to spend more time with his family, especially his young son, and working the 10:30 P.M.–6:30 A.M. graveyard shift in West L.A. allowed him to do that. The regular hours also gave him time to help set up a neighborhood watch program on his street in the Leimert Park district, where he and his wife owned an attractive and meticulously maintained Spanish-style home they'd purchased eleven years earlier. He also established a buddy-system program for local schoolkids to walk to school together, spoke frequently to classes at his children's school, was the assistant coach on his son's soccer team, and never missed a game. And he went back to working part time as a uniformed security guard.

Dedicated father, faithful husband, community leader, good cop: that was the David Mack that most of the world saw, the face that most of the people who knew him remembered.

But like any good undercover cop, Mack had an almost amazing ability to show the face that he wanted people to see, to appear to be something that he was not. And although most people didn't realize it, by 1997, if not earlier, Mack had gone back undercover—with a twist.

Before, David Mack had been a cop working undercover as a gangster.

Now, he was a gangster working undercover as a cop.

✦ ✦ ✦

After breaking the bad news to the Robbery-Homicide captain at Parker Center, Detectives Tyndall and Grant went back to the interview room where Errolyn Ramirez was waiting quietly with Special Agent Brenda

Cotton. Fingering her longtime lover had seemed to drain her emotionally. She was unresponsive, didn't want to answer any other questions. No, she said, she didn't know who the second man in the bank robbery was, and she didn't want to talk about it anymore. What she wanted to do was talk to her mother.

By this time, Ramirez's mother and cousin had showed up at Parker Center in response to Tyndall's earlier call; they were waiting downstairs. Brenda Cotton and the detectives talked it over outside the interview room. The detectives escorted Ramirez's mother and cousin up to RHD and let them talk to her alone in the interview room—without mentioning that the discussion was being taped. (It was perfectly legal; there is no expectation of privacy in a police interview room.)

Unfortunately, they didn't come through. Mom and the cousin advised Ramirez to shut up and get a lawyer. They seemed to already know the basic details of what had happened at the bank; Ramirez apparently had confided in them after the robbery. And they also seemed to intuitively understand more about the real David Mack than Ramirez did.

"Errolyn, your life's going to be in danger," her mother said. "Our lives are going to be in danger."

"He's not going to hurt me," Ramirez insisted. "He's just going to end up going to jail. He's not going to hurt me and he's not going to hurt you. Mother, I've been seeing David for so long . . .

She let the sentence trail off, as if it spoke for itself.

When Ramirez came out of the interview room, she told Tyndall, Grant, and Cotton that she wanted to speak with an attorney. Grant gave it one last shot, telling her that once she got an attorney, they, her good friends in the FBI and Robbery Homicide, wouldn't be able to help her anymore. But Ramirez wasn't buying. As a formality, they read her her rights again and asked if she wanted to make a statement. She declined.

And then they let her go. Although her statements were incriminating, she hadn't exactly directly confessed—yes, I did it, I was involved—and her identification of Mack as the robber would have to be corroborated. But they didn't want to lose track of her either; she left Parker Center with a crew from the LAPD's Special Investigations Section (SIS), the department's top surveillance team, quietly on her tail.

Meanwhile, Brenda Cotton and two other RHD detectives sped down to the Bank of America on Jefferson with a six-pack photo array with David Mack's picture in it. They showed the six-pack to LaPortia Davis and Rhea Edwards, the two bank employees who'd been in the vault counting room when Mack burst in with a gun. Both women quickly picked out Mack as the robber.

"I won't ever forget his face," Davis said.

A check of department records showed that Mack had been off work on November 6, the day of the bank robbery, and for several days thereafter, allegedly because of a family illness. Ramirez's statements and the ID by the bank employees, along with the apparent lack of an alibi for Mack, was enough. An SIS team sat on Mack's house until seven-thirty that evening, when they saw him come out of the driveway in a black Chevy Blazer. They followed him to a Ralph's supermarket, and when he came out ten minutes later the SIS guys, with Tyndall and Grant standing by, put him under arrest. Errolyn Ramirez was arrested by another SIS team at her apartment at about the same time.

Mack didn't resist, didn't argue, didn't say, "What's this all about?" as they took his gun and shield and put him in handcuffs. His demeanor was cold, arrogant, defiant. When they read him his rights and told him the charges against him, all he said was, "Give it your best shot." Tyndall and Grant loaded him into their car and headed for Parker Center.

Even though it was a high-profile case, the detectives took no pleasure in the arrest. They were cops of the old school, veterans of a department that, while frequently criticized for its aggressiveness, its willingness to kick ass and take names, had for the past half century been remarkably clean in terms of criminal financial corruption in the ranks—or so it was thought. Having a fellow cop arrested for a crime—an armed bank robbery, for God's sake—was for those two good detectives an embarrassment, a disgrace, a kind of failure.

They put Mack in an interview room at RHD and tried to get him to talk about it, half-hoping that he'd come up with some reasonable explanation, that maybe there'd been a mistake, that he wasn't a dirty cop. But Mack refused to say anything, except when they told him they were going to search his house. Mack told them to go ahead, and added, in voice full of contempt, "Just don't treat my family like a bunch of niggers."

But it wasn't enough for Detective Grant, like Mack an African American, not too much older but somehow of another generation. As he was taking Mack downstairs to the Parker Center lockup to be booked, he tried again, unofficially, for his own peace of mind, to understand the why of it.

David, he said to Mack, just between you and me, I gotta know something. If I had come into that bank during the robbery, and you knew I was another cop, would you have shot me down?

David Mack just snickered—and Greg Grant's blood went cold. He realized at that moment that he wasn't dealing with a cop anymore. David Mack may have been a fellow cop once, may even have been a good cop. But now he was just another sullen, handcuffed, fuck-you gangster on his way to jail.

Later that night a virtual swarm of FBI agents, RHD detectives, and LAPD Internal Affairs officers searched Mack's house. They found $2,600 in fifty-dollar bills ($150,000 of the stolen money was in fifties), an M-11 9-mm machine pistol and a shoulder rig similar to the one used in the robbery, a bank statement showing a deposit of $7,000 on the day of the robbery, and, hidden under the carpet in a closet, receipts for $22,000 in recent cash purchases. A search of Ramirez's apartment turned up nothing. Wherever Mack had hidden the bulk of the stolen cash, we couldn't find it.

The next day the story hit the press.

"Officer Charged in Bank Heist That Netted $722,000," said one *Los Angeles Times* headline. "Robbery Suspect Called LAPD Leader," said another.

To those who knew Mack, or thought they did, it was unbelievable. It must be a mistake, they said, or even a frame-up—maybe a racially based frame-up. Support for Mack poured in from friends, neighbors, teachers, community leaders; they bombarded the court with letters attesting to Mack's honesty and good citizenship.

Even most of his fellow officers, who knew damn well that Robbery Homicide wasn't about to arrest a cop without overwhelming evidence of guilt, reacted more with shock than anger.

"He was well thought of and liked by colleagues," West L.A. Division Captain John Leap told the *Los Angeles Times*. "People here feel saddened and disappointed." "It strikes you right in the heart," said

LAPD Deputy Chief Martin Pomeroy. "He was a good guy," said Dave Hepburn, president of the LAPD Police Protective League (in essence, the police union) and a former supervisor of Mack's. "But we hire from the human race, and . . . occasionally we get a bad apple."

Meanwhile, the detectives and FBI agents on the case were trying to figure out just how bad an apple Mack was. And the David Mack they discovered couldn't have been more different from the David Mack everybody was saying so many nice things about.

They found that Mack had always kept to a tight circle of friends within the department, most of them young African Americans: Officer Rafael Perez, Mack's partner during the shooting on Cambridge Street, was one; Sam Martin, one of Mack's early partners from patrol, and Kevin Gaines, another undercover cop from Narcotics Division, were among the others. There was nothing necessarily unusual or sinister about that. However well members of different races might work together, social cliques tend to separate along racial lines. Walk into any office building cafeteria in America at lunchtime and you'll see that phenomenon in action.

But while he might not have shown it to his white colleagues, there had always been a touch of racial militancy to David Mack, a chip-on-the-shoulder sensitivity to perceived racial slights that dated back to his days on the Oregon track team. Before joining the LAPD, Mack reportedly flirted with the black separatist Nation of Islam, but he found the movement's strict rules about drinking and womanizing too confining for his taste. Still, there seemed to be a sense of racial anger lurking inside him—just as there was in the LAPD at large.

Although the department had come a long way from the time when black officers and white officers weren't allowed to ride in the same patrol car, the polite fiction that "LAPD cops only come in one color—blue" belonged more to Jack Webb and *Dragnet* than to anything in the real world. Black LAPD officers often complained of unequal treatment in assignments and promotions, while the consent decrees of the early 1980s, which required more hiring and promotion of females and minorities, rankled some white officers, who complained of preferential treatment for blacks.

Meanwhile, the same racial discord that racked the city as a whole also divided the LAPD. The Rodney King case, the 1992 riots, the O. J.

Simpson acquittal—black cops and white cops often responded to those events the same way as the civilian population did, with diametrically opposed opinions based on their race. And six months before Mack robbed the bank, a violent and bizarre incident involving Mack's friend, Kevin Gaines, brought the racial animosity within the department boiling to the surface.

In March 1997, Gaines, still working undercover in the Narcotics Division, got into an off-duty traffic beef with another motorist. Gaines, driving an SUV, was dressed in his undercover "uniform" of shaved head, goatee, and gang-banger-style nylon running suit—cops called it a "two-eleven suit," since it was currently the fashion trend among gang member armed robbers. The other motorist, driving a Buick Regal, was a pony-tailed, mustached white guy who looked for all the world like a charter member of the Aryan Brotherhood. During the confrontation, Gaines pointed a .45-caliber handgun at the white guy and shouted, "Punk, I'll put a cap in you"—at which point the white guy drew his own .45 and fired twice, killing Gaines.

What Gaines hadn't known was that the white guy was also an LAPD cop, an undercover Narcotics Division detective named Frank Lyga. And Lyga hadn't known that he was shooting another cop.

Lyga was cleared in the shooting—it was ruled self-defense—but the killing of a black undercover officer by a white undercover officer exacerbated the racial tensions in the department. The black officers' association demanded that Gaines be given a full-dress department funeral, which is usually reserved for officers killed in the line of duty; white officers argued that a cop shot while brandishing a gun in an off-duty road rage incident hardly constituted an honorable line-of-duty death. In the end, Chief Willie Williams, himself an African American, agreed to (and attended) a semiofficial funeral for Gaines–a compromise that satisfied absolutely no one. The killing of Officer Gaines reinforced the idea among some black cops, Mack included, that the department was institutionally racist.

But Gaines's death also revealed some disturbing evidence of corruption and links between police officers and street gangsters. Investigators discovered that the SUV Gaines was driving when he was shot was owned by Sharitha Knight, Gaines's girlfriend and the estranged wife of Marion "Suge" Knight, founder of Death Row Records, which produced violent—and notoriously anti-police—"gangsta rap" music. Knight, who was then serving a prison sentence for assault, had reportedly been a member of the Mob Piru Bloods in Compton, and the record company was said to have strong ties to various South Central gangs.

Without department approval, Gaines and other black cops—including David Mack—had been providing personal and site security for Death Row Records personnel and events. For department investigators, the idea of cops guarding gangsta rappers with suspected ties to gang murders and the dope trade was more than a little troubling. And other aspects of Gaines's lifestyle were suspicious, too. He drove a black Mercedes with a vanity plate that said: ITS OK IA—"IA" referring to the LAPD's Internal Affairs Division—and among his belongings investigators found credit card receipts for thousand-dollar dinners at high-end West Side restaurants. The guy was living way beyond his visible means.

So was David Mack. As FBI and LAPD investigators looked into Mack's background, they discovered that he had always been a player, a guy who liked the finer things in life. Even before he joined the LAPD, Santa Monica Track Club coach Joe Douglas had noted Mack's taste for fine clothes and fine restaurants and beautiful women—and was concerned enough about it to warn him that his "playboy lifestyle" could endanger his track career. Throughout his LAPD career, Mack had continued to wear designer suits and hang out at nightclubs and take expensive vacations, often with other young cops. And while Errolyn Ramirez was the most long-lasting, she wasn't the only young woman Mack was seeing on the side. Mistresses are expensive—and beautiful ones tend to be even more so.

Sure, a single guy making $55,000 a year, as Mack was, might have been able to pull it off, if he was also bringing in a little extra moonlighting or overtime money. But Mack had a wife and two kids and a mortgage, and there are only so many moonlighting and overtime hours in a week. Inevitably the question arose: Where was this guy Mack getting his cash?

No one ever proved that Mack had been guilty of corruption before the bank robbery, even while he was working narcotics. Still, for any cop who's inclined that way, in any police department in America, narcotics is the place to be.

After all, there's not much corruption potential when you're working murders or robberies or sexual assaults or patrol. What are you going to do, lift the corpse's wallet? Pilfer the rape victim's purse? Shake down a random motorist who just might turn out to be the mayor's sister's cousin? But when you're chasing dope dealers, the opportunity for corruption can be as close as your next bust. You take a drug dealer's money and who's going to know? The dealer sure as hell isn't going to file a complaint—and even if he did, who's going to believe some low-life crack-dealing scumbag?

It's even easy to rationalize, if rationalizing is what you need. Here I am, making forty or fifty grand a year putting my ass on the line, jacking up dope dealers in some godforsaken hellhole, and for what? If I arrest this guy, if I take him off this corner, another one just like him will be standing there five minutes later. What difference will it make if I take his money and his product and kick his sorry ass loose?

Again, nobody ever proved that Mack was running drug deals while he was with the LAPD—although his buddy Perez certainly was, at the same time he and Mack were hanging out together.

But it was clear to everybody who looked that even before the bank robbery, Mack was spending more money than an honest cop was likely to make—and even then it wasn't enough. At the time of the bank robbery, Mack was $20,000 in debt to the IRS, he had $17,000 on plastic, and he was starting to miss mortgage payments. And despite Mack's public image as a dedicated husband and father, his wife, by all accounts an honest and decent woman, was well aware of his outside romantic interests. There was talk of a costly divorce.

And there was something else that was suspicious about Mack, something that led investigators to conclude that the bank job hadn't been Mack's first foray into crime. Although most of the people who knew him were genuinely shocked at his arrest, and couldn't believe that he would have ever done anything illegal, there were some people who weren't surprised at all.

Mack had come a long way from the streets of Compton, yet he had always kept in touch with some of the homeboys from his old neighborhood. And after Mack's arrest, in an effort to work his way out from under a state charge, one of Mack's homeboys—we'll call him Darren—told us a story.

Darren said that before the robbery, Mack had boasted to him that he had a "bitch" who was going to make him rich by setting up a score at the bank she worked at. Darren had known Mack for his entire life, and he wasn't surprised that Mack was planning a stickup. But he was surprised that Mack had the girl involved in it. According to Darren, Mack had always said you should "never trust a bitch."

Mack offered Darren $10,000 to steal a getaway car for him, which he did, boosting a white Windstar van from a Budget Rent-A-Car lot. The day before the bank robbery Darren delivered the van to Mack's house, and Mack said he would pay him the $10,000 the next day—a delayed payment program that displeased Darren considerably. As a kind of gangster collateral, Mack explained the score: At 9:00 A.M. the next morning, an armored car was going to deliver almost $1 million in cash to a bank, and he and two other guys—he didn't identify them, although he indicated it was a "family thing"—were going to walk in and take it; it was all set up. Mack showed him the M-11 assault pistol and the shoulder rig, and talked about how he would hide the weapon under his suit. It was going to be easy, he said.

And it was. The next day, three hours after the bank robbery, Mack stopped by Darren's house and, good as his word, paid him $10,000 in fresh fifty-dollar bills.

No, Darren said, Mack didn't seem upset or nervous after committing the bank robbery. He seemed calm, at ease, not at all what you might expect if Mack had been a previously honest cop who was unaccustomed to committing felonies, and who had just committed a huge one a few hours before. If Mack felt any remorse, he didn't show it.

In fact, he was going on vacation.

During the search of Mack's house, his wife had told the detectives and FBI agents that in early November Mack had taken a trip to Las Vegas and had come back with stories about winning big at the craps tables. The winnings were bullshit, but the Vegas trip was real. Two days after the bank robbery, Mack and his old friend Officer Perez, along with Perez's mistress (a convicted cocaine dealer) and LAPD Officer Sam Martin, drove to Vegas and checked into Caesar's Palace. Over the next two days they dropped $20,000 on rooms, gourmet meals, champagne, and gambling.

Later investigators would find a photo of Mack and Perez taken outside a restaurant in Caesar's. There was Perez, handsome in a double-breasted blue suit, and Mack, decked out in a red suit and a red derby hat, a fat ring on his finger, a gold bracelet on his wrist, both of them holding Panama cigars and smiling happy smiles.

It was a picture of gangsters on holiday.

And Errolyn Ramirez? Where was she while Mack and his buddies were spending the cash from the bank robbery she had helped set up? She was at home—waiting for her lover to call.

On Thursday night, seven days after the robbery, Mack finally showed up at Errolyn's apartment. Ramirez later claimed that she had been furious with him, that she hadn't believed he would actually rob the bank. Mack had told her to calm down. And he gave her a warning.

"You know what happens to people who talk too much," Mack told her.

Maybe so. Maybe Ramirez really was mad at Mack, maybe he did threaten her. But if she was angry, she quickly got over it. A few nights later, on her twenty-sixth birthday, Mack took Ramirez out to dinner at a Benihana restaurant in Marina del Rey. Afterward they checked into a hotel and made love.

I'm an FBI agent, not a therapist or a daytime talk show host: I don't know much about the psychology of women. I can't say if Ramirez feared Mack, or loved him, or both. But I've loved the same woman for thirty years, and I know that Mack never felt toward Errolyn Ramirez anything that could realistically be called love. She was useful, and convenient, and ego-enhancing, and Mack had probably whispered sweet I-love-you's in her ear. But no man who truly loved a woman could have ruined her life as coldly and callously as Mack did Errolyn Ramirez's.

That callousness was on parade the day after they were arrested, when Mack and Ramirez were taken to federal court to be arraigned on federal bank robbery charges. Mack had spent the night in Parker Center, while Ramirez was held in the lockup at the LAPD 77th Division station—not a pleasant experience for anyone, and certainly not for someone who had never been arrested before. Sitting in the custody section of the courtroom, Ramirez was a mess—unshowered and unkempt, dressed in a baggy blue jail jumpsuit, her only jewelry the handcuffs on her wrists, she was a portrait of misery.

Mack, also handcuffed, in a jail jumpsuit, was sitting in a row in front of her. He was still cocky and defiant, not at all the usual hangdog picture of a disgraced cop. He turned around and spoke to Ramirez.

He didn't say, "I'm sorry I got you into this," or, "Don't worry, baby, it'll be okay," or even an empty "I love you." Not even close. Instead, he looked at her jail jumpsuit and said:

"You know I don't like you in blue."

He never spoke to her again. Soon enough, he'd be trying to figure out a way to kill her.

✦ ✦ ✦

David Mack's open transformation from cop to gangster, which began when he was arrested, continued in jail. Eventually he started wearing red socks, a red handkerchief "do rag," anything red he could get his hands on—the "colors" of a Bloods gang member—and began telling fellow prisoners he was with the Mob Piru Bloods of his old Compton neighborhood. It may have simply been a jailhouse defense strategy; in jail, gang members are respected, and feared, far more than ex-cops. But as he did with any role, Mack played it convincingly.

Immediately after his arrest we kept him in the police lockup in Montebello, a small suburban city southeast of downtown. The choice of jails was based largely on Mack's own security; he might have already rejected his police background, but that wouldn't necessarily guarantee his safety from other prisoners in a hard-core jail. The Montebello jail had a reputation as a "snitch jail," a place where police and federal agents could safely stash away informants—and in Mack's case it lived up to its reputation.

Shortly after Mack was locked up, a snitch told us that he had gotten friendly with him, and that Mack had boasted of the bank robbery. Mack told him the "bitch" (Ramirez) had agreed to help him with the bank robbery if he would finally leave his wife, but no, she wasn't getting any of the money. The only way anybody would find the missing money, he said, was "if a dog or a cat dug it up." Mack also bragged that he was going to beat the rap—and even if he didn't, he'd do his time and have the money waiting for him when he got out.

"The bitch is the only one who can do me," Mack told the snitch. "The only other thing they have is a glimpse of me on film. So I'm gonna fuck the bitch."

Of course, a hit on a witness wasn't the sort of thing you could safely plan over a jailhouse phone, so Mack told the snitch that one of his "homeboys" was going to get himself arrested in Montebello and be brought to the city jail to meet with Mack. Sure enough, two days later the homeboy, a career criminal and lifelong friend of Mack's, got arrested for petty shoplifting at the Montebello Mall and was brought in.

"I told you my boy would be in," Mack told the snitch. "That's the guy who's going to handle the bitch." Mack and the homeboy spent several hours in close conversation.

Fortunately for Ramirez, who had bailed out of jail after her aunt put her home up as collateral, the homeboy got cold feet and told his lawyer about the alleged plot, and the lawyer notified police. There wasn't enough evidence to charge Mack with conspiracy to commit murder—but he was moved to the more controlled "high-power" lockup at county jail.

As it turned out, Mack didn't need to kill Errolyn Ramirez to keep her quiet. Even though she could have greatly reduced her potential prison time by agreeing to testify against Mack, Ramirez—and her attorney—wasn't interested. She would take her chances in court.

Their trials had been separated, and Mack went first. Even without Ramirez's testimony, it was a strong case. Assistant U.S. Attorney Stephen Wolfe methodically went through the identification of Mack by the other bank employees, and his sudden infusion of cash after the robbery. Mack didn't testify in his own defense, but his attorney, the prominent L.A. criminal defense lawyer Donald Re, gave it his best shot, attacking the witness IDs and trying to explain away the money.

But the jury wasn't buying. In March 1999, after one day of deliberations, they came back with guilty verdicts against Mack for armed robbery, conspiracy, and use of a firearm to commit a crime of violence. Mack, dressed in an expensive suit (he saved his gangster pose for jail), showed no reaction as the verdicts were read.

Ramirez went on trial two months later. She'd caught a legal break from the presiding judge, Robert Takasugi: he had thrown out the incriminating statements she had made to Special Agent Cotton and Detectives Tyndall and Grant, on the grounds that she hadn't been read her rights—this despite the fact that she'd been Mirandized before her polygraph test prior to the interview. It made for a tougher case.

And Ramirez was a sympathetic defendant. On the witness stand, dressed in a dark blue suit and speaking in a low, unemotional voice, she put it all on Mack—knowing that with Mack already convicted, what she said about him now couldn't hurt him. She denied that she had known in advance about the robbery, or that she had ordered the extra cash shipment so that Mack could steal it. She was surprised when he came into the bank that day, she said, and astonished when he showed the gun and ordered her to open the bandit barrier door.

"He looked strange," Ramirez said. "His face was darker. I believed at the time that David would have shot somebody in the lobby or have killed me." Fearing for her life and the lives of others, she said, she let Mack into the vault—and she insisted that as he ran out she had activated her remote alarm button.

And afterward, why didn't she tell anyone that it was her boyfriend who had robbed the bank?

"I was afraid he would kill me," Ramirez testified. "If he thought I would say anything he would kill me—there was no doubt in my mind that he would. I believed that if I didn't say anything, he wouldn't do anything to me."

It had always been like that, she said. Throughout their seven-year relationship he had always controlled her, dominated her, made her fear him. Once when she tried to break up with him, she said, "He told me I would end up like Nicole Brown.

"He was always telling me that he would kill me if I tried to leave him, that I was his, he had created me, nobody else could have me." That was why she hadn't told anybody that he was the bank robber—because she was afraid.

Bullshit, Special Agent Brenda Cotton thought.

As the case agent, Brenda sat at the prosecution table throughout the trial. Watching Ramirez on the witness stand, Brenda had the same take on the situation as she'd had that day eighteen months earlier when she sat in the interview room with Ramirez at Parker Center. All the mention made about being afraid of Mack was her attorney talking, Brenda thought. Yes, David Mack was a dangerous man, and yes, he had plotted to kill her from jail. But Ramirez hadn't agreed to the bank robbery, or protected him afterward, because she'd been afraid of him.

She did it because she loved him. And watching her, and knowing a little bit about women and men, Brenda decided that despite all the misery David Mack had brought her, a part of her loved him still.

Eleven twelfths of the jury apparently agreed with Special Agent Cotton. They didn't buy that Ramirez was unaware in advance of the robbery or that fear alone had kept her quiet. Eleven jurors voted to convict, but the twelfth, a male social worker, wouldn't budge. The trial ended in a hung jury.

Two months later, after the U.S. Attorney's office agreed to reduce the charges in a plea bargain, Errolyn Ramirez pleaded guilty to one count of conspiracy. Judge Takasugi was merciful, sentencing her to just two and a half years in prison. Given the circumstances, the fact that she'd been a law-abiding person lured by love and foolishness to help rob a bank, no one took excessive pleasure in the conviction; everyone concerned hoped that when she got out she could salvage her damaged life.

Her former lover fared less well—although not as badly as he should have. In September 1999, Mack appeared for sentencing, and Judge Takasugi asked him if he cared to say what happened to the rest of the stolen $722,000. Through his attorney, Mack said no, he didn't care to say where the money was; nor did he care to finger his still unidentified accomplices, or to say anything on his own behalf. Takasugi sentenced him to just over fourteen years in federal prison—and also ordered him to pay Bank of America $722 per month for a thousand months, if and when he gets out.

Bank of America is not holding its breath that it will ever see the money.

✦ ✦ ✦

Although Mack was on ice, his legacy hovered over the LAPD like a bad smell. There were still unresolved questions as to what other criminal activities Mack had been into, and with whom. What no one expected was that eventually Mack's bank robbery would prove to be a portal into one of the biggest police corruption scandals in LAPD history—a scandal that Mack actually had nothing to do with.

Ever since they found out about the high-rolling trip to Las Vegas, investigators had been curious about Mack's pal Rafael Perez, who after his undercover narcotics work with Mack had transferred to Rampart Division CRASH (Community Resources Against Street Hoodlums), the elite group of hard-charging cops tasked with combatting gang-related street violence and drug dealing. They wondered how an honest cop could drop that kind of money—or even watch his friend drop that kind of money. Although there was nothing to link Perez directly to the bank robbery—he didn't match the surveillance photo of the layoff man, and no prints or other evidence put him inside the stolen van—there was something hinky about the whole situation.

It got even hinkier. In March 1998, four months after the bank robbery, three kilos of cocaine came up missing from the LAPD Property Division, which stores evidence in criminal cases. Surprisingly, the property room worked largely on the honor system: If a cop needed evidence for a court case, he came in, showed his badge, signed for the evidence— a murder weapon, seized drugs, whatever—and then when he was through with it he brought it back. Problem was, the cop who signed for the three keys of dope never brought it back, and the name he signed turned out to be phony. All the property clerk could remember was that he was a young African-American looking officer who spoke Spanish.

Gosh, the detectives wondered, who do we have who fits that description—and who just happens to be best friends with a crooked cop who robbed a bank? Perez was put under surveillance, and the task force discovered that, like Mack, he was a high roller living beyond his visible means, with nice cars, two homes, and a taste for beautiful mistresses. Through phone records, task force investigators tracked the coke stolen from the property room back to Perez's mistress, a convicted cocaine dealer; they also discovered that in addition to stealing those three keys of coke, Perez had been routinely checking cocaine out of the property room, replacing it with "bulk" (usually Bisquick) and checking it back into the evidence room. Through his mistress he would put the real stuff out on the street—again.

They still couldn't connect him to the bank job, but Perez, who had spotted the surveillance on him, assumed that was what they were after. When he was served with a search warrant, his first words were: "This is about the bank robbery, isn't it?"

Well, yes and no. A cop committing a bank robbery is bad enough, but in the pantheon of police department nightmares, a cop stealing and dealing dope from the police evidence room is even worse; it not only looks awful in the newspapers, but it can throw a wrench into scores, even hundreds of past and future criminal prosecutions.

Perez was arrested, but unlike his pal David Mack, eventually he was willing to talk. In return for a reduced sentence on the cocaine thefts, and immunity on other crimes he committed, he would reveal widespread corruption within the LAPD. Some investigators figured he would put Mack in the bag for dope rip-offs, other robberies, maybe even contract murders.

But when it came time for Perez to play Queen for a Day, he didn't want to talk about David Mack, a man Perez had idolized ever since the 1993 shooting on Cambridge Street. Perez insisted that he himself had played no role in the bank heist, and claimed that he'd been shocked—shocked!—when Mack was arrested for the bank job. As far as he had known, Perez swore, Mack was an honest, dedicated police officer.

No, the tale Perez wanted to tell concerned corruption in the Rampart Division CRASH unit—a tale of out-of-control cops beating and planting evidence on suspects, using throw-downs to cover up bad shootings, and routinely perjuring themselves in court to send innocent men to prison. In short, he wanted to talk about what became known as the Rampart Scandal, one of the worst police brutality scandals in the modern history of the LAPD.

A close look at the scandal is beyond the scope of this book. But before it was over, based almost entirely on Perez's allegations, scores of criminal convictions were overturned, a blizzard of lawsuits were filed, tens of millions of dollars were paid out by the city in damage awards, and thirteen Rampart CRASH officers were fired or resigned. Ever since Rodney King, Los Angeles had been a city at odds with its own police department, and Perez's allegations seemed to confirm every suspicion that the department was riddled with corrupt, brutal cops.

But as time went on, some task force investigators came to believe that Perez had manipulated them, that he was a master liar and con man, steering them away from crimes committed by David Mack and his other friends by laying brutality charges on other cops he didn't care about.

If so, it worked. Amid the political turmoil of the Rampart Scandal, Mack, who had never worked in the Rampart CRASH unit, largely faded into the background.

True, there were still rumors, suspicions, loose ends. After Mack was already in prison, a former girlfriend of Perez's told FBI and LAPD task force investigators that she had seen Perez and Mack murder a drug dealer and his mother in a Rampart Division "crash pad" used by off-duty officers to party and hang out with women, and that the bodies had been dumped in Tijuana. The FBI spent three months and $350,000 digging through a garbage-filled Mexican ravine, looking for the bodies, before the woman admitted she made the whole thing up to get even with Perez for jilting her. Even her own attorney described the woman as a "stupid little brat"—a description that the garbage-covered Special Agents on the task force thought was overly charitable.

Other suspicions about Mack, though, had a little more meat on them. One unsolved crime that investigators looked at was the March 1997 murder of rapper Biggie Smalls, aka Notorious BIG, aka Christopher Wallace, a twenty-four-year-old former New Jersey crack dealer who was a star for the East Coast–based Bad Boy Records, run by rap mogul Sean "Puffy" Combs. Smalls had been gunned down in the Wilshire District of L.A. while riding in a motorcade of gangsta rappers after the Soul Train Music Awards. The speculation was that the hit on Biggie Smalls was payback to Bad Boy Records by Death Row Records for the murder of Death Row's star rapper, Tupac Shakur, in Las Vegas in 1996, a shooting in which Death Row Records founder Suge Knight was wounded. If so, it wouldn't have been unusual; the long-running feud between the two gangsta rap record companies was believed to have already resulted in a dozen murders. (Interestingly, before his death Shakur had starred with Jim Belushi in a film called *Gang Related*, in which Shakur portrayed a corrupt LAPD cop who was shaking down drug dealers.)

There was some circumstantial evidence that possibly linked Mack to the Smalls killing. The shooter's car was described as a dark Chevy Impala, the same kind of car Mack drove, and when showed Mack's picture, some witnesses placed him at the scene. Mack's reported security work for Death Row Records and his connections to slain Officer Kevin Gaines also fueled suspicions. Nobody who knew him—really knew him—doubted that Mack would have been capable of a contract hit.

But that was as far as it went. Mack's possible role in the Biggie Smalls murder was widely speculated about in the news media; there were even allegations in the press that the new LAPD chief, Bernard Parks, mindful of the racial politics involved, had blocked deeper investigation into what could have turned out to be a cabal of African-

American gangster cops in the department—allegations that the chief strongly denied. Whatever the reasons, no one ever conclusively put the Biggie Smalls murder in Mack's lap—or anything else for that matter. In the end, the bank robbery was at all that Mack had to answer for.

But the bank robbery was enough.

Mack hasn't done well in prison; ex-cops seldom do. Shortly after his sentencing, while being held at Greenville Federal Correctional Facility in Illinois, Mack got into a fight with some convicts from L.A.'s 18th Street gang and took a shiv in the chest, collapsing a lung; he only narrowly survived. Whether the beef was because Mack was an ex-cop or because he'd been calling himself a Blood isn't known, but the fight cost him some of his "good time"—and his dreams of having all that money to spend when he gets out inched that much further away.

And even if he survives prison, even if there's not another shiv waiting for him on his next walk across the prison yard, think about what's really waiting for him when he gets out.

No one ever thought that Mack had divided the robbery take equally, but his layoff man and the getaway driver probably got at least $100,000 between them as their part of the take. Subtract what he blew on Vegas and other frills before he was arrested, and wherever the money is, there's probably not much more than half a million left.

Half a million may sound like a lot of money. But over the fourteen years he'll spend in prison, Mack could have earned more than that as a cop—an honest cop, with a wife and children who loved him, and friends who trusted him.

So why did he do it? Why did David Mack throw his life away, along with Errolyn Ramirez's, to do a bank lick? Was he always a dirty cop, or did he only gradually become that way? Did he spend too long working undercover, posing as a gangster, and somehow lose his way? Or was he born with a gangster's soul, and was everything good that he did in his life just a sham, an undercover operation on the world?

I don't know—and no one else who knew him, or thought they knew him, can really know for sure, either.

But I do know this: as bad a cop as David Mack was, he was an even worse bank robber. He should have studied the genre more carefully, should have shown a little more respect for those of us who work bank robberies for a living—and he should have better understood the nature of his accomplice and lover, the woman he'd been sleeping with for seven long years. He should have known that we'd easily be able to figure the bank robbery out, that everything would point back to her, and that being the kind of person she was, she'd never be able to hold up under a criminal investigation.

David Mack should have known that inside bank jobs almost never work.

No matter how much the insider loves you.

6

SHOOT-OUT
IN NORTH HOLLYWOOD

The bank robbers had made a fatal error. Despite all their planning, all their knowledge, all their attention to the professional requirements of the bank robbery trade, they made the biggest mistake that a bank robbery crew can make.

They stayed too long in the bank. And I knew they were going to bleed for it.

It had started off well enough. Wearing body armor and ski masks and carrying automatic weapons, they had taken over the bank and ordered everyone to the floor, flex-cuffing the security guards, grabbing the manager's vault key, one of them keeping the lobby under control while another opened the vault and started stuffing the cash into canvas duffel bags. It was a huge take, $12 million in fact, and if they'd been out of there in under two minutes they might have gotten away with it. After two minutes you're into the danger zone, the point at which the cops are realistically able to respond to a two-eleven silent alarm, and every second after that the danger increases.

These guys were deep into the danger zone. Minutes were ticking by, and when the bandits finally made it out of the bank, dozens of armed police were waiting, crouched behind their black-and-white patrol cars. Seeing them, the bandits opened up with their fully automatic weapons; the uniformed police officers, although seriously outgunned, fired back with their semiautomatic pistols and shotguns. It was a maelstrom of gunfire, a blizzard of zipping lead. Car windows exploded, black-and-whites riddled with rosettes of bullet holes slumped to the ground as their tires burst, hundreds of expended brass casings skittered on the sidewalks. Windrows of cops fell wounded and dead as hysterical bystanders ran screaming, trying to get away.

It was madness, mayhem. Watching it unfold, seeing the blood and hearing the screams, I thought, This can't be happening, this isn't the way bank robberies are supposed to play out. Something has gone wrong.

Then I reached for another handful of popcorn.

It was a movie, of course, a 1995 release called *Heat*—and a fine movie it was. But it was still a movie, with all the compromises of drama over reality that film requires. And like every other bank robbery movie I'd ever seen, it made the armed bank robbery business appear a lot more glamorous and exciting—and easy—than it really is.

The film industry has always had a thing for bank robbers; it has lionized them in a way that would be unthinkable for murderers, rapists, burglars, counterfeiters, shoplifters, or almost any type of criminal. It's hard to think of a major movie star who hasn't, at one time or another, portrayed a bank robber: Paul Newman (*Butch Cassidy and the Sundance Kid*, *Where the Money Is*), Steve McQueen (*The Getaway*, *The Great St. Louis Bank Robbery*), Al Pacino (*Dog Day Afternoon*), Tom Hanks (*Road to Perdition*), Warren Beatty and Faye Dunaway (*Bonnie and Clyde*) Clint Eastwood (*Thunderbolt and Lightfoot*) Robert Redford (*Butch Cassidy*), Robert De Niro (*Jackie Brown, Heat*), George Burns, Art Carney, Lee Strasberg (*Going In Style*), Bruce Willis and Billie Bob Thornton (*Bandits*). The list goes on.

Even John Wayne, as Marshal Rooster Cogburn in *True Grit*, admitted that in his younger days he had robbed a bank. He downplayed the criminal element of the heist by saying that it wasn't like he had stolen a man's watch.

Which pretty much sums up Hollywood's attitude on bank robberies: it hardly even seems like stealing. Even the violence comes without pain. When your extras and bit players get shot—the faceless uniformed cops, bank or armored car guards, hapless bystanders—they don't fall screaming in agony and fear; they fall quietly, with hardly a sound, and the plot rolls happily onward. Even if the hero—which is to say, the bank robber—gets killed in the end, it somehow seems glorious and fitting, a man (or woman) dying doing what he loved to do. The movies gloss over the fundamental reality of the bank robbery trade: that bank

robbers' lives are either exceedingly short, or exceedingly long and boring, spent largely behind bars.

Technically, the movies miss the mark as well. Conceived and committed in a fantasy world, by guys who have probably never picked up
a real gun, most bank robbery movies pay little if any homage to the
realities of the modern-day bank robbery business: police response
times, dye packs, electronic tracking devices, the physical properties of
large amounts of cash, the uncontrollable vagaries of chance—the passing patrol car, the traffic jam on the escape route, whatever. In Hollywood, even the most outlandish robbery schemes work flawlessly. It
may be entertaining escapist fare when Bruce Willis and Billie Bob
Thornton do a bank lick and escape from a police cordon by staging
their own deaths with the aid of exploding blood packs, and then unzip
themselves from body bags on the way to the morgue. But it ain't bank
robbery.

Heat was actually better than most. Directed and produced by
Michael Mann, and starring Robert De Niro as the leader of a professional robbery crew (Val Kilmer, Tom Sizemore) and Al Pacino as an
obsessed LAPD Robbery-Homicide lieutenant, the film follows De Niro
and crew as they pull off a series of well-planned heists while being
relentlessly pursued by Pacino. Moody and dark, shot in deep shades of
L.A. blue, it was both an action movie and a study of the psychological
similarities between the hunter and the hunted, the professional criminal and the professional cop. And unlike most bank robbery movies,
Heat at least tried to pay attention to the details and realities of the professional robbery business.

But it was a still a movie, and I was an FBI agent who had spent
decades studying real-life bank robberies. As I watched it, I was like a
doctor watching an emergency-room show: even though I enjoyed the
movie, I couldn't help picking it apart.

For example, that opening scene where De Niro and crew smash an
armored car with a stolen semitruck and then steal a shipment of bearer
bonds? Excitingly done, but why steal bearer bonds that you're going to
have to lay off at 20 percent of face value, and leave the cash behind?
Real-life bandits don't work that way. Why use that delayed-fuse incendiary device to torch the stolen ambulance they had used as a getaway
vehicle? Yes, it makes for a satisfying film explosion, but it draws atten-

tion to the cold car you're switching to, and besides, the explosion won't necessarily destroy everything you've left behind.

And how about Al Pacino's character, the Robbery-Homicide lieutenant? Pacino's a fine actor, but your real-life RHD lieutenant is not a street detective but an administrator, a guy who spends his days behind a desk, up to his ass in paperwork. Unlike Pacino, your real-life RHD lieutenant doesn't have time to sit on stakeouts and meet with informants in dark bars at 2:00 A.M. and get into shoot-outs with bank robbers while he's also breaking up with his wife. Oh, and the $12 million in cash they stuffed into two duffel bags and carried out of the bank? Sorry, but twelve mil in standard bank denominations wouldn't fit into two duffel bags, and even if it could, each bag would weigh over 300 pounds.

But it was the climactic gun battle itself, the one described above, that really left me shaking my head. It was just too big, too dramatic, with too many rounds fired, too many cops involved. It doesn't happen that way. Over the years FBI agents and local police have gotten caught up in numerous gunfights with bank bandits, most often when the bandits walked into a staked-out bank. I'd been involved as a street agent in a stakeout shooting that left one bandit dead and two others seriously wounded, along with an unlucky civilian who got wounded in the leg in the cross-fire.

But having De Niro and crew walk into an impromptu ambush of dozens of uniformed police officers and then wage a firefight with hundreds of rounds fired? C'mon. Bank bandits aren't Delta Force commandos; they don't carry that kind of ammo. Besides, getting a dozen or two patrol cars to a single location is going to take at least ten, maybe fifteen minutes, and no bank bandits are stupid enough to spend that much time in a bank. If they do, it's not going to be a bank robbery anymore; it's going to be a hostage situation, with the bandits holed up inside and the police surrounding the building.

As good as *Heat* was overall, the gun battle scene seemed like pure fiction.

It was only later that I realized I'd been wrong.

What I didn't know, as I sat in the theater, munching popcorn and shaking my head, was that somewhere in Los Angeles two mismatched social misfits with big dreams and violent tendencies and lots of guns were watching the same movie I was. And for them, *Heat* wasn't just a movie. It was a map, a blueprint, a guidebook for the short remainder of their weird little lives.

Just over a year later they would become two of the most famous—and overrated—bank bandits in history. Dressed up in body armor and comic book–style black Ninja outfits, armed with fully automatic weapons, they would walk out of a bank and into a small army of LAPD cops. For almost forty minutes, while circling TV news helicopters captured the scene live and beamed it around the world, the two men in black would fight a ferocious gun battle with outgunned police officers, firing more than 1,000 rounds of ammunition and shooting a dozen police officers and civilians before they themselves wound up dead on the asphalt.

The shoot-out was the climax to their movie, their version of *Heat*—except that unlike De Niro and Sizemore, they acted out their roles with real bullets, and real blood, on the streets of North Hollywood.

✦ ✦ ✦

If anyone could be said to have been born to be a criminal, Larry Eugene Phillips, Jr., was probably it. After all, this was a guy who was conceived on the run from the law, and born under an aka.

He had his father to thank for it; young Larry was an acorn that hadn't fallen far from the tree. Phillips's father, Larry Senior, was a two-bit criminal with a record for a gas station robbery and, believe it or not, corpse desecration; for reasons even he probably couldn't fully explain, he and some drunken teenaged buddies had dug up a body in a Colorado cemetery and tried to cut off its head. Sent to a youth reformatory, Larry Senior had escaped and spent the next seven years on the lam, working as a printer under the alias Daniel Ira Warfel. When his son, Larry Junior, was born in L.A. in 1970, the last name on the baby boy's birth certificate was his dad's alias, Warfel.

Only later would Larry Junior learn that his real name was Phillips—although with Phillips, it was always hard to say what was real and what was not. Over his short life he would accumulate a long list of "also known as": Larry Phillips, Larry Warfel, Dennis Franks, Mark Wright, Genis Franks, Larry Martinez, Patrick Davis, Joseph Battaglia; at any given moment, he could be almost anybody.

At his daddy's knee, young Larry developed a hatred of cops, federal agents, and authority in general, counterbalanced by admiration for men who operated on the other side of the law. One of Larry's most vivid memories was from when he was six years old. FBI agents showed up at the family's house in Denver and hauled Dad away in handcuffs on a federal fugitive warrant. Larry Senior, of course, blamed the agents, not himself.

"He hated cops because of what they did to me," Larry Senior later told the *Los Angeles Times*. "He knew that every time I came in contact with police, something bad happened."

Something else "bad" happened when Larry was thirteen, and his dad got mixed up in a bone-headed counterfeiting scheme that came apart when federal agents found a bag of bogus bills with the name of Larry Senior's printing shop conveniently tucked inside. Still, Larry admired his pop, and adopted his attitudes; he became the kind of guy who never used the word "cops" without putting "fucking" in front of it.

By all accounts Larry Junior was a smart enough kid, although not a well-educated one; after moving back to Los Angeles from Colorado with his mother, he dropped out of school after the ninth grade and never went back. A devotee of muscle magazines since his early teens, he started pumping iron, dreaming of becoming the next Arnold Schwarzenegger or Hulk Hogan. Six feet tall and 210 pounds, with dark brown hair and black eyes—a legacy of his Mexican-American mother—Phillips developed the thick, sloping neck and 20-inch biceps of a professional bodybuilder, but overall he didn't have the looks or the style to make a living at it. It was another unrequited fantasy, one of many.

Honest work held no appeal, either. Dirt-poor all his life, Phillips had always nursed dreams of being a big shot, with nice clothes and cars and pockets full of money. As a teenager he would drive around the swanky sections of L.A., through Bel Air or Holmby Hills, to stare at the mansions and envy the people inside them.

"He despised being poor," his half brother would later say. "For him to see people who were wealthy, and he wasn't, he couldn't accept it. Larry didn't just want a first-class seat on an airplane; he wanted his own Learjet. He didn't just want a mansion in an expensive neighborhood, he wanted his own island, with a castle."

They were big dreams for a poor boy, the sort of dreams that found nurturing on late-night get-rich-quick TV infomercials. Phillips was especially drawn to the infomercials featuring Tom Vu, a strange Vietnamese-American man who made his televised pitches from the deck of a yacht, surrounded by babes in bikinis, exhorting his viewers to sign up for his no-capital-required, make-a-bundle-in-real-estate courses. In broken English he challenged his viewers: "You no make money with me, you a loser!" Inspired, Phillips, age twenty and with a pregnant girlfriend to take care of, decided to go into real estate.

He passed the state real estate test, but before he got his license the real estate board discovered that Phillips had a criminal record for boosting $400 worth of suits from a Sears store—suits that Phillips had thought he needed to look the part of a real estate whiz. The misdemeanor conviction, which had cost him a fine and three days in the jug, prevented him from getting a license. Phillips was furious, blaming the system, not himself, for his problems.

But he went into the real estate business anyway, setting up a shell company called Capital West Investments and using forged documents to sell phony discounted second mortgages without the property owners' knowledge. When confronted by one of his scam victims, Phillips acted the tough guy, claiming he worked for some big, bad people and telling the victim to keep his mouth shut. The victim didn't buy it—Phillips was just a kid—and called the cops. Phillips slipped away that time, but later he was busted in Orange County for a similar scam; when arrested, he was carrying a 9-mm Glock in his waistband. Phillips narrowly managed to avoid criminal prosecution, but he did wind up with a $140,000 civil judgment against him—that was never paid.

The experience didn't set him straight, though. He moved back to Colorado and started a new scam, renting out vacant houses and apartments without the owners' knowledge, and pocketing the deposit and first month's rent he collected from the unsuspecting renters before disappearing. He was busted for that one, too, and eventually he pleaded guilty to one felony count. It was a pissant crime, officially known as "larceny by trick," but then Phillips made it worse. Before he was sentenced, while he was out on bail, he went on the lam—again, like father, like son—and headed back to L.A.

In Denver, he left behind his girlfriend and their two young children, who never saw him again. But he took with him Jeanette Federico, a young woman who had known him since he was a kid, and who had a baby daughter of her own. Back in L.A., living under a variety of aliases, Phillips hooked back up with an old buddy of his—a huge, lumbering, Baby Huey–type Romanian immigrant named Emil Decebal Matasareanu.

In a sense, Matasareanu had started his early life on the run, too. His mother, Valerie, was a Romanian opera singer who defected to the West with her husband and young son while on a concert gig in Italy. Eventually the family arrived in Altadena, an L.A. suburb in the foothills of the San Gabriel Mountains, where they bought a Mediterranean-style home that they turned into a "residential board-and-care facility" for developmentally disabled young adults. State welfare agencies paid the Matasareanus an average of $2,000 per month per patient to keep them in their home.

It was a strange situation for a boy to grow up in, living and working in what was essentially a small mental institution, and Emil was a strange and unusual boy. Socially maladroit and chronically overweight—as an adult he stood six feet tall but at one point weighed in at an astonishing 340 pounds—he suffered from a mild form of epilepsy that caused blackouts. An only child, lonely and friendless, his interests centered on guns, of which he had several, and computers. After high school he got a degree in computer technology from DeVry Institute, a chain technical college that advertised heavily on late-night TV. He tried to start a computer programming business, but couldn't drum up much business and started getting deep into credit card debt. Mostly he worked around the board-and-care home under the direction of his mom—Dad was out of the picture by then—a shrill, now mostly toothless woman who nagged him relentlessly. There was never enough money, and the state inspectors were constantly on their backs, complaining about the care afforded the patients and threatening to shut the place down—which eventually they did.

At age twenty-four, Emil managed to get married, traveling to Romania and returning with a young and pleasant-looking wife, Cristina; Emil must have looked a lot more prosperous and sophisticated by Romanian standards than he did by American ones. The young couple moved in with Emil's mom and the developmentally disabled adults under her care, while Emil kept trying to scratch out a living.

Moody and brooding, he was given to depression and resentment; this was a guy who would turn a speeding ticket into proof that "the system" was out to get him. He was also capable of violent outbursts. Once he threatened an eighty-one-year-old neighbor with a chain saw in an argument over the neighbor's dog; and later, state investigators would kick him out of the board-and-care home for roughing up a patient.

Meanwhile, he was continuing his lifelong battle against obesity. After being picked on in school for most of his young life, chubby Emil, a fan of muscle magazines, had started working out at Gold's Gym in the L.A. beach community of Venice, a mecca for serious bodybuilders. He was too much the endomorph to ever get truly buffed out, but he hardened up somewhat, and his sheer bulk made him stand out.

It was at Gold's Gym in 1989 that he had first met Larry Phillips— the only friend that Emil would ever have.

Outwardly, they might have seemed mismatched—the young, buffed-out hustler and the older, obese computer geek—but actually they had a lot in common. They both came from strange, disjointed families, both had wives and kids that they really couldn't support. Both were failures in business—and for Phillips, a failure in two-bit crime as well. They were immature, self-centered, given to fantasies of muscles and money and power; they loved playing video games and watching action movies, and taking their guns out to the mountains to squeeze off rounds. They were the sort of guys who read *Soldier of Fortune* magazine and survivalist manuals, guys who dreamed of becoming mercenaries or professional hit men—or armed robbers. And they both nurtured boiling resentments against representatives of "the system"—cops, federal agents, state inspectors, the real estate licensing board, prosecutors, judges, all the people who had picked on them and kept them down. They hated them all.

Separately, they might never have become a real danger. Despite his criminal record, Phillips had never impressed anyone as a violent type, and despite his violent outbursts, Matasareanu had never impressed anyone as a truly criminal type. But together they fed each other's fantasies and resentments, and inspired each other's dreams and hatreds. As a pair, they were more dangerous, and more evil, than the sum of their parts.

People who knew them later assumed that it was Phillips, the natural leader of the two, who first came up with the idea, but no one knows for sure. Somehow, by 1993 they had decided that the path to success didn't lie in real estate or computer programming or running a group home or pulling off two-bit white-collar scams. If they wanted big money, they were going to have to take it.

So they set out to become bandits—just like in the movies.

✦　✦　✦

They pulled their first job in Littleton, Colorado, Phillips's old stomping grounds, in 1993, hitting a Wells Fargo armored truck that was making a delivery to a bank. Armed with a handgun and a rifle, their faces dusted with theatrical makeup to make them appear older, they had accosted the armored truck hopper at gunpoint, grabbed a bag containing $23,000 in cash, and taken off in a stolen getaway car.

It wasn't exactly a masterpiece of crime. They let the hopper walk into the bank with $192,000 in fresh, crisp, shrink-wrapped bills, and then hit him on the way out when he was carrying nothing but "discard cash"—worn or mutilated bills that the bank was returning to the Federal Reserve to be exchanged and then destroyed. I can almost see the "aw shit" looks on their faces when they opened the bag and found nothing but bills so old and limp that they got probably got an argument from the clerk at the 7-Eleven every time they tried to spend one.

They might have tried to improve their luck soon after—$23,000 wouldn't have lasted them very long—except that they got caught playing soldier.

In October 1993, a few months after the Colorado heist, a cop in Glendale, a suburb just north of Los Angeles, pulled over a maroon T-bird for speeding. Phillips was driving, Matasareanu was in the passenger seat; it was ten o'clock at night. It was the standard drill: The cop saunters up to the window, asks for license and registration. But even when it served his purpose, Phillips couldn't hide his contempt for cops of every stripe.

Don't have it, Phillips tells him.

What's your name, then? the cop says.

I'd rather not say, Phillips tells him.

You'd rather not say? The cop backs up, hand on his service weapon. Okay, buddy, out of the car. He pats Phillips down and finds a 9-mm Glock in his waistband. He calls for backup, and pretty soon Phillips and Matasareanu both have their hands in the air. The cops toss the car and—holy shit!—they find an arsenal right out of *Soldier of Fortune*: a

.45-caliber semiautomatic pistol, a MAC-90 semiauto assault rifle, an AK-47, two black ski masks, two sets of body armor, police scanners, stopwatches, three sets of California plates, smoke grenades, spray-on gray hair coloring, hairpieces, and more than 2,500 rounds of ammo in various calibers. They also find on Phillips a California driver's license identifying him as one Dennis Franks.

It was a classic "robbery kit," and Phillips and Matasareanu were immediately arrested on suspicion of robbery—even though the police had no idea what, if anything, they had robbed. Their booking mug shots show Phillips, six feet and 210 pounds, with close-set, guarded brown eyes and buffed-out shoulders that stretch the limit of his jail coveralls. Matasareanu, six feet and a whopping 340 pounds, with greasy long hair and hazel eyes, looks like a little kid, even though at twenty-seven he's four years older than Phillips.

Why they were driving around with all that stuff stashed in the trunk, just waiting for some suspicious cop to find it, is hard to figure; it wasn't as if they were on their way to hit a bank or an armored car—not at ten o'clock at night. Professionals would have kept that stuff stashed at home until they were ready to use it; but Phillips and Matasareanu weren't professionals.

The mistake should have been enough to put Phillips, at least, on ice for the next two or three years. Although at the time no one had connected him or Matasareanu to the Denver armored car job, Phillips already had the phony rentals felony conviction and fugitive warrant from Colorado hanging over his head; a simple check of the NCIC (National Crime Information Center) computers after the Glendale arrest should have kicked it out.

But somehow the Colorado warrant hadn't made it into the NCIC. And when the Glendale cops sat down with the L.A. County District Attorney's office and tried to figure out what to formally charge these guys with—the feeling was, with all that stuff in the car they had to be guilty of something—the most they could come up with were some low-level conspiracy and weapons charges.

And even those charges eventually got bargained down in the inevitable winnowing process of an overworked justice system. Matasareanu copped to weapons charges and got seventy-one days in jail with three years probation. Phillips finally pleaded guilty to felony "false personation" and carrying a concealed weapon charges; he got three years probation and ninety-nine days in jail. During his stretch in custody, Phillips married Jeanette Federico, who at the time was nine months pregnant with his son. The ceremony was performed by a judge in a Pasadena courtroom; Phillips honeymooned alone in Men's Central Jail.

And here's the kicker: After their release, a judge ordered the Glendale Police Department to give Phillips and Matasareanu most of their stuff back: the body armor, the ammo, the ski masks, even most of the guns. It makes you wonder if justice is not only blind but stupid.

Still, the Glendale arrest seemed to give pause to Matasareanu, if not Phillips. His mother, the dominant woman in his life, had never liked Larry Phillips, and over the next several months she relentlessly nagged her boy to break away from his friend. Here he is, twenty-seven years old, with a wife and two kids, and his mother is treating him like he's six—although her instincts about Phillips were right. Finally, Emil promised his mother that he wouldn't see Phillips anymore. But he was lying; he kept seeing his buddy on the sly.

In the meantime, state inspectors ordered Emil out of Valerie's group home after he roughed up a patient in a fit of anger. His share of the cash from the Denver armored car robbery, which wasn't much to begin with, was long gone. He and his family moved into a rental house in Pasadena, paid for with money from Mom from a refinancing on the group home residence.

Phillips, for his part, went back to his little real estate business, peddling discount second mortgages—some legit, some not, although he wasn't caught for it. He and the missus and their two young children (their son and her daughter by a previous relationship) were living in an apartment on Coldwater Canyon Avenue in the San Fernando Valley. They'd rented it under the name of Lawrence, although they were also using the names Joseph and Madeline Battaglia; Phillips was so secretive that even Emil's wife, Cristina, thought Phillips's wife's name was Madeline.

As far as the county probation office knew, Phillips and Matasareanu were staying out of trouble. But Phillips, especially, was congenitally unable to go straight, and where Phillips went, Matasareanu was sure to follow.

This time, though, they wouldn't be satisfied simply with an amateurish, bungling robbery like the one in Colorado. This time they turned it into an amateurish, cold-blooded murder.

On June 14, 1995, a Brinks armored truck was making its regular route stop at a Bank of America on Roscoe Boulevard in Canoga Park. The hopper, a man named Herman Cook, had just walked out of the bank carrying a bag of cash and opened the side door of the armored truck. Suddenly Phillips and Matasareanu, both armed with .223-caliber assault weapons, rose up from behind a 4-foot-high concrete block wall that lined the bank parking lot and started firing armor-piercing bullets at him. There was no warning, no "Don't move!", no "This is a robbery!" The armor-piercing rounds, made of jacketed tungsten-carbide, not lead, cut through Cook's protective vest like it was butter. He probably never even knew what hit him.

Struck three times, Cook fell to the ground, mortally wounded; he would die at a hospital several hours later. When Cook fell, Phillips, wearing body armor but no mask, hopped over the wall and ran toward the armored truck. Locked inside the front cab of the armored truck, the driver drew his pistol and started firing at Phillips through one of the gunports in the door.

Meanwhile, Matasareanu, wearing a mask and body armor under a windbreaker, remained behind the wall, still firing armor-piercing .223 rounds at the armored car. The rounds easily penetrated the inch-thick Plexiglas truck window, wounding the driver. With the driver down, Phillips stepped over Cook's body, reached into the open side door of the armored truck, and grabbed the bag containing $122,000 in cash before he and Matasareanu ran to a nearby Chevy Celebrity and took off.

It was a successful robbery, in that Phillips and Matasareanu got away with the money—far more than they'd gotten in the Colorado heist. But it was also brutal and utterly without finesse, nothing more than a senseless bushwhacking and cold-blooded murder of a good man. Herman Dwight Cook was a soft-spoken fifty-one-year-old man who loved to hunt and fish, and read western novels, a man whose life centered on his wife and their two teenaged children. An employee at a San Fernando Valley aerospace firm, he'd been caught in the defense industry downturn of the early 1990s and, like many others, was laid off. To make ends meet, Cook had taken a stop-gap job as an armored car guard with Brinks, protecting other people's money. While it didn't pay much—at the time, armored car guards were starting at about nine bucks an hour—he liked the work. After five years on the job, he was robbed one time—the day he was murdered.

It was a contemptible crime. I'd encountered plenty of professional bandits who would kill if they thought they had to, if a guard drew on them or if a victim resisted. But Phillips and Matasareanu weren't forced by changing circumstance to shoot Herman Cook; they had planned it that way from the start.

By long-standing agreement, the FBI and the LAPD's Robbery-Homicide Division shared jurisdiction on armored car heists inside the L.A. city limits, just as we did bank robberies in the city—and since this one had happened outside a bank, it was immediately on the center of my radar screen. Unfortunately, no one had gotten a plate number on the getaway Chevy, and although we papered the entire West with tele-types and bulletins, looking for any crimes with a similar M.O., noth-ing kicked back. (The Colorado armored car heist was too old to jog anybody's memory, and the Glendale arrest was a run-of-the-mill local weapons case that didn't ring anybody's bell.)

The well-publicized $100,000 reward offered by Brinks and Bank of America didn't help, either—retrospectively, for obvious reasons. Rewards work in direct proportion to how talkative the criminal is, and how many friends he has. A primary purpose of a reward is to make greed overcome friendship, and inspire a friend or relative to drop that all-important dime. But Phillips and Matasareanu were loners, with no friends except each other; even their wives honestly didn't know what they were up to. The hundred thousand could have been $100 million and it probably wouldn't have made any difference.

But we still wanted these guys badly; even without the murder of Herman Cook, this would have been a high-profile crime. The body armor, the assault weapons, the armor-piercing rounds, the willingness, even eagerness to shoot first and rob later—it was excessive for the task at hand. And the balls-out boldness of the robbery was scary. It was car-ried off in broad daylight, in front of a dozen witnesses who were in the bank parking lot or at the gas station next door. At one point, as he was firing from behind the low wall, Matasareanu had turned to the civil-ians at the gas station and shouted, "Get down and don't look!" before he started firing at the armored truck again.

Given the weaponry involved, and because of occurrence of several such incidents in the Midwest and Northwest, I couldn't discount the possibility that Phillips and Matasareanu were urban terrorists or right-wing militia types, robbing to finance their political movements.

But based on my experience and intuition, I wasn't convinced. I had no idea who they were, not yet, but I suspected that these guys weren't just in it for the money but for the thrill of the thing, the sheer joy of the sound of gunfire and the acrid smell of cordite, the boyish excitement of playing commando with an audience watching. If my instincts were correct, Phillips and Matasareanu were doubly dangerous. Guys who are in it for the money are to some extent predictable: they rob when they need the dough, and they'll do it the easiest and most effective way they can. But thrill bandits, guys who are in it for the fun, are capable of almost anything.

And there was something else. They had shot Herman Cook without warning, for no good reason, and yet they hadn't harmed any of the civilian witnesses, even the ones who got a good look at them; they hadn't even pointed their weapons at them. Cook wasn't a cop, of course, but he was wearing a uniform. Was it the uniform they were shooting at? In their minds, did they see civilians as bystanders, but uniforms as open game?

In the months ahead, Phillips and Matasareanu would prove my hunches right. Their contempt for uniforms—which is to say, cops—would become dangerously apparent. And their robberies would grow increasingly strange, even spooky: robberies that defied logic and common sense. Rather than get better at their profession, they got worse. It was as if they were following some kind of weird scenario where the robberies were ends in themselves, and the money was secondary.

I didn't make the connection until later, and while I can't prove it, I knew it in my bones. From that point on, these odd young misfits were no longer modeling themselves after movie bandits and action figures in general, but after a particular movie.

From now on, they would be acting out their favorite scenes from *Heat*.

They had watched it again and again, first in the theater, later on videocassette. After they were dead, amid all the other evidence of their violent temperaments and childish fantasies—the exotic weapons and ammo, the Ninja outfits, the bodybuilding magazines and survivalist books—FBI agents and cops who were searching their homes would find several VHS tapes of *Heat*. A source would later describe it as, hands down, "their all-time favorite movie."

I can almost see them watching it in the movie theater, munching their popcorn—double butter for Matasareanu—with Phillips imagining himself as the dark, cool, steely-eyed Robert De Niro, Matasareanu picturing himself as Tom Sizemore, De Niro's big, burly, affable-but-violent right-hand man. I want to be like him, they're thinking; I want to be just like him.

It seems ridiculous: two grown men—Phillips was twenty-five, Matasareanu twenty-nine—men who have already committed murder, sitting in the dark and fantasizing over a movie. But Phillips was a guy who dreamed of Learjets and islands and castles, and Matasareanu a man everybody agreed had the social and emotional maturity of a teenager. They were guys who spent their days and nights mooning over muscle magazines and dropping quarters in video arcades, zapping space invaders next to thirteen-year-olds. Let's face it, the prisons of America are full to bursting with childish men, there for committing stupid, puerile crimes.

I'm not suggesting that *Heat* sent Phillips and Matasareanu down the road to robbery and murder; they had hit that highway long before the movie came out. And I've never believed that violent movies are *the* root cause, or even *a* root cause, of violence and crime by anyone.

But no matter who we are—cops, FBI agents, husbands, wives, lovers, bandits, whatever—movies and popular culture subtly affect us, help determine how we dress, how we talk, what we think is glamorous or romantic or exciting. And throughout my career I'd seen case after case where a movie about bank robbery inspired the weak of mind, the overactive of imagination, and the already criminally inclined to try to play out in real life what they had seen on film, to model themselves after the "heroes" up on the screen.

There were the young gang-bangers from South Central L.A. who admitted that they had decided to hit a bank after watching a videotape of *Set It Off*, a 1996 release starring Queen Latifah, Jada Pinkett, and Elise Kimberly as three South Central L.A. women who try to escape the ghetto by staging a series of takeover bank robberies. As in the movie, the gang-bangers stormed into the bank with guns blazing; unlike in the movie, the poor woman they shot down and killed in front of her ten-year-old son was a real person.

Or take for example the husband-and-wife team in Las Vegas who obsessively watched *Bonnie and Clyde* on the home VCR. Over the course of a year they drove their BMW down to Los Angeles fourteen times to commit armed bank robberies, a string of cross-border crimes that ultimately ended in a highway gun battle that left both car and bandits riddled with bullets.

Then there was the nineteen-year-old former high school cheerleader in Orange County who, with her equally young and foolish husband, decided to rob a bank using the 1991 movie *Point Break*—starring Patrick Swayze as the leader of a bunch of surfers who exploit bank robberies to finance their round-the-world surfing safaris, and Keanu Reeves as an FBI agent who is pursuing them—as a guide.

I knew from painful personal experience that as a bank robbery training film, this was a particularly unfortunate choice. Before *Point Break* was filmed, I was told by the Special Agent in Charge to take Keanu Reeves, a pleasant but somewhat spacey young man, under my wing and give him some pointers on how to portray an FBI agent chasing bank robbers. Unfortunately, none of those pointers came within a million miles of the finished film.

In real life, FBI agents do not actively participate in armed bank robberies in order to infiltrate a bank robbery crew. And unlike Special Agent Keanu Reeves, seldom does a real FBI agent jump out of a plane—without a parachute—to pursue a fleeing bank bandit. For weeks after *Point Break* premiered, I had to endure a daily ration of grief from my bank squad buddies, who held me personally responsible for what surely was one of the dumbest bank robbery movies ever made.

What works on the screen doesn't necessarily work in real life. Certainly this was true with Phillips and Matasareanu's next armored car job.

On March 27, 1996, shortly after 9:30 A.M., a Brinks armored truck with a driver in front and two armed guards in the rear compartment was heading north on Fallbrook Avenue in the San Fernando Valley after making a cash delivery at a Bank of America. Nothing unusual, just the standard run. The armored truck driver didn't pay much attention to the red Ford Econoline van heading toward him in the opposing traffic—or at least he didn't pay much attention until the passenger in the red van, wearing a black ski mask and holding an assault rifle, leaned out from the open passenger side window and let loose a half dozen shots: *Bam! Bam! Bam! Bam! Bam! Bam!*

This guy is a good shot. The van is moving at about 30 mph, the armored truck is moving at about the same speed in the opposite direction, and still the shooter hits the truck with five armor-piercing rounds. Three of them penetrate the windshield of the armored truck and then rip through the armor plating inside, wounding the driver with flying glass and metal shards. But the armored truck keeps going, the wounded driver still at the wheel, so the van turns and starts chasing it—in broad daylight on a busy urban street.

Finally, after several blocks, the van breaks off the chase; the bandits had probably guessed, correctly, that the armored car driver had radioed in, and that the cops would be on the way. The bandits pull the van into an alley and light a crude timed incendiary device—a jug of gasoline with a fuse made out of matchheads—in the back and then race up the alley, carrying their guns with them, to a getaway car they have stashed there. Moments later the gasoline goes up and the van bursts into flames—just like the opening scene of *Heat*. Later, we found a charred police radio scanner and a battery-powered bullhorn left behind in the van.

We knew these were the same guys who had killed Herman Cook; the recovered rounds from the armored truck told us that much. And now the question for us was: What in the world were these men thinking? How could they have possibly believed that this lame-brained scheme was going to work?

Consider: These are two guys in a 3,000-pound van trying to take down three armed guards in a moving 10,000-pound armored truck. They can't stop the truck by ramming it, like the bandits in *Heat*: the armored truck would have rolled over the van like an SUV rolling over a squirrel. Sure, if they had killed or seriously wounded the driver, as they tried to do, that would have stopped the truck. But then what? How do they get inside to get the money? They can't blow the doors with an explosive shape charge, like the bandits in *Heat* had—Phillips and Matasareanu didn't have the training, or equipment, for anything like that.

The only thing we could figure, based on what they left behind in the van, was that they had planned to kill or disable the driver and then stand outside the truck and use the bullhorn to order the guards in back to open up—and if they didn't open up, our guys would riddle the Plexiglass windows with armor-piercing rounds.

It was going to be a robbery by bullhorn.

Pause for a moment and savor the idiocy of that picture: It's nine-thirty in the morning, on a busy city street, and our guys are going to be standing there in black ski masks next to a bullet-riddled armored car, using a battery-powered bullhorn audible over a six-block radius to scream at the armed men inside—who as far as they know may already be dead or incapacitated from the rounds they've already fired—"*Open the door and come out with your hands up or we'll shoot!*"

And if they don't come out, if the guards stick shotguns out the gunports and start blasting away, what are they going to do? Fire up the truck? Kill the guards? That's fine, you geniuses. But then who's going to open the goddam door? And meanwhile, dozens of civilian witnesses are driving by, almost every one of whom has a cell phone fully capable of reaching 911. Hell, our guys wouldn't have needed that police scanner to track the approach of responding police cars; they could have simply listened as the sound of screaming sirens came closer.

It was worse than amateurish; it was more a thrill game than a serious attempt at robbery, more a wild E-ticket ride than a rational crime. It was like something out of . . . a movie.

In one sense, Phillips and Matasareanu had been lucky. Nobody got a description or a plate number on the getaway car they had stashed in the alley, and except for the bullhorn and the scanner, the torched van didn't produce any clues.

But they hadn't gotten any money; as armored car robbers go, these guys were having a bad career. In three armored car attacks over three years, they had netted a grand total of $145,000—roughly twenty-four grand apiece per year. By the standards of that criminal genre it was a chump change, "You want fries with that?" level of income. Certainly it wasn't worth the risks they had taken, not to mention the loss of an innocent man's life.

Nevertheless, if they'd been ordinary bandits, they probably would have stuck with armored car jobs. Robbers, however inept they may be, tend to stay with what they know, or think they know.

But our guys weren't ordinary bandits. And now, just like the crew in *Heat*, who went from armored car jobs to bank jobs, it was time for Phillips and Matasareanu to move on to the next scene.

✦ ✦ ✦

Monsters, some of the victims called them. Huge, ski-masked, black-clad, lumbering monsters, like something out of a horror movie.

They had strolled into the Bank of America in Van Nuys, in the San Fernando Valley northwest of downtown L.A., just after 10:00 A.M. on May 2, 1996, five weeks after the botched armored car hit. Both carried holstered pistols and AK-47–style assault rifles with folding metal stocks and 75-round drum magazines; both wore black ski masks with shades underneath to hide their eyes, and they had stopwatches sewn into the wrists of their black gloves—just like the crew in *Heat*. Big men to begin with, with the body armor and ammo-bearing "combat vests" they wore under windbreaker-type jackets, the vests laden with extra drum magazines, they looked like giants.

"All you motherfuckers hit the floor!" Phillips yelled, sweeping the barrel of the AK-47 back and forth. "Get on the fucking floor or we'll kill you!"

Some thirty people—employees, customers, and customers' children—were in the bank. As they dropped to the floor, Matasareanu walked up to the Plexiglas bandit barrier door and sprayed it with fully automatic fire. More than forty .223-caliber armor-piercing bullets cut through the Plexiglas like cheese and destroyed the locking mechanism. Matasareanu then easily kicked in the door.

At the sound of the gunfire, people started screaming and children started wailing. Mothers on the cold tile floor were dragging their children under their bodies, trying to shield them, while Phillips shouted: "Shut up! Shut those fucking kids up!" Both bandits went behind the counter and screamed at the tellers lying on the floor: "Where's the manager? Don't make us kill you!" The branch manager, a woman, raised a hand, and the bandits pulled her to her feet. They dragged her to the vault, forcing her to open the day gate.

"Where's the money Brinks just delivered? Don't make us kill you!"

The manager motioned to the double-locked steel vault boxes, called Burgher boxes, where that morning's armored car cash shipment had been broken down and stored. The manager started unlocking them.

While Matasareanu stayed in the vault, loading the cash into a large duffel bag he had brought with him, Phillips went back out and patrolled the lobby, slowly walking back and forth and shouting at the whimpering victims to "Shut the fuck up!" For the victims proned out on the floor and praying for their lives, it seemed to last forever.

Finally Matasareanu came out of the vault, dragging the bulging duffel bag behind him, and both bandits headed out the door—but slowly, deliberately, as if they weren't in any particular hurry. In the parking lot there was a Chevrolet Celebrity, unoccupied, with the motor idling and the driver's side door open. It was the same Chevy they'd used in the first L.A. armored car job, now repainted white; they must have figured it was their lucky getaway car, because they would use it in every one of their robberies. They tossed the duffel bag in the back, climbed in, and slowly drove away.

As soon as the call came in, we knew they were our armored car bandits, now moving up to bank robbery; the weapons, the outfits, the car, and the physical descriptions made that clear. And in contrast to their armored car jobs, they had pulled off an excellent score, getting away with $750,048 in cash, one of the biggest takes ever in an L.A. bank robbery.

But as in the armored car jobs, Phillips and Matasareanu had made mistakes—strange, frightening, spooky mistakes that defied all logic.

There was the getaway car, for one thing, the white Chevy left idling in the parking lot. A truly professional crew would have had a getaway driver, and if for some reason they couldn't find one, pros never would have left a car with the keys in it and the engine running. This is L.A.: there are thieves everywhere, car thieves included. The last thing you want to do is come out of a bank and find yourself afoot.

There was also the ammo situation. From the surveillance photos, we could see that in addition to the 75-round drums locked into their assault rifles, each of these guys was carrying two or three extra drums attached to their combat vests. Add to that the body armor, the sidearms, and the rifles themselves, and these guys were each carrying more than 60 pounds of extra weight when they walked into the bank. It was like doing a robbery carrying a fully loaded military field pack. What was the point of all that weight and ammo?

But the car and the surplus ammo were insignificant compared with the really spooky thing about this bank lick.

A video surveillance camera with date-time capability on an ATM outside the bank had caught a shot of the bandits entering and a shot of them exiting. When I first saw the recorded times of both shots, I assumed the video camera was malfunctioning. But the timer was accurate: it indicated that our bandits had spent six minutes inside the bank.

Six minutes.

It doesn't sound like much time, but in the context of a bank robbery it's an eternity. If you don't think so, take a look at the clock on the wall and watch as the second hand sweeps slowly around the face, six times. Think about how long that really is, and what can happen in that amount of time. Every professional bank robber—and even most amateurs—knows that the instant it becomes clear a robbery is taking place, someone in that bank is going to hit a two-eleven silent alarm button. No matter much how much you shout, no matter how much you threaten, there's no way to stop it; there are just too many alarm buttons, and too many people with access to them, especially since the advent of the remote alarms bank employees carry with them. Even if by some miracle nobody hits a silent alarm, there's no way for the bank robber to know that. You damn well better assume the alarm has gone out.

And from that moment you have 60 to 120 seconds, tops, of relative safety before the alarm can go to the bank's central security office and then be forwarded to the appropriate local police dispatcher, who will put out a two-eleven-in-progress call to police patrol cars. How soon a black-and-white arrives on the scene after that is a matter of luck; it can be ten seconds if a unit happens to be close by, or ten minutes if all the available units are in another sector or tied up on calls. But every second past two minutes that you stay inside the bank takes you deeper and deeper into the danger zone and makes it more likely that you're going to run into armed police and have to either give it up or try to shoot your way out—and no rational bank robbery crew wants to shoot it out with cops. It's dangerous, and bad for business.

In a way, time is a bank's best defense against robberies—or at least against high-loss robberies. That's why they spread their cash out in locked boxes inside the vault, because it will take robbers too much time to gather it all—more time than any rational robber would be willing to invest. Rational robbers wouldn't have had time to load up anywhere near the three quarters of a million these guys got.

But Phillips and Matasareanu weren't rational robbers; they weren't worried about time. They had stopwatches to count down the seconds, but they never even looked at them; the watches seemed to function primarily as fashion accessories. In the bank, the two bandits were utterly unhurried, moving virtually in slow motion. It was a miracle of sorts that the police response had been so slow, that the first black-and-white didn't get to the bank until after the bandits were gone. If a couple of cops had arrived any earlier, with just pistols against body armor and automatic weapons and men who were demonstrably willing to kill, they would have been dead on the ground.

By bank robbery standards, the whole thing was insane—so insane, in fact, that we wondered if a certifiably insane former bank robber had played a role in it. Remember the West Hills Bandits, the "Messengers from God" who ran the home fudge-making business and took to robbing banks to finance Armageddon against the Luciferians? The guys who had an underground bunker full of assault weapons and 27,000 rounds of ammo? As you'll recall, one of them, James McGrath, went down for fifteen years in prison, but the other, Gilbert Michaels, was ruled mentally incompetent and was released under psychiatric supervision. We hadn't heard from him since, but given the firepower in this bank job and the armored car robberies, and the insane way the robbers were acting, we wondered if crazy Gilbert had come out of retirement and was back to battle the Luciferians once again.

But after we put him under close surveillance for a week, we had to rule him out. Poor old Gilbert was living in a community mental health center, spending his days feeding the ducks at a local park and wandering around the neighborhood babbling to himself. He really didn't have the wherewithal to be pulling these bank and armored car jobs—and besides, he just didn't seem to fit the profile in this case. Gilbert and McGrath had always been polite during their bank robberies, calling out, "Thanks everybody!" as they made their getaway; there was none of the foul language that these guys were fond of. More important, as crazy as Gilbert and his partner had been, they'd never been so crazy as to spend more than 120 seconds in a bank.

Even though Gilbert didn't work out, we still figured we'd have some time to work this case, maybe to find these guys before something really bad happened. After all, your average bank robbers, fresh off a three quarters of a million dollar score, are going to lie low for a while and enjoy their money. No matter how free you are with a buck, it's going to take a while to burn through that kind of dough.

But again, Phillips and Matasareanu were working against the norm. Just four weeks after the Bank of America job, they hit another B of A on Roscoe Boulevard in Canoga Park—the same bank where they had gunned down the Brinks courier Herman Cook a year earlier.

It was the same drill as the first bank robbery: ski masks, body armor, AK-47s, tons of ammo, *Heat*-style stopwatches, everybody on the floor, then a burst of automatic fire at the door to the Plexiglas bandit barrier, people screaming, and the bandits telling them to shut up or be killed. They forced the manager and assistant manager to open the vault and the reserve cash boxes and then loaded the money into a collapsible suitcase and walked out, this time with $795,000. They fled in the same white Chevy that was sitting in the parking lot with its motor running. Two bank employees had been cut by flying Plexiglas shards, and one older customer who was lying on the floor with his dog on a leash next to him was slightly injured when he desperately tried to keep the terrified dog from barking at the robbers and the dog bit him on the hand.

It had been a terrifying experience for everyone in the bank. When I got there twenty minutes later, the smell of gunpowder still hung heavily in the air and the floor was carpeted with expended brass cartridges. The victims were still crying and hugging each other in terror and relief.

Once again, everybody noticed how strange these guys were, how slowly they moved, almost like robots; even when they were cursing at them, the robbers' voices sounded dull, unexcited, lifeless, almost as if they weren't connected to what was going on. A witness outside the bank also noticed that as they were pulling slowly out of the parking lot in the white Chevy, still wearing their black ski masks, the driver was careful to put on his turn signal when they turned right onto Winnetka Avenue.

Imagine it. These guys are decked out like Ninja warriors, armed to the teeth, they've just robbed a bank in broad daylight—and they're careful not to violate the Vehicle Code as they're making their getaway.

And once again, one factor in the bank robbery defied any rational explanation: This time, Phillips and Matasareanu had spent *eight full minutes in the bank.*

In thirty years of chasing bank robbers, I had never seen anything like it. It was as if they *wanted* the police to show up, *wanted* to get into a shoot-out with them, *wanted* to cap off their bank robbery by capping a couple of cops—for the fun of it, the thrill of it.

Fortunately in this case, Los Angeles is a sprawling city, with police units spread thinly over a wide geographic area, especially during the generally low-crime day shift. It was just the luck of the draw that at this particular time the nearest black-and-white was miles away, and didn't arrive at the bank until the bandits were already heading out the back door, unseen, and making their getaway.

But that sort of luck couldn't hold. If these bank robberies kept up, sooner or later a couple of cops were going to walk into these guys— and given the bandits' superior firepower, chances were the cops would lose. We couldn't just wait around and let that happen.

Finally, the FBI and the LAPD decided to set up one of the most ambitious bank stakeout efforts ever attempted.

In the old days we would have put undercover teams inside the banks, posing as loan officers or tellers, with shotguns ready at hand, and when the bandits came we'd give them a nanosecond to surrender and then blow them away. I'd been involved in one such stakeout in 1970 that left a crew called the Dashiki Bandits bleeding on the linoleum. It was an effective technique, but in modern times it was considered too dangerous for bank employees and customers—not to mention too likely to produce lawsuits from customers emotionally traumatized by having some bank bandit's blood splattered all over them.

Instead, we would put rolling surveillance teams outside banks all across the San Fernando Valley, backed up by SWAT teams from both agencies and helicopter air support. The rolling surveillance teams would cruise around the targeted banks and try to spot the bandits before they entered, and then have SWAT teams with body armor and heavy weapons take them down when they came out.

It wasn't an ideal situation. Since there probably wouldn't be enough time to get everybody in place to confront the bandits before they got into the bank, by necessity we'd most likely have to let the robbery go down, with all the potential dangers that involved for the people inside—and we might wind up getting sued for that, too. But it was the best anybody could do.

Now the question was, which banks do we surveil? There are dozens upon dozens of banks in the San Fernando Valley; we couldn't cover them all. We'd have to narrow it down to the most likely targets. That was where I came in.

With only two bank robberies under their belts, these bandits hadn't had time to establish much of a pattern. And they'd already exhibited unpredictable, even aberrant behavior in their robberies, which made them especially hard to predict. Still, it appeared that they preferred the Bank of America, specifically larger branches equipped with bandit barriers; they probably assumed, with some justification, that the bigger and more secure the bank, the more cash there would be on hand. There were fourteen banks in the Valley that fit that profile; those were the ones we'd surveil most intensely.

But when would they hit? With junkies, you can figure the time between robberies: they'll rob when they need their next fix. Even pro-fessional bandits sometimes take on kind of a rough schedule, depend-ing on how fast they run through money. But with these guys there was no telling.

Still, they'd waited a month between their two robberies; another month until the next one was as good a guess as any.

So, four weeks after the second Bank of America robbery, more than a hundred FBI agents and LAPD officers fanned out through the San Fernando Valley to sit on our targeted banks. They sweated in the backs of vans, circled the banks all day in Corvettes or old station wagons, stood around the SWAT teams' command post, suited up and ready. Civilians and the news media, if they'd heard about it, which of course they didn't, would have been amazed at the army of law enforcement deployed in their midst. We were confident that if our bandits hit any of our targeted banks, they would wind up arrested, or dead.

But they didn't. Day after day went by, with nothing.

No large-scale stakeout operation can continue indefinitely. With every passing day without success, the guys behind the desks at the FBI field office or Parker Center start to wring their hands and calculate the man-hours and fret about overtime costs; in law enforcement, the budget trumps patience every time. After two weeks, the higher-ups pulled the plug.

It was frustrating, but in hindsight it was the right decision. As it turned out, we had picked exactly the right bank to surveil—the Bank of America in the 6600 block of Laurel Canyon Boulevard in North Hollywood. We were just doing it at the wrong time.

What we didn't know, couldn't have known, is that while we were busy staking out the banks, one of our bank robbers was having a bad headache.

✦ ✦ ✦

After the two Bank of America robberies, Phillips and Matasareanu were sitting on just over $1.5 million in cash. Literally sitting in it.

Actually, there's not much else you can do with that kind of cash. In large quantities, cash is pretty hard to spend, given the fact that federal anti–money-laundering laws require the reporting of all cash transactions over $10,000; you certainly can't deposit a million cash bucks in a bank account without somebody wondering where the hell you got it. You can't buy a house with cash, can't invest it in the stock market; it's not going to get you a platinum credit card, at least not a legitimate one. Professional criminals, guys with organized crime or underworld connections, would have access to money-laundering operations, ways to convert the paper into seemingly legitimate numbers in a financial account and then move it offshore or plow it into real estate or stocks. But Phillips and Matasareanu didn't have those kinds of contacts or organization. They were loners, trusting only each other.

It was ironic. Phillips had always wanted to be rich, to have the things that rich people had—and more. But with all the cash he had, he still couldn't have most of the big-ticket items that money can buy. Island and castle purchases generally are handled by check.

So they put the cash in a home safe and lived well, but not big. Phillips bought nice suits, a Rolex watch, a diamond ring—the small, flashy outward signs of success. They kept the house Emil had been renting in Granada Hills as a kind of staging area, a place to stash their weapons, ammo, and the white Chevy Celebrity they'd used in the robberies. According to neighbors, they were occasionally joined there by women not their wives, prostitutes most likely; Emil especially wasn't exactly a babe magnet.

Meanwhile, they moved their families farther out into the suburbs, and a little up in the world. Matasareanu rented a nice house in Rowland Heights, a middle-class area in the San Gabriel Valley, for himself and his family. Phillips rented a pleasant but not ostentatious house for $2,000 a month in Anaheim Hills in Orange County—he and Jeanette called themselves Patrick and Sandra Davis on the lease—and enrolled Jeanette's daughter in a $5,000-a-year private school. Phillips and Matasareanu both paid all of their bills with money orders, and kept to themselves. They were the quiet bank robbers living next door.

They might have hit another bank sooner, might have walked into one of our stakeouts, except for Matasareanu's headaches. All his life he had suffered from seizures, small fadeouts and blackouts that came suddenly, without warning. Doctors had prescribed phenobarbital, but Matasareanu refused to take the medication—although, as we'll see, the phenobarbital came in handy for other purposes.

In the weeks after the May bank robberies, Matasareanu was suffering from a series of blinding headaches and fadeouts. At the end of June 1996, while we were staking out the banks in the San Fernando Valley, Matasareanu had taken his wife out for dinner at a Denny's—he's got three quarters of a mil in cash, and Mr. Big Spender takes the wife to Denny's—when he suddenly collapsed, out cold. Paramedics showed up and transported him to a hospital, where a CAT scan showed a right temporal hematoma, a blood-filled swelling in the brain. Doctors strongly recommended surgery to relieve the pressure, but Matasareanu, childish as ever, blew them off, checking out of the hospital against the doctor's advice.

But the headaches and fadeouts continued, and finally a neurosurgeon convinced him that if he didn't get the surgery, his next coma might be his last.

Of course, Matasareanu didn't have any health insurance; he didn't even give the doctor or the hospital his real name. But he gave them a $15,000 down payment in money orders on the $45,000 procedure, and foolishly, the hospital and the doctor trusted him for the rest. In July, the neurosurgeon drilled a hole in his skull and repaired the lesion on his brain. Matasareanu spent a week in the hospital recovering from the operation, with his mom, who claimed to be his aunt, sleeping in the room with him. After he checked out, Matasareanu's doctor prescribed Dilantin to control any future seizures, but Matasareanu again refused to take his meds, and the seizures continued. The doctor described his patient as "intelligent but extremely immature." He was also cheap; he stiffed the doctor and the hospital on the remainder of his bill, and finally the account was turned over to a collection agency. It was, of course, never paid.

The upshot was that for months, until he finally got straight on his meds and got the seizures under control, Matasareanu was in no shape to do a bank lick—and Phillips had no one else he could depend on. So they waited.

As time went by without another hit, I assumed that these guys had either made their nut and retired or else moved on to somewhere else—although our nationwide alert hadn't turned up any bandits with a similar M.O. anywhere else. We still wanted these guys, badly; they had a lot to answer for. Unlike other cases, though, we weren't hoping they would pull another job so we'd get another shot at catching them; it was too dangerous. But in the meantime we had nothing on them, not a clue as to who they were—no leads, no tips, nothing.

So they could have gotten away with it, probably could be walking around alive and free today. By February 1997, they still had at least several hundred thousand dollars, maybe even more than a million, left over from their robberies the previous spring. They didn't need more money, at least not yet.

But they decided to do another job anyway—because it wasn't just about the money.

And this time, they were doomed from the very start.

Friday, February 28, 1997, 9:17 A.M. LAPD Officers Martin Perello and Loren Farrell are on routine patrol in North Hollywood, cruising along Laurel Canyon Boulevard in their black-and-white, when Perello sees something he can hardly believe. Two large men in black ski masks and Ninja-style outfits, carrying assault weapons in their hands, are walking into the front door of a Bank of America, pushing ahead of them a customer who had been making a withdrawal at the outside ATM machine.

You see that? Perello says to Ferrell. But the Ninja boys are already in the bank, out of view.

See what?

Those two guys—they're robbing the bank!

Ferrell gives Perello one of those "Are you sure you're seeing what you think you're seeing?" looks. But Perello isn't kidding around.

Call it in!

And pretty soon it's crackling over the radios of every LAPD car in the division: Two-eleven in progress. Officers need assistance. This time Phillips and Matsareanu won't have two minutes before they're in the danger zone. They don't know it, but they're in the danger zone right now.

Inside the bank, it's the same drill as always. They push the ATM customer down and shout out: "This is a robbery! All you motherfuckers hit the floor!" It's a big bank, and it's crowded on a Friday morning—almost fifty employees and customers, men, women, and children, are inside. They all drop, except for one guy who just stands there, seemingly frozen in shock. Phillips looks at him, says "Oh fuck!" but doesn't kill him or knock him to the ground; he leaves him standing there. Matasareanu walks over to the bandit barrier door and fires a fully automatic burst of .223-caliber armor-piercing rounds into it, smashing the Plexiglas. That's when the screaming starts—inside and outside the bank.

Outside, Officers Ferrell and Perello are doing what they're supposed to do: waiting for backup. As a cop, you don't walk into an armed bank robbery in progress; it's too dangerous for the civilians inside. The last thing you want is a gun battle indoors, with bullets flying and ricocheting around. But when Ferrell and Perello hear the automatic weapons fire—it's so loud that at first they think it's coming from somewhere outside the bank—they're wondering if a gun battle has already started. They're on the radio again, shouting.

Shots fired, shots fired! Officers need assistance! And now every black-and-white patrol car and detective sedan in the Valley is screaming code three for the 6600 block of Laurel Canyon. In minutes there are at least a dozen of them staggered around the bank building, cops standing behind them with 9-mm sidearms and 12-gauge pump shotguns loaded with buckshot trained on the bank doors. More cars, more cops are arriving every minute. Ambulances, LAPD helicopters, and

SWAT teams have been called and are on their way. Overhead, TV news helicopters have picked up the chatter on their police scanners and are racing to the scene.

Inside, Phillips and Matasareanu's stopwatches are clicking down the seconds and the minutes, completely ignored; as usual, they're acting like they've got all the time in the world, walking around almost in slow motion. Phillips stays in the lobby, lumbering about, weighed down by the extra ammo drums hooked to his combat vest and 43 pounds of body armor that covers him from ankles to neck. He points his AK-47 this way and that, telling the terrified customers to "Shut the fuck up." Behind the bandit barrier, Matasareanu starts searching for the man-ager—more seconds are ticking by—then finally finds him and drags him to the vault. "Open the gate or I'll fucking kill you!" Inside the vault, he starts to load cash into the collapsible suitcase he brought in with him.

But it's not enough.

Phillips and Matsareanu don't know it, but they're victims of their own successes. After the huge losses in the two earlier robberies, Bank of America had designated every one of its banks in the San Fernando Valley as a "high-risk" bank, which mandated changes in the cash con-trol policies. Simply put, they had started keeping less cash in the vault, so if they got hit again, there'd be less of it on hand to steal. On this par-ticular day, there's only $330,000 in the vault and the tellers' drawers. Matasareanu is shouting, threatening, but there's nothing the manager can do. The money simply isn't there.

It's eight minutes into the robbery now—eight minutes. Matasareanu is still back in the vault, screaming for money that doesn't exist, when Phillips decides to look outside. Slowly, slowly, he walks out the front door—and suddenly he sees the cops lined up outside like God's own firing squad. One of the cops who sees him—huge, bulging with body armor, the dark glasses under his ski mask giving him a bug-eyed insect look—thinks, "Wow, these guys are monsters!"

The cops don't fire—Phillips is framed against the glass doors, and there are civilians inside—and Phillips doesn't fire either. He turns and walks, slowly, slowly, back into the bank.

Inside, he and Matasareanu are pissed off. It's not enough money. They want more. It's unbelievable: Here they are, surrounded, doomed, and instead of worrying about how they're going to escape, or survive, these guys are still trying to do a bank robbery. They herd most of the customers and employees into the vault, then haul the manager across the lobby to a door that opens onto a small utility room behind the outside ATM machines; it's the room where the bank employees can access the machines and fill them up with cash. The manager opens the locked door and they order him to punch in the combination on the backs of the ATM machines.

He does, but there's a problem. There are thousands of dollars in crisp twenties inside the machines, but again, Phillips and Matasareanu's earlier successes have worked against them. As a "high-risk" bank, the ATMs have had time delay locks installed, which means that after you punch in the combination, you have to wait ten minutes before the machines will open. The time delay locks still allow employees to have access to the machines when they run out of cash, but the ten-minute wait discourages robbers—what bank robbers in their right minds are going to wait ten minutes for the goddamned thing to open?

Matasareanu is furious now. Standing in the tiny room, he cranks off thirty rounds of armor-piercing .223s into the ATMs. Fragments of plastic and steel and tungsten-carbide bullets are flying everywhere; people on the floor in the lobby are screaming and crying again. But it's no use, the machines won't open. With their locking mechanisms shattered, the locking bolts are frozen in place.

Finally, Phillips and Matasareanu realize it's no use. It's time to go. It's been fifteen minutes since they first entered the bank, and by now there are about two dozen black-and-whites and God only knows how many unmarked police sedans lined up around the bank, with more still on the way. That's what Phillips and Matasareanu are going to walk into, like Butch and Sundance wading into the Bolivian army.

But there's one more indignity waiting for them, one more example of just how badly they have screwed up this robbery. After the robberies in May, every Bank of America branch manager in the Valley started putting dye packs in their vault cash, salting the stacks of legitimate currency with small bundles of bogus cash containing packets of explosive dye. As Matasareanu drags the suitcase with the $330,000 in cash toward the front door, an electronic transponder hidden near the door sends out a signal that arms the dye packs inside the suitcase.

Ten seconds later, just as Phillips and Matasareanu are walking out the front door, three dye packs inside the suitcase go off—*pop! pop! pop!*

Wisps of red dye waft out of the seams and zippers of the suitcase, and inside the dye stains every stack of bills a deep red, ruining them forever.

Phillips and Matasareanu hear the pops, see the smoke; they can figure it out. They're about to die for absolutely nothing.

Standing by the doorway, Phillips cranks off burst after burst of automatic fire at four cops who have taken cover behind a keymaking kiosk in the parking lot across the street; 150 rounds punch through the kiosk, wounding two of the officers and sending them all fleeing for better cover. Cops and civilians are crouched behind cars in the parking lot, but the armor-piercing rounds punch through them like cardboard. Windshields are exploding, tires bursting, cops and civilians are bleeding on the pavement.

After several minutes of constant firing, Phillips and Matasareanu, still shooting, start moving slowly away from the bank door toward the parking lot around the corner of the bank, leaving the suitcase of ruined money behind. The cops are firing back now, with sidearms and shotguns, and they're getting hits, but the "monsters" are unaffected: they stagger slightly from the impact when the police bullets hit their body armor, but the rounds don't penetrate. The cops are flipping out; they can't believe these guys aren't going down. Police are trained to aim for the center of the body mass, but now a new order crackles over the radios: "Go for the head. Go for the head."

In the bank parking lot, the white Chevy Celebrity is sitting there with the engine running. Matasareanu climbs in behind the wheel, but Phillips just stands there, spraying the area with automatic bursts. Matasareanu is firing bursts through the passenger side window at anything that moves.

No one has ever seen anything like it—but everyone in America who has the TV on is seeing it now. TV news helicopters are circling overhead, beaming the firefight live across the nation; at one point Phillips raises his automatic weapon and fires a burst at them. On camera you can see Phillips taking more bullet hits in the body—if the police are aiming for his head, they're missing—but he sloughs them off and returns fire, reloads, returns fire again.

Finally, after five minutes of this, they start to move—but slowly, Matasareanu steering the Chevy out of the bank parking lot at three miles an hour, Phillips walking beside the car, using it as a shield and firing over the roof. Suddenly, inexplicably, Phillips breaks off away from the car—no one will ever know why—and Matasareanu keeps going, rolling along at three or four miles per hour on Archwood Street, a residential street lined with close-set bungalow-style homes.

Phillips ducks behind a parked semitruck, still firing his AK-47, but suddenly it jams and he can't clear it. He drops the rifle, pulls out his 9-mm Beretta pistol, and starts walking along a hedge, firing at a knot of cops at the corner. Then a police bullet hits the Beretta, knocking it from his hand. Phillips bends down, picks it up, puts the muzzle under his chin, and—*bam!*—he blows his brains out on live television. As he falls backward, a police bullet catches him just above the armor vest, hitting his spine and blowing out the back of his neck.

Both the self-inflicted head wound and shot to the neck are fatal—and actually superfluous. Phillips had already taken another hit just above the vest that had severed his subclavian artery. He would have bled to death in a little while anyway. The police swarm in and, following procedure, cuff his dead hands behind his back.

Matasareanu, meanwhile, is still rolling slowly along Archwood Street in the white Chevy, all the tires blown by gunfire, the trunk open and flapping up and down. Amazingly, civilian cars are also moving along the street; he tries to make a couple of them stop, pointing a rifle through the window, but they steer around him. Finally, he stops next to a Jeep pickup whose driver has bailed out and run away. He gets out of the car and slowly, deliberately, as if he's in no hurry at all, starts transferring his weapons from the Chevy to the pickup. He actually climbs into the driver's side of the pickup before he notices that the fleeing driver has taken the keys with him. He climbs back out, a huge, lumbering fat man, limping a little; he's already been hit.

Suddenly, Matasareanu sees a black-and-white screaming down the street toward him: it's full of cops, including some SWAT guys armed with .223-caliber AR-15s. He crouches behind the white Chevy, firing bursts at the cops with his AK-47. The cops bail out of their car, using it as a shield, and return fire, shooting under the cars and hitting Matasareanu in the legs; other cops, on foot, are coming up from Matasareanu's left, firing at him. Matasareanu throws his hands up, then drops them, grabs the rifle again. There are more shots, and at last Matasareanu slumps to the ground. The SWAT guys move in, rifles ready, kick his rifle away, and kick him over on his belly. An LAPD detective runs up and snaps handcuffs on him, then rolls him up into a sitting position.

Thirty-five minutes after the bank robbery began, it's over.

A few minutes later, when the scene is under control, the detective crouches down next to Matasareanu and asks him: "How you doin'?"

"Fuck you," Matasareanu says. "Shoot me in the head."

The detective doesn't do that, of course. He doesn't need to.

Emil Matasareanu bleeds to death on the asphalt.

Hundreds of LAPD officers would spend the next ten hours searching the neighborhood for other suspects. It's indicative of the confusion present in any firefight that some officers firmly believed that three or even four people had been involved in the robbery and shoot-out. Given that report, the search was sound tactics. But I knew they were wasting their time.

I was miles away when the firefight broke out, in Ventura County, firing my quarterly weapons qualification on the FBI range. I was immediately summoned back to the L.A. FBI headquarters, and like just about everybody else I watched the remainder of the action unfold live on TV. The only things I shot that day were paper targets. But I recognized the pair instantly from their previous jobs. I knew that they worked alone.

The dead robbers were quickly identified from the fingerprints from the Glendale arrest: Larry Eugene Phillips, Jr., age twenty-six, CII (Criminal Identification and Investigation) No. A09065810. Emil Decebal Matasareanu, age thirty, CII No. A10886261. FBI agents and RHD detectives fanned out to find out more about who they were, or had been, and what had happened to the money from the earlier robberies.

Meanwhile, the LAPD was busy counting up the score.

More than 1,700 shots had been fired in the shootout, at least 1,100 of them by the gunmen, almost all of them armor-piercing high-velocity rifle rounds, the rest by the police, mostly 9-mm pistol rounds and shotgun buckshot. (In a highly publicized ironic twist, during the gunfight a group of police officers had raced to a civilian gun store to borrow some high-velocity rifles that could penetrate the robbers' body armor, which the owner gladly handed over. But they didn't make it back in time to use them.)

Nine LAPD officers were wounded by gunfire, as were three civilians and one dog that was grazed on the nose; all recovered. It was generally considered a miracle that nobody was killed. Twelve LAPD cars had been completely destroyed by gunfire, and eighty-five civilian vehicles were damaged. The day after the shoot-out, after the yellow police tape had been taken down, the site was swarmed by tourists who fingered the bullet holes in building walls and picked up shell casings and fragments of bullets as souvenirs. Later, seventeen LAPD officers and detectives would receive well-deserved Medals of Valor for exceptional courage in battling the gunmen and rescuing the wounded.

The LAPD, beset by bad press ever since the Rodney King case, was initially lauded in the news media for its performance in the shoot-out—but as every law enforcement officer knows too well, press appreciation is fleeting. Within days the news media, ever eager to second-guess cops from the safety of their word processors, started raising questions about whether police had intentionally allowed Matasareanu to bleed to death—a touching show of concern for a guy who had helped murder one man and easily could have killed dozens more. Later, an L.A. attorney, Stephen Yagman, who had made a career out of suing cops, filed a federal civil rights lawsuit against the LAPD and two officers on behalf of Matasareanu's two children. Given Matasareanu's murderous behavior, you'd think the jurors in the ensuing civil trial would have tossed out the case and asked the judge to have Attorney Yagman publicly flogged. But amazingly, they deadlocked. The lawsuit was finally dropped.

Searches of Phillips and Matasareanu's homes yielded up a few things. The Granada Hills safehouse contained some ammunition, manuals, and equipment for converting semiautomatic weapons to fully automatic, some bodybuilding magazines and copies of Soldier of Fortune. Matasareanu's house in Rowland Heights also contained a few weapons, some survivalist books, and $20,000 in stolen cash; Phillips's Anaheim Hills house had a safe with $280,000 in stolen bank cash in it. And again, at all the houses there were those much-watched VHS copies of Heat.

(A search of a commercial board-and-care building that Matasareanu and his mom owned in Pasadena also turned up a forty-four-year-old mentally ill woman locked in a room with no toilet or water, reeking of urine and feces. Matasareanu's mother was later charged with felony abuse of a dependent adult.)

What happened to the rest of the stolen money, though, is anybody's guess. RHD Detective Tom Gattegno, who handled much of the follow-up investigation, is convinced, as I am, that neither man's wife knew anything about the robberies, or where the money went. Phillips and Matasareanu were too secretive, too caught up in their own little fantasy world, to share that kind of information. On the morning of the robberies, they had told their wives they were going to an out-of-town "business meeting" or "real estate seminar" and would be back Saturday. Like everybody else, the wives saw the shoot-out on TV, but the first they knew of their husbands' involvement in it was when they saw their mug shots flash across the screen! Phillips's wife quickly fled the state, but she left behind the safe with the $280,000 in it; if she'd been in on the game, she surely would have taken the cash with her.

Yet there must have been more money, somewhere. Phillips and Matasareanu may have pissed away hundreds of thousands of dollars of the $1.5 million they stole, on guns and cars and Phillips's suits and jewelry, but they probably couldn't have spent it all. I suspect it's buried somewhere, or that it sat in bank safe deposit boxes under phony names until the box rent was long overdue and the money was escheated to the state. Whatever happened, no one ever found any financial records, or any indication of where the stolen money was.

Phillips and Matasareanu, of course, were in no condition to say. Still, the dead men's bodies were telling some tales.

Three days after the shootout, Phillips's refrigerated body was stretched out on a stainless-steel table in the county coroner's office, to be weighed and measured, sawed and sliced apart, his wounds tracked and catalogued. On the slab he measured five foot eleven and weighed 193 pounds; the pathologist described the body as "lean and very muscular," with the chest hair shaved in bodybuilder fashion. He was wearing 42 pounds of body armor, including an armor vest and leg and arm armor that had been fashioned out of cut-up pieces of Kevlar fastened together with Velcro strips. It was no wonder he had taken so many hits without falling: he was swathed neck to ankle in armor. In fact, as the morgue workers undressed him, spent bullets and shotgun pellets that had been stopped by the armor fell out of his clothing.

Despite the armor, Phillips had been wounded nine times, including the self-inflicted shot to the head. Amazingly, none of the other wounds were head-shots, despite the police orders to "go for the head." But a head is a pretty small target, especially in the heat of a firefight. At least two of the other wounds would have eventually proved fatal. Not surprisingly, the official cause of death was listed as "multiple gunshot wounds."

Matasareanu was autopsied the same day. On the slab he measured six feet and weighed 283 pounds; although the pathologist still described him as "markedly obese," he had actually slimmed down some after his brain surgery. Unlike Phillips, his only body armor was a vest; apparently his legs and arms were too fat to carry the armor and still allow him to move. That was fatal: his armor vest had taken several shots that didn't penetrate, but he was badly chewed up on the arms and below the waist, with no less than twenty-nine bullet wounds. His cause of death was also officially listed as "multiple gunshot wounds."

There was something else that the autopsies revealed. In each of their three bank robberies, witnesses had commented on the slow, lumbering, unhurried way they had moved, as if they'd been in no hurry—the antithesis of every other bank robber I'd ever encountered. It was a mystery—until the autopsy analysis of their blood showed that both Phillips and Matsareanu had ingested some of Matasareanu's prescribed phenobarbital before the North Hollywood robbery, and presumably before the other robberies as well. Phenobarbital is a barbiturate that is used to treat epilepsy. It acts by partially blocking nerve impulses in the brain, and in sufficient doses, it can produce a staggering gait, an inability to think clearly, and a slowed sense of time, as well as suppressing the natural fear instinct. (Matasareanu's body also showed levels of Dilantin, like phenobarbital a treatment for epilepsy, and one that produces similar potential effects.)

The drugs fit the psychological profile I had developed for these guys: although they may have styled themselves as big, brave bandits, they were cowards, little boys who needed doses of pharmacological courage to pull off their jobs. The drugs could also partially explain why they stayed so long in the banks; the pheno may have given them an altered sense of time.

But it's not the entire answer. All along I had thought that these guys were looking for a shoot-out with police, a chance to battle it out with the authority figures that Phillips in particular so deeply hated. They weren't looking to kill just anybody; if they had been, they could have slaughtered dozens of civilians in the banks. No, they wanted cops. (Again, Brinks guard Herman Cook was a civilian, but he carried a gun and wore a police-type uniform.)

Of course, if killing cops was all they wanted to do, they could have simply ambushed some on the street. Obviously, they wanted the money from the bank robberies, too—and despite Phillips's suicide when all was lost, they weren't suicidal; they had wanted to get away. But somehow a gun battle fit in with their fantasies of what bank robbery was all about. After all, it's a feature of almost every bank robbery movie, and their movie wouldn't have been complete without one. Their mistake was to give police time to assemble in overwhelming force—and to think that, as in the movies, they could win against the odds.

In the immediate wake of the shoot-out, just about everybody made the movie connection, noting that the shoot-out in North Hollywood seemed more like a film than real life—and most commentators specifically mentioned *Heat*. Even before anyone knew very much about Phillips and Matasareanu, the social commentator Neal Gabler made the point in the *Los Angeles Times*.

"It seems likely that the North Hollywood robbers had rented 'Heat,'" Gabler wrote. "It was too coincidental: the black body armor, the automatic weapons, the daytime sally. But the most telling sign that they were in thrall to the movies was the way one gunman calmly strolled down the street to his fate, dying in a fusillade of bullets. It was a scene that could have only happened in the movies—or to someone whose faith in the movies was absolute."

Gabler was right. Phillips and Matasareanu were in thrall to the movies; their childish faith was absolute.

But the movies had lied to them, and to everyone else who might think that bank robberies are what they see on the screen. In real life, Phillips and Matasareanu's bank robberies weren't glamorous, and they didn't end with the credits rolling and the lights coming up. In real life, their bank robbery movie ended with two dead men lying on a slab, naked and cold, eviscerated.

Without so much as a single island or castle to their names.

EPILOGUE

Finally, after more than three decades of chasing bank robbers in the bank robbery capital of the world, it was time to say good-bye to the FBI.

I was already a year past the mandatory FBI retirement age of fifty-seven, and I couldn't put it off any longer. I filled out reams of paperwork, broke in my replacement, cleaned out my office and, with a lump in my throat, I walked out of the bank squad office for the last time.

It was over. I had responded to my final two-eleven silent. Now the only remaining crime-in-progress I had to respond to was my FBI retirement party.

I'd had a good run, better than I ever would have dreamed back when I was a fresh-faced young kid at the Academy. For all its faults and frustrations, the FBI had given me a chance to see a world that few people ever see, to do things that few people ever do. For thirty-three years I had actually looked forward to going to work every day—and for that I was grateful.

I wasn't under any illusions, of course. Despite the thousands of cases I worked on, the hundreds of bank robbers I helped send to prison, the many bank robberies that my efforts may have helped prevent, I didn't walk away thinking that I had permanently altered the face of bank robbery, or crime in general. As long as there is money there will be people eager and willing to steal it, and any lawman who thinks he can fundamentally change that is looking for a broken heart, and a bitter retirement.

And yet, I could look back on my FBI career with an enormous feeling of satisfaction. Because in just about every bank robbery case, I—we, the FBI—had won. Even when we didn't win, even when the bank bandits got away from us, they didn't really win either.

And they won't win in the future.

Some readers may wonder if I've given away too much information, if I've revealed too many secrets about the business of bank robbery, if somehow this book might actually encourage someone to rob a bank and make it easier for them to do so. The answer is no. For one thing, almost everything I've discussed here is already common knowledge in every extension school of crime in every cellblock in every jail and prison in America. I haven't told criminals anything they don't already know, or can't readily learn elsewhere. Besides, what I've covered here does not reveal every secret about the art and science of catching bank robbers.

As for amateur would-be bank robbers, ordinary citizens who might read this and decide that robbing a bank is an easy or smart thing to do, they're missing the point. They should look beyond the mechanics of the bank robbery trade and consider the underlying theme that runs through every line and story and chapter in this book.

That theme is: Sooner or later, bank robbers always lose.

Think about it. Poor Smitty in Cleveland tossed away his freedom for sixteen hours of not feeling sick and a wad of bills that he never even got to spend. Eddie Dodson stole more than a quarter of a million dollars in seven months and then stood before the judge a pauper, the money having literally gone up in smoke; it cost him ten years of his life, and then he did it again—because bank robbery, like drugs, is an addiction. Robert "Casper" Brown had the brains and the charisma to be somebody, to rise above the streets, but he made the mistake of thinking that he was smarter and tougher than the law; his career ended at age twenty-three, and he'll be a middle-aged man before he ever breathes free air again.

Yes, the Hole in the Ground Gang got away with their bank vault tunnel jobs, but even then they didn't win: they struggled and sweated in the dirt for months for what turned out to be chump change. David

Mack threw away his honor, his family, and his freedom to rob a bank, all for less than what he could have made as an honest cop; and Larry Phillips and Emil Matasareanu wound up rich but dead, riddled with bullets and stretched out naked in the county coroner's office.

In the end, they were losers, just like almost all of the countless other bank robbers I had dealt with in my career. They were living proof—or dead proof—that the famous line about bank robbery really isn't true, that even the title of this book is laden with irony.

For bank robbers, in the long run, banks aren't where the money is. They're where the money isn't.